*International
social welfare*

# International social welfare

**WALTER A. FRIEDLANDER**

*Professor Emeritus of Social Welfare*
*University of California at Berkeley*

**Prentice-Hall, Inc.,** *Englewood Cliffs, New Jersey*

*Library of Congress Cataloging in Publication Data*

FRIEDLANDER, WALTER A
  International social welfare.

  (Prentice-Hall sociology series)
  Includes bibliographies.
  1. Social service—International cooperation.
2. International agencies.  3. Social work education.
I. Title.
HV41.F67     361     74-13146
ISBN  0-13-470906-3

Printed in the United States of America

10  9  8  7  6  5  4  3  2  1

Prentice-Hall International, Inc., *London*
Prentice-Hall of Australia, Pty. Ltd., *Sydney*
Prentice-Hall of Canada, Ltd., *Toronto*
Prentice-Hall of India Private Limited, *New Delhi*
Prentice-Hall of Japan, Inc., *Tokyo*

# Contents

# International
## social welfare

# *Brief history of international social welfare*

The incentive for international cooperation in the area of social welfare arose in the mid-nineteenth century, from the desire of private charities and public welfare and correctional agencies to confer with each other, and by sharing their experiences to improve their methods of providing charitable and relief services, preventing delinquency, and rehabilitating criminals. The first two such international conferences met in Paris (1849) and Brussels (1851); later conferences took place in Rome, Vienna, St. Petersburg, and other central European cities. The congresses included the International Congress of Charities, Corrections, and Philanthropy; the Paris Sanitary Convention of 1851; the Penitentiary Congress; the International Penal and Prison Congress; the Universal Congress for the Improvement of the Fate of the Blind; and the International Congress for the Protection of Discharged Prisoners.

The effect of the international conventions was rather limited: they did not find much publicity beyond the narrow circles of their delegates, and they did not include representatives of the objects of their discussions—the poor, the ill, convicts, and released prisoners. The members of religious and private charities and the officials of public institutions were anxious to impress other countries' delegates with descriptions of the high quality and success of their services. However, no attempt was made to provide the convention delegates with the opportunity to meet people of other social classes, particularly the persons to whom the various social services were giving help, so that the delegates might evaluate the results of the charitable activities.

### The International Red Cross

In 1861, shortly after the first international social welfare convention, the International Red Cross was founded, the first large-scale, international social welfare organization. It was the work of a young Swiss banker, Jean Henri Dunant of Geneva. On a business trip in northern Italy in 1859, he arrived by accident at the battlefield of Solferino, where thousands of wounded and dying Italian, French, and Austrian soldiers were lying without any care. Shocked, Dunant left his carriage and tried with the help of his valet to dress the wounds of some of the soldiers and to bring water to the thirsty. He encouraged the frightened peasants in a nearby village to help him, but the small number of people were unable to give adequate assistance. A few days later, Dunant related his experience to the commanding general of the Italian and French armies and persuaded him to send soldiers to look for the wounded still on the battlefield. After returning to Geneva, Dunant wrote a book, *Un Souvenir de Solferino,* which aroused public opinion in several European countries and at several courts. With the moral support of the empress of France and the queen of Prussia, the Swiss government decided to invite representatives of 17 countries to an international convention in Geneva, to provide for the humane treatment and medical care of soldiers wounded in battle and to protect the persons administering such services, so that doctors, nurses and other attendants, hospitals, clinics, and ambulances would be treated as neutrals rather than as enemies. These principles were embodied in the constitution of the International Red Cross Convention which met in Geneva in 1864.

The executive organ of the International Red Cross is composed only of Swiss citizens. Authorized to recognize national societies as members of the International Red Cross, it encourages civilized nations to join its organization and attempts to secure the observance of the humanitarian objectives of the agency. It also arranges international relief actions in peacetime to aid victims of severe natural disasters, such as volcanic eruptions, earthquakes, tornadoes, and floods; in wartime, it provides medical care for wounded soldiers and civilians, relief for civilian populations, and communication with and help for prisoners of war, including the sending of letters and parcels from their families and the inspection of prisoner-of-war camps. When the International Red Cross was founded in 1864, the United States Congress refused to join the organization; however, urged by the American Red Cross Society under the leadership of Clara Barton, the United States became a member of the International Red Cross in 1882.

During the First World War (1914 to 1918), British and American Red Cross Societies conducted large-scale relief actions in France, Belgium, Italy, and Greece. They built and equipped hospitals, convalescent homes, dispensaries, and infirmaries; evacuated civilians from war-devastated regions; fed women and children; and provided medical treatment and resettlement services. Undernourished and sick children were brought to Switzerland for recuperation, and child care centers, summer camps, and numerous schools were established, partly under the auspices of the International Red Cross.

### Other Relief Organizations

A number of other relief agencies joined the Red Cross Societies in this necessary work, among them the British Service Committee (Quakers), the American Friends Service Committee (founded by the Quakers in Philadelphia in 1917), the American Joint Distribution Committee (AJDC), the American Relief Administration, the Near East Foundation, and the International Save-the-Children Fund (founded in England but headquartered in Geneva, Switzerland, and now called the International Child Welfare Union after its merger with the International Child Protective Society of Brussels).[1] In 1919, after the First World War, the League of Red Cross, Red Crescent, and Red Lion and Sun Societies was founded to allow the national societies a major role in Red Cross work. It consists at present of ninety countries, with a membership of over 170 million persons. Its headquarters are in Geneva, Switzerland.[2]

Between the First and the Second World Wars, these and several other international philanthropic agencies developed welfare and health services, mainly for women and children, in Ethiopia, Greece, and the Balkans, setting up hospitals, clinics, orphanages, and schools. The American Joint Distribution Committee provided medical care and children's services, mainly for people in Eastern Europe, and assisted in the establishment of the OSE, an international federation for the training of Jewish physicians, nurses, and health personnel, in the establishment of hospitals and dispensaries, and in the founding of ORT, an international organization for the vocational training of Jewish adolescents to prepare them for emigration and resettlement, particularly in Israel.

During the First World War, and again during the Second World War, the World's Young Women's Christian Association (World's YWCA), founded in 1894 in England, organized services and set up recreational facilities for refugees and evacuees in France and Belgium and assisted in emigration activities. It also founded, in 1921, a non-denominational International Migration Service, with headquarters in Geneva and New York. Now called the International Social Service, it is particularly active in administering adoption services for children of various nationalities, uniting separated families, and providing services for American servicemen and their foreign brides.[3]

The major religious faiths in the United States are engaged in international social services. The Church World Service, an organ of the National Council of Churches of Christ, organizes the activities of 34 Protestant and other evangelical commissions. Several other denominations have individual foreign departments, such as the Lutheran World Relief, the American Baptist Relief, and the Seventh Day Adventists Welfare Service. The Catholic Relief Services, working under the auspices of the National Catholic Welfare Conference, give relief and technical assistance to numerous countries. The international services of the American Joint Distribution Committee, mentioned earlier, are connected with the Hebrew Immigrant Aid Service (HIAS), OSE, and ORT. The international services of the American Friends Service Committee (Quakers) are also significant. Similar nonsectarian services are carried on by the Unitarian Service Committee, with headquarters in Boston, which specializes in giving medical aid, teaching physicians and other medical personnel, training social workers in African and European countries as well as in Korea and Venezuela, and giving grants to physicians and social workers of those countries who want to study in the United States.

*The League of Nations.* Another international social welfare program was established at the end of the First World War, in 1919, in the framework of the League of Nations. The League established a standing committee on social welfare for the discussion of pressing social problems, and the secretariat of the League organized a Section on Social Questions and Opium Traffic, its primary concern to protect women and children against kidnapping or seduction for prostitution (the "white slave traffic") and to protect the member nations of the League against the smuggling of dangerous drugs. The Section also developed guidelines for child labor, and made suggestions for the protection of youth in periods of unemployment and against the influence of obscene publications. Its reports on childhood marriage, the status of illegitimate children, child welfare councils, and institutional and foster care of children were distributed to the member nations of the League.[4] In cooperation with an already operating International Office of Public Health in Paris, the Health Organization of the League published current information on epidemics and communicable diseases and set up special bureaus for preventive health services in Singapore and in Rio de Janeiro. Through its permanent, worldwide service of epidemiological information and warnings, the Health Organization of the League assisted member governments greatly in the development of efficient public health systems. It also provided for the interchange of experience in conferences and for the delegation of experts and technical health personnel to countries in need of information and help.

### The United Nations Relief and Rehabilitation Administration

*Organization and Functions*

The most dynamic element in the development of international social welfare services was the United Nations Relief and Rehabilitation Administration (UNRRA). Founded in Washington, D.C., on November 9, 1943, two years before the establishment of the United Nations itself, UNRRA was organized by 44 nations to solve the tremendous relief problems caused by the invasion of 35 countries by the Axis powers in the Second World War.[5] These countries in Europe and Asia were left with their political systems and economies destroyed and their populations semi-starved; ravaged by hunger, disease, epidemics, and despair; without sufficient food, clothing, housing, and medicine; and in dire need of care for their sick and homeless. Large masses of people had fled or had been forced into slave labor in other lands. Among the free nations of the world, there was a consensus that the task of helping the victims of the war and of restoring normal living conditions, morale, health, and hope after the liberation of the occupied countries could be achieved only through the cooperation of all countries.

Even before the foundation of the UNRRA, in August 1940, Winston Churchill had promised that after the defeat of the Nazis, food, medicine, raw materials, and the means of reconstruction would be provided through interallied collaboration to the liberated countries. An Allied Committee on Post-War Requirements (the so-called Leith-Ross Committee) was established in London to prepare relief and rehabilitation in Europe and North Africa. The committee established the Middle-East Relief and Refugee Administration (MERRA) with headquarters in Cairo and set up camps in Egypt and Palestine for refugees from Poland, Greece, Czechoslovakia, and Yugoslavia.

In the United States in 1942, shortly after the declaration of war by Japan and Hitler's Germany, President Franklin D. Roosevelt established the Office of Foreign Relief and Rehabilitation Operations (OFRRO) within the Department of State, under the leadership of Herbert Lehman, a former governor of New York. OFRRO cooperated with the British Leith-Ross Committee in organizing relief operations for civilians in North Africa in connection with the Allied armies.

With the foundation of the UNRRA in 1943, the peoples of the countries invaded by the Axis powers, as well as the resistance groups in these countries, found new hope that they would be liberated and would receive help from the free nations of the world. The planners of the UNRRA had the advantage of learning from the experience of the Leith-Ross Committee and the Office of Foreign Relief and Rehabilitation Operations. This was particularly helpful in the difficult task of selecting the staff for the UNRRA headquarters in Washington and London. The UNRRA was also assisted by the Bouderau Committee, a group of American experts in international relations. The UNRRA's policy was to select personnel on the basis of high quality and competence rather than of nationality. However, the appointment of staff members other than British and Americans proved difficult, because until the liberation of the occupied Western European countries in 1945, the governments in exile had very few capable persons available, and the Soviet Union did not permit the UNRRA to recruit in Russia. Despite these obstacles, the UNRRA attempted to assure international composition by recruiting personnel in Canada, North and Central America, India, the Southwest Pacific, and South Africa, as well as in Europe after the end of the war. Russian staff members were appointed upon suggestion by their government. The recruitment of the staff proved to be one of the most arduous tasks of the entire operation.[6] Recruitment of additional personnel needed for the large displaced persons program was easier after the end of the war, when more people were available because of the demobilization of substantial parts of the Allied armies. In several European countries, nominations to the UNRRA staff were made as rewards for service in resistance groups; however, only in France were a number of unqualified persons temporarily employed in UNRRA services.[7]

Another difficult assignment for the UNRRA was the proper and timely information of its member countries about the operations of the agency, and the explanation to the countries which received UNRRA assistance of what supplies could be provided, particularly if this assistance could not fully meet the countries' requests. The UNRRA's Public Information Division tried to announce the actual relief operations to the receiving countries to avoid dramatization and boasting, and to work in friendly cooperation with its member governments, but it was unable to prevent hostile press releases and criticism within the contributing countries, especially when the relief operation in Asia and the assistance to displaced persons began.

Until the end of the war in 1945, it was uncertain what supplies the occupied countries needed for the first emergency relief. At that time, military shipping and supplies had priority over all civilian requests, including those of the UNRRA. Thus, after the end of the hostilities, the UNRRA had to distribute relief supplies cautiously, following a carefully prepared program. In all countries receiving relief, the UNRRA did not assume the task of full industrial rehabilitation, but limited its efforts to the restoration of the most-needed public services—water, sanitation, gas, electricity, and transportation—and the rehabilitation of such industries which were producing relief supplies. Its industrial rehabilitation program gave preference to those countries which had suffered most from enemy occupation and devastation as a consequence of their active resistance against the occupying forces.

UNRRA rehabilitation activities also included the establishment of medical and social services, the assignment of experts in the fields of health care, social welfare, and agricultural and industrial reconstruction, and technical training for the citizens of the liberated countries. In 1945, the actual delivery of relief supplies started in Greece and Yugoslavia, followed by relief to Czechoslovakia and Poland. Despite this beginning, several European countries complained that they were not equitably considered; however, the imbalance was caused by the lack of suitable port facilities and by a number of unfortunate dockworkers' strikes in the United States.

Procurement of food was the most important part of the UNRRA relief program, requiring nearly half of all UNRRA resources. Food relief consisted mainly of grains, oils, meat, dairy products, fish, and fats. In 1945, the UNRRA was able to ship food in large quantities to the liberated countries; the peak of the deliveries was reached in the summer of 1946. The UNRRA Council had recommended that food consumption in these countries be raised to 2,650 calories daily per capita, but the UNRRA was unable to realize the goal: in 1947, several countries were still short of a daily ration of 2,000 calories. The deficiencies in food provisions were caused partly by unexpected crop failures and by lack of cooperation of several food-supplying governments, including that of the United States, where soap industries influenced Congress to prevent the stockpiling of fats for UNRRA war relief, and used them instead for soap production. In 1946, a worldwide food shortage prevented the UNRRA from obtaining some of the food it needed for its relief operations, and the difficulties were aggravated by the reluctance of the Allies' Combined Food Board to allocate needed supplies to the UNRRA, by the refusal of some governments to deliver the promised supplies, and by a shortage of funds, as several governments refused to allocate the necessary contributions for the purchase of food and other supplies. Even in the United

States, the late appropriation of funds for the UNRRA delayed the procurement of food for the relief program, and storage space for the food was inadequate. Canada, however, proved to be more cooperative and less bureaucratic. In the first food shipments to Europe, in 1945, there was a shortage of protein foods—meat, cheese, dried eggs, margarine, milk in all forms, and fish—while bread grains were available in abundance. (Military requirements were still very heavy at this time.) To improve this condition, the UNRRA established an Emergency Food Program that aimed to prevent serious nutritional defects and health damage.

Another troubling problem arose in late 1945, when the threat of a severe famine in India caused the UNRRA to send emergency relief there, creating serious food shortages in the displaced persons operations in Germany and in Japan.

During the period of its operations, the UNRRA was the largest exporter in the world. Most of the relief materials were transported by ship. But until the end of the war, military priorities made it difficult to obtain sufficient tonnage for UNRRA supplies, and thereafter, seamen's strikes and the facts that harbors in many countries were still mined or severely damaged, that railways were blocked or destroyed, and that trucks were in short supply delayed deliveries longer than the organization could have forseen, with the result that supplies could not reach their destination.

The arrangement for the delivery of UNRRA relief and rehabilitation supplies was that they would be provided without a claim for payment in foreign exchange against the invaded countries, within the limits of the UNRRA's financial resources. The receiving governments took title to the supplies on their arrival and distributed them according to the resolutions of the UNRRA Council. The UNRRA was to be informed of the distribution procedure and was to establish in each country a UNRRA mission responsible for the administration and supervision of the relief distribution. Local labor used in the distribution process was to be paid for from the proceeds of certain supplies permitted to be sold by the UNRRA. The distribution of relief supplies was to be conducted without discrimination as to race, religion, or political affiliation, but the independence and sovereignty of the receiving countries were to be fully respected. Relief activities were conducted by the UNRRA in 17 countries.

*Medical Program of the UNRRA*

The health program of the UNRRA served first as an emergency service for the liberated countries. It had the advantage of preparation by the OFRRO in Washington and by the Technical Advisory Committee on Medical Supplies and Services of the Inter-Allied Committee in London. Among its leading medical experts were Dr. Walter A. Sawyer, director of the International Health Division of the Rockefeller Foundation in New York; Dr. Andrew Topping, deputy medical officer of Health of the London County Council; Dr. M. T. Morgan, president of the International Office of Public Health in Paris; and Dr. Melville D. Mackenzie, chairman of the Inter-Allied Technical Advisory Committee on Medical Supplies and Services.

After the First World War, in 1919 and 1920, more people died because of epidemics and communicable diseases than had lost their lives in combat and through military operations during the war. After the Second World War, the UNRRA and measures taken by the liberation armies of the Allies prevented a repetition of this sad experience.

The UNRRA's program of medical aid and sanitation pursued four goals: (1) rehabilitation of basic health services, hospitals, clinics, dispensaries, and laboratories; (2) prevention of epidemics; (3) restoration of the drug and pharmaceutical industries; and (4) provision of special assistance to war victims.[8]

UNRRA medical services made substantial contributions to the standard of medical care in the receiving countries, especially in Yugoslavia, Poland, China, and India. Most medical supplies came from the United States, Great Britain, and Canada, although Mexico later provided hospital textiles and equipment. Large quantities of drugs including penicillin, sulfa drugs, insulin, aspirin, diphtheria toxoid and antitoxin, and typhus serum were used to prevent the outbreak of epidemics. Malaria swamps in several countries, in particular Greece, Italy, and North Africa, were sprayed by aircraft, and epidemics were prevented in the displaced persons camps in Germany, Austria, and Italy. In Yugoslavia in 1946, a threatening outbreak of diphtheria was curbed by the vaccination of 3.5 million children. In 1946 in Italy, Poland, and China, vaccination programs against typhus, cholera, and the plague for children and adults, along with rat poisoning and sanitation provisions, prevented menacing major epidemics. In all countries invaded during the war, venereal diseases threatened to approach epidemic proportions; the UNRRA's medical services provided penicillin and arsenicals so that substantial improvement was achieved, although not all patients could be cured. The incidence of tuberculosis had increased greatly during the war, but toward the end of the war, streptomycin was developed and the UNRRA was able to send modest quantities to European countries to help fight tuberculosis. When infantile paralysis broke out in Czechoslovakia in the autumn of 1945, the UNRRA was able to ship fifty iron lungs from London, thus helping to save many patients. The UNRRA also trained medical personnel from liberated countries in England, Canada, Sweden, Switzerland, and the United States.

The importance of these health services was evident from the decision of the UNRRA Council that they should be extended, in the spring of 1946, even to the enemy and ex-enemy countries.

*Industrial Rehabilitation Under the UNRRA*

The UNRRA's aid in industrial rehabilitation consisted primarily of the reconstruction of transportation facilities; provision of equipment for railways, highway reconstruction, bridges and water transport materials (including coal and fuel in countries short of them); delivery of materials for the restoration of public utilities, gas and electricity, and telephone equipment; and the restoration of a few basic industries to enable the liberated countries to rebuild their normal economic functions. Some coal and other fuel was brought from Europe, but most was shipped at considerable cost from Canada and the United States. For inland transport, trucks, trailers, and motor vehicles were bought, largely from military surplus materials of the Allied armies. Gasworks, electric power plants, power generating stations, and water dispensation materials were provided as vitally necessary for the welfare of the civilian population. Mining machinery was supplied to European and Asian countries to enable the resumption of mining operations. Another urgent requirement was the restoration of housing.

*Agricultural Rehabilitation Under the UNRRA*

The UNRRA delivered to the liberated nations seeds, fertilizer, and agricultural equipment, which had to be timed to arrive before the seeding season. This was frequently very difficult, especially in mainland China, because of transportation problems. In most of the invaded countries, tractors and draft animals had been stolen or destroyed by the occupying armies. Seeds and most of the fertilizer were supplied from European countries, although some were shipped from Latin America. Pesticides were needed mainly in Italy and Greece, where production of them had been disrupted by the war; they were produced primarily in England. Fisheries in all the liberated countries were in severe need because their fishing fleets had been either destroyed or stolen. The UNRRA had to purchase fishing boats and fishery equipment from Europe and the west coast of the United States.

Among the UNRRA staff, there was no consensus on whether the UNRRA should set up professional schools and research institutes in the liberated countries. In the spring of 1946, however, the UNRRA Council decided that educational materials for schools and training facilities in health, social welfare, and agricultural and industrial construction should be supplied by the UNRRA to the liberated countries as a part of its rehabilitation services.[9] These supplies, the nucleus of the educational and training activities in several countries, were transferred to UNESCO and voluntary agencies when UNRRA operations ceased.

### UNRRA Social Welfare Services

Although several members of the UNRRA Council believed that all the relief and rehabilitation activities of the organization were concerned with welfare, in early 1946 the Council approved a special standing committee on welfare and added a welfare division to its administrative headquarters to serve as liaison with UNRRA missions, field offices, and voluntary agencies cooperating with the UNRRA. In March 1946, the welfare division was merged with the rehabilitation division in London. During the following years, the division was occupied primarily with aid to displaced persons in Germany, Austria, Italy, Greece, and North Africa, and later in China. The welfare staff of the UNRRA provided food, medical services, and transportation to the displaced persons and assisted local public and private agencies which also served these unfortunate victims of the war. The UNRRA established training programs in Central Europe, Italy, and Greece, and later in China, for the displaced populations. Its relief activities included child feeding, child care centers, and protective services for children and orphans.[10] At the conclusion of UNRRA services, these activities were transferred to the United Nations International Children's Emergency Fund (UNICEF), which was established by the United Nations at the urgent request of UNRRA and was originally financed by the transfer of remaining UNRRA resources.

In 1946, the welfare division of the UNRRA suggested the establishment of a fellowship program under which selected persons from the liberated countries and from Italy, Austria, and Albania were invited to England, Canada, the United States, and Switzerland to receive training in the fields of health services, welfare, public administration, agriculture, and industrial rehabilitation so that they could supplement UNRRA aid processes on returning to their native countries.

### Voluntary Agencies and the UNRRA

The cooperation of voluntary religious and humanitarian agencies with the UNRRA was an essential element of its services. Such organizations made substantial contributions to its supplies and personnel, and supplemented UNRRA activities with their own programs, particularly in the field of aid to displaced persons. It was agreed that foreign voluntary agencies should operate within the UNRRA program only with the consent of the director-general of the UNRRA. At the outset, negotiations about the methods of cooperation were difficult, since several governments preferred to make their own arrangements with the private organizations rather than to work within the international framework of the UNRRA. After the establishment of local UNRRA missions, however, reasonable cooperation was achieved.

The most elaborate use of foreign voluntary agencies was made in Germany in the program for the millions of displaced persons, after the Allied armies delegated that responsibility to the UNRRA in 1944. In these operations, the British, French, Belgian, and Dutch Red Cross Societies remained largely independent; the American National Red Cross withdrew its personnel, but transferred some to the UNRRA. Serious political disagreements about the use of voluntary agencies developed with the Soviet Union and the newly constituted communist governments in Eastern Europe, forcing the UNRRA to discontinue its cooperation with private agencies in those countries.

In general, however, the cooperation of the UNRRA, as an international government agency, with private, voluntary welfare organizations was a remarkable success. American organizations which participated include the Red Cross, Roman Catholic agencies, the Unitarian Service Committee, the Congregational Christian Service Committee, the American Friends Service Committee, the American Joint Distribution Committee, and the Brethren Service Committee. Cooperation with private social agencies also succeeded in England, Canada, the Latin American countries, Czechoslovakia, Hungary, Poland, Italy, and Greece, and later in China. It substantially increased the aid available to the deprived native populations and especially to displaced persons in these countries.[11]

### Field Operations of the UNRRA

While UNRRA relief operations were limited primarily to Allied countries which had been invaded by the Axis powers, the UNRRA Council decided in 1946 to give assistance to some of the former enemy countries, mainly Austria and Italy. Western European countries which had been occupied by the Nazis—France, Belgium, the Netherlands, Denmark, and Norway—were still in the possession of foreign exchange and did not apply for UNRRA relief.[12]

The first major field operation of the UNRRA in Europe developed in the Balkan countries. The UNRRA took over from the Middle East Relief and Rehabilitation Agency the responsibility for providing relief to local agencies in Greece, Yugoslavia, and Albania. The relief included medical services for the prevention of epidemics, welfare services, and repatriation of the many displaced persons. It was also necessary to ship special supplies to prevent black market exploitation of the desperate, starving population and to start emergency rehabilitation of agriculture, industries, transportation, and public utilities. Greece, a largely agricultural country which depended on imports, had been devastated by the Nazi and Italian occupation and conflict with resistance groups. Its vital shipping industry had been deprived of 75 percent of its vessels; its finances were ruined; its populace was politically divided; and shortly after liberation from the enemy forces, in December 1944, civil war broke out. Despite these conditions, the UNRRA began relief operations immediately. But as a neutral, impartial international organization, it faced hostility from all factions and received little support from the changing governments, which tried to use UNRRA supplies to bribe their supporters. The UNRRA mission assisted the destitute population by distributing food and clothing, since the native authorities were unable to handle this relief. Agricultural rehabilitation was encouraged through the import of mules, donkeys, horses, cows, and agricultural equipment such as tractors, seeds, fertilizer, and pesticides. Welfare services in Greece included the repatriation of numerous refugees from Palestine and North Africa. Health services needed total renewal: there was a great need for physicians, nurses, hospitals, dispensaries, and clinics as well as for medicines and supplies. UNRRA opened child care centers, schools, hospitals, and clinics and developed training courses for doctors, nurses, and auxiliary personnel.

Four years of Nazi occupation and ferocious civil war had destroyed most of Yugoslavia when Marshal Tito liberated that country in late 1944. The people in the mountainous regions faced starvation because the Nazi and Italian forces had destroyed farms, railroads, bridges, and water mains and had stolen livestock and machinery. UNRRA relief operations were delayed by political suspicion; Yugoslavia requested no services, only supplies. Nevertheless, the UNRRA carried out a successful campaign against malaria and typhus, established hospitals and clinics to provide plastic surgery for war victims, and rebuilt the transportation system, which was a prerequisite for the industrial reconstruction of the country. Large quantities of foodstuffs, clothing, coal, coke, and oil brought in by the UNRRA ended the starvation of people and animals which had occurred during the first year of liberation.

Similar conditions were faced by the UNRRA in Albania. Here, the

UNRRA mission faced even more hostility from the communist government and part of the population, which delayed effective relief action. A
crisis arose in November 1946, when two members of the UNRRA mission were wrongly accused of participation in an act of sabotage at the
Lake Maliq. Only after a strong complaint by mission chief Peter Floud
to the prime minister, in which Floud threatened to withdraw the entire
UNRRA mission, was the dispute settled. UNRRA medical services prevented a typhoid epidemic and fostered agricultural rehabilitation in
Albania.

Poland was the most ravaged European country at the conclusion
of the Second World War. Its railroads, power stations, highways, and
bridges had been destroyed, its ports made unusable, its factories
stripped of machinery or burned, its livestock killed. Over six million
Poles had died in the war, and at least as many had been deported as slave
laborers to Germany and to concentration camps. Almost the entire
Jewish population had been murdered by the Nazis. The eastern part of
Poland was annexed by the Russians. The western (German) provinces
of Pomerania, Silesia, Poznan, and part of East Prussia were transferred
to Poland as compensation for its loss of the eastern provinces, but most
of the German population had fled. At the time of its liberation, Poland
was occupied by Soviet armies. The first request for UNRRA relief had
been made by the Polish government-in-exile in London; but the establishment in July 1944 of a communist government in Warsaw with the
support of the Russian army made it difficult for the UNRRA to set up
relief activities without violating neutrality. In the fall of 1945, a UNRRA
mission under Canadian brigadier Charles Drury was begun in Warsaw,
and food shipments, medical supplies, trucks, and transportation materials started arriving from the port of Constanza on the Black Sea. After
the restoration of the Baltic ports of Danzig, Gdynia, and Stettin, transportation of relief supplies became easier. Large numbers of displaced
Poles were repatriated from Germany and Austria. Difficulties arose when
the Polish vice-premier, Wladyslaw Gomulka, accused the UNNRA of
using its food distribution as a political weapon.

To prevent widespread starvation, the UNRRA brought large
masses of bread grains, fats, meat, oils, and dairy products to Poland,
restored the railroads and the destroyed bridges, and raised the barges
sunken in the rivers. It supplied thousands of trucks and trailers, mainly
from Canadian army surplus, enabling Poland to use the rich coal fields
of the newly acquired province of Silesia for the reconstruction of its
destroyed industries.

During the winter of 1945–46, UNRRA medical services prevented
a threatened typhus epidemic and enabled Polish physicians to become
acquainted with newly developed medicines. There were some difficulties

caused by the lack of adequate storage facilities for the medicines, linguistic problems in identifying proper medicines, and mix-ups in transportation of supplies (for example, deep-sea diving material was sent to an inland hospital which had no use for it).

The major task of social services in Poland was to assist in the repatriation and resettlement of the many refugees and displaced persons, even though the Polish government had originally felt that it would not need UNRRA help in this task.[13] In 1946, the UNRRA welfare division created a Coordinating Committee of Foreign Voluntary Relief Agencies for Poland which organized a special program of child care services.

In the Soviet Union, the Ukraine and the Belorussian Republic had suffered destruction like that in Poland and Czechoslovakia during the war. Forced to flee, the Nazi armies had demolished industries and agriculture with scorched-earth tactics, flooded large parts of the country, exploded the mines and the railroads, and looted and burned the villages. Despite the obvious need for help, the establishment of UNRRA missions in Russia was delayed by the hesitancy of the Soviets to issue visas for its personnel, as most staff members were American citizens. Finally, two missions were set up for the Ukraine and Belorussia, their major function to supervise the delivery of relief supplies. Technical advice for rehabilitation was neither requested nor accepted, and field inspections were difficult because of the wide expanse of the territory and the lack of transportation. Food was distributed in the cities because the rural villages were soon considered self-supporting; it was given primarily to pregnant and nursing women, war veterans, and children. Tractors were delivered to state tractor stations, while the local soviets distributed supplies to widows, war veterans, and factory workers. Because of the threat of tuberculosis, the UNRRA distributed drugs, medicines, chemicals, and hospital equipment. Obtaining proper publicity for the UNRRA program proved to be difficult because the authorities did not wish to give credit to the international help. The UNRRA program in Russia terminated in June 1947.

In Italy, an Axis country during the war, the Allied armies defeated Benito Mussolini's troops in Sicily and Southern Italy in 1944; they advanced to the Pisa-Rimini line, but the northern part of Italy was still held by the Nazi armies. In February 1944, the UNRRA decided, upon the request of the United States and Great Britain, to undertake the responsibility for displaced persons held in camps in Southern Italy. UNRRA observers reported in the summer of 1944 the need for food and medical services among refugees, displaced persons, and nursing and expectant mothers and children in the Italian population, as well as the need to secure the repatriation of the displaced persons. UNRRA Council members Russia and Yugoslavia objected strongly to any aid to the "enemy country," but the Council overruled them and voted to start a relief program in Italy. Spurgeon Milton Keeny, who had served under President Herbert Hoover as head of the American Relief Administration in Poland and Russia, was appointed chief of the UNRRA mission in Rome. The UNRRA relief program in Italy included food for mothers and children, medical services, and repatriation of refugees and displaced persons. During the war, lack of food had severely increased infant mortality and tuberculosis. Welfare agencies had been destroyed, their personnel and funds dispersed. The UNRRA established a large feeding program in cooperation with local and provincial Italian committees. The program prevented widespread starvation and malnutrition; however, it was extremely difficult to obtain shipping space because the Allied armies still needed all available tonnage.

UNRRA programs rebuilt Italian hospitals, clinics, and sanitation facilities, provided medical supplies and instruments, and helped, with support from the Rockefeller Foundation, to eliminate malaria in Sardinia. In 1946, the UNRRA assisted the returning Italian refugees whose houses had been destroyed to build new homes in rural districts, and cared for more than 100,000 displaced persons until the Italian program terminated in the summer of 1947. Keeny, the UNRRA mission chief, remained in Rome as the head of the newly created International Refugee Organization of the United Nations.[14]

Austria had been invaded by Nazi Germany in 1938 and made a part of the German Reich. Even though it was therefore an enemy country, the UNRRA Council in 1943 recognized that it was a victim of Hitler's aggression and should be considered one of the "liberated countries" after the defeat of the Nazis. When in November 1945 a new Austrian government was established and recognized by the Allies, the Austrian population was in dire need of relief. In January 1946, the UNRRA sent a mission to Vienna under Brigadier R. Parminter. The agency had to borrow food supplies that spring from the armies of the United States and Russia, and had to prevent the confiscation of all oil supplies by the Soviets, who considered them war reparations. For nearly a year, the mission chief also had to administer the displaced persons program in Austria and to face substantial difficulties: for example, the need to dismiss former Nazi collaborators; the problems caused by the joint military occupation by Britain, France, the United States, and the Soviet Union; and the inefficiency, corruption, lethargy, and maladministration among Austrian and Allied officials. Despite these problems, the UNRRA obtained food and clothing from Italy, Yugoslavia, Czechoslovakia, the United States, and Russia, after the mission and the mayor of Vienna had applied to the UNRRA for a special emergency food program. A major part of UNRRA medical supplies was used for the displaced-persons camps. Other supplies enabled Austrian physicians to resume normal operations in hospitals, clinics, and private practice. Lack of adequate transportation resulted in food being stored in warehouses instead of distributed to the suffering population; some food was stolen. Population statistics, needed for the administration of the program, were unavailable, as the Nazis had taken them to Berlin.[15]

During the war, malnutrition had tripled the incidence of tuberculosis in Austria and had greatly increased infant mortality. The UNRRA faced great caloric deficiencies in its food program. In the field of industrial rehabilitation there were also problems. Italian textile industries objected to the restoration of Austrian competitors and therefore refused to provide badly needed clothing and footwear. Even Austrian merchants held back farm machinery in warehouses in Vienna to prevent their free distribution by UNRRA to farmers in the provinces; UNRRA was finally able to enforce their distribution in the spring of 1947. Black market swindlers tried to profit by selling UNRRA supplies until the mission interfered.

Ethiopia had suffered six years of Italian aggression and occupation. Peasants had been driven from their land. The country needed agricultural and industrial reconstruction and the restoration of its educational system. After long consideration of the chances for a successful relief program in Ethiopia, the UNRRA Council decided in May 1945 to try a health and welfare training plan. Not until July 1946 was agreement reached with the Ethiopian government. The program was primarily to train hospital aides and sanitary inspectors. Relief supplies were delayed by the breakdown of the Italian-built railroads and by international dockworkers' strikes. But the UNRRA rebuilt the transportation system, restored children's institutions and hospitals, and trained agricultural experts. At the end of the mission in 1947, the UNRRA personnel were transferred to the United Nations World Health Organization.

The northwestern part of Finland—Lapland—had been invaded by a Nazi army of 200,000 men who not only did much damage but also refused to leave after an armistice had been concluded among Great Britain, Russia, and Finland. Thus, the small Finnish army was forced to evacuate the Nazi German troops in the spring of 1945. Most of the Finnish civilian population had fled before this time: 56,000 refugees to Sweden, and the remainder to southern Finland. All of them wanted to return to Lapland when it was freed in the summer of 1945. In January 1946 a UNRRA mission arrived in Helsinki, headed by Irving Fasteau, a professional American social worker. It received support from the British and United States embassies, but not from the Russian delegation. The Swedish International Relief, a Finnish relief agency (Suoma Huolto), and the Swiss International Aid (Don Suisse) also supported UNRRA relief activities in Lapland. Clothing, footwear, fishing equipment, agricultural machinery and tools, and transportation facilities were distributed or restored before the severe winter of 1946. Destroyed boats and railroads were replaced. Medical supplies helped to mitigate malnutrition, and food programs for preschool and school children were carried out, receiving some supplies from Russia.[16]

Hungary had been occupied by the Nazi armies in 1944 as a result of an insurrection against Hitler's Germany. In February 1946, upon Hungary's appeals to Washington, London, and Geneva, the UNRRA Council approved emergency relief for the liberated section of Hungary. The Jewish population of Hungary, part of which had escaped mass murder by the Nazis, was in a desperate condition. The entire Hungarian population had suffered the ravages of the war, the bombing of the cities, and the loss of livestock in the rural regions. When the UNRRA mission under the leadership of Stanley Sommer arrived in Budapest in April 1946, food rationing was necessary in the cities. UNRRA supplies helped feed pregnant women, nursing mothers, children, and the aged, and later those who did heavy labor. Medical supplies were distributed to hospitals and clinics. Clothing for the destitute Jewish citizens was brought in by the American Joint Distribution Committee.

### The Far Eastern Relief Program

China relief started in November 1944, when a small UNRRA staff group was sent to Chungking, China's temporary wartime capital, during the Japanese occupation. In November 1945, the first relief supplies arrived in Shanghai. The territory occupied by the Japanese armies was about as large as that occupied by the Axis powers in Europe, but the Chinese population affected by the occupation was much larger. During the Japanese occupation of Manchuria in 1931, the Chinese population had suffered from famine, epidemics, and civilian strife. During the war, millions of Chinese were forced to flee from their homes and provinces, large areas of China were flooded as a result of Japanese military actions, food shortages assumed famine dimensions, and railways, roads, bridges, and waterways were destroyed.[17]

UNRRA relief operations were directed mainly toward the 260 million people in the Chinese provinces which had been occupied by the Japanese armies. There was acute danger of mass starvation, and no relief organization existed which could prevent a disaster. There were neither trained personnel nor any operating institutions. Before the UNRRA relief operation began, the Chinese government (Kuomintang) requested relief supplies amounting to $945 million and 2,200 foreign experts. These demands far exceeded the UNRRA's resources. In 1945, the Kuomintang organized the Chinese National Relief and Rehabilitation Administration, modeled on the UNRRA, to coordinate UNRRA operations in China. After the outbreak of civil war in China, the communist forces established a rival Communist Liberated Areas Relief Administration for their territories; UNRRA, as a neutral organization, had to cooperate with both agencies. Voluntary relief agencies of several countries helped with emergency relief operations in China. The first emergency supplies were flown from India over the Himalaya mountains; after the sudden end of open hostilities in August 1945 (after Hiroshima), the UNRRA was able to send by sea larger supplies of food, clothing, textiles, medicine, and equipment for agricultural and industrial rehabilitation.[18] Some relief supplies were purchased from the United States Navy and Army in the Pacific area. Shanghai was the first and Hongkong the second port of entry, with other ports used later.

Transportation facilities had to be rebuilt as the first step of relief distribution. The lack of a rationing system in China and the inexperience of Chinese government officials with such a relief operation, forced the UNRRA mission to arrange for widespread free distribution of food to prevent famine and starvation.

Besides the difficulties of securing transportation, the greatest problem was the task of avoiding discrimination, after the civil war, between the population in Kuomintang and in the Communist territories, both of whom vied for UNRRA relief. Numerous UNRRA staff members were lent to the China National Relief and Rehabilitation Agency as distribution officers for the relief operations. An equitable division of relief supplies was nearly impossible, because there was no reliable estimate of the populations concerned, of the varied needs of the provinces, or of the amount of war destruction and the disruption of transportation. Particularly in the provinces of Hunan and Kwangsi, the countryside was so devastated that immediate emergency measures were necessary to avoid mass starvation. In Manchuria, clothing was badly needed to protect the people against the severe winter; industrial rehabilitation was also necessary. In the Communist territories, medical supplies, food, clothing, and transport equipment were low. Distribution of relief was severely impeded by the civil war, as was a restoration of normal economic conditions. There was rapid inflation and the entire population, most of whom were farmers, was impoverished. The eight years of the Japanese war, 1937–1945, involving military and terrorist actions, had caused enormous suffering, misery, disease, and death. About 30 million refugees had fled their homes, many having to move again and again as the Japanese armies moved forward.

Because of its limited resources, the UNRRA had to concentrate its relief operations on the most urgent needs in several provinces. Food, clothing, and medical supplies were needed most critically, especially by the masses of refugees. Group feeding stations and clothing distribution centers, temporary refugee camps, and medical dispensaries were established. But all these arrangements could not meet the tremendous needs of the people. Work relief projects played an important role in the relief operation. Over two million people were employed in river dam work, railroad restoration, and rebuilding of highways and housing projects; they were usually paid in food rather than in money. Flood control, irrigation, and drainage operations reclaimed large land areas.

UNRRA health services tried to restore public health and to open the medical schools, hospitals, and public health stations which had been closed by the Japanese. Medical supplies, including instruments, pharmaceutical production equipment, laboratories, and medical textbooks helped to restore health facilities. Even though the UNRRA could recruit for its staff only 189 of the 885 persons it needed for the medical section of the mission, it succeeded in reestablishing medical facilities and in preventing epidemics of cholera, plague, and malaria.

Industrial rehabilitation in China involved the restoration of the fishing and shipping industries. Agricultural rehabilitation was undertaken with the distribution of seeds, farm tools, fertilizer, insect control, and livestock. Internal transportation had to be restored. Food control, especially in the Yellow River Valley, was one of the most significant relief activities of the UNRRA mission. During the war, Chinese military units had blown up the southern dike of the Yellow River, drowning thousands of farmers and destroying about six million homes. After the UNRRA mission arrived, the Chinese requested that the old Yellow River bed be restored and the flooded lands reclaimed. The task would have been difficult and time-consuming even under peaceful conditions, but the outbreak of the civil war made it virtually impossible. Using 200,000 peasant workers paid with UNRRA food, the agency attempted to do the job after persuading the communist armies to let the work be done, as most of the territory was under communist control. However, the UNRRA could not complete the planned comprehensive reclamation of the valley because the communist troops would not allow the final stages of the reclamation.

At the end of UNRRA operations in China, in 1947, the agency transferred its remaining materials and personnel to the United Nations World Health Organization, International Refugee Organization, and United Nations International Children's Emergency Fund.[19]

Japanese occupation had devastated a large part of the Philippines, leaving many thousands of families without shelter, in rags, and facing starvation. The obstacle to UNRRA relief here was the fact that the United States Congress considered the American government responsible for the rehabilitation of the Philippine Islands. The United States Army had started a $100 million relief program with the assistance of the United States Foreign Economic Administration, which organized the Philippine War Relief of the United States with support of the American National Red Cross. However, in July 1945, General Douglas MacArthur informed the head of the UNRRA Southwest Pacific Area Office, Frank S. Gains, that the army wanted the UNRRA to take over the task of civilian relief. The Philippine government's inability to pay for relief put the UNRRA in a delicate position, fearing that the United States Congress would refuse to allocate the urgently needed funds for UNRRA operations, but the problem was finally solved by negotiations. The UNRRA assumed the distribution of food, clothing, footwear, textiles, and medical and sanitary supplies, and organized the restoration of the fishing industries and agricultural production.

Although Korea had not been directly involved in the fighting, it had been occupied by Japanese troops before the war and had suffered under the occupation. Thus the UNRRA approved an emergency relief operation for Korea, and a UNRRA mission arrived in Seoul under Clyde S. Sargent in June 1946. North Korea, under Russian occupation, did not permit UNRRA staff to visit that country. Emergency supplies distributed in South Korea included food, clothing, footwear, medical equipment, and tools for agricultural and industrial rehabilitation.[20]

### The UNRRA Displaced Persons Program

One of the most important UNRRA operations was caring for refugees and displaced persons. During the Second World War, in Europe alone about 21 million people had been forced to flee their native countries, had been taken by the Nazis to Germany or Austria as prisoners or slave laborers, or had been interned in displaced-persons camps. About the same number had found refuge in their own or other countries. In China and the Philippines, refugees numbered additional millions.[21]

In May 1944, when the UNRRA assumed from the Middle East Relief and Refugee Administration (Cairo) responsibility for refugees, it had to care for 40,000 Greek, Yugoslav, and Polish refugees who had escaped from the onslaught of the Axis armies in their countries. In 1945, at the end of the war, the UNRRA was responsible for over 8 million refugees and displaced persons after the first groups of them had been repatriated by the Allied armies. The major task of the UNRRA program for displaced persons was to repatriate them.

At the end of the war, almost 6 million displaced persons, slave laborers, and refugees returned on their own, often traveling long distances on foot, to their former homes. The UNRRA assisted them by establishing transient camps and providing food, clothing, and medical services. Involved nations sent repatriation officers to help the returnees. The Soviet Union and other communist countries tried to force the UNRRA missions to pressure the displaced persons to return home, but the UNRRA refused, even though this caused internal tensions with the repatriation delegates from the communist states.[22] More than half a million refugees refused to return to Russia and other communist states. Many Poles and former citizens of the Baltic states disapproved of the new communist governments and feared reprisals if they returned to Poland, Estonia, Latvia, and Lithuania. Polish Ukrainians refused to return to Russia, which had taken over the formerly Polish part of the Ukraine, because they feared punishment or even execution. Many Jewish refugees wanted to go only to Israel, since anti-Semitism in Russia, Poland, and the Baltic states would endanger their lives. Other displaced persons had married while in the camps and wished to remain in their spouses' countries. The UNRRA tried to persuade some of these refugees to return to their home countries by offering to give them food and clothing for two months after their repatriation, but had limited success.[23] Friction and disagreements between part of the UNRRA staff and the repatriation officers of several of the Allied powers resulted in disputes about the desirability and legality of enforced repatriation. However, in general, the UNRRA performed its assignment of assistance to the displaced persons with remarkable success, achieving their human rehabilitation, self-government in the refugee centers, medical care, educational progress, training, and recreation after years of terrible suffering and dehumanization.

To reunite disrupted families, the UNRRA established a central tracing bureau in Germany. The organization also provided medical services, hospitalization, and psychiatric treatment for numerous displaced persons and organized several children's centers for orphans and lost children, including those who had been taken from their parents and placed in Nazi families.

*Present-day refugee problems.* Refugee problems in the Near East and in Asia remain unsolved. The fate of the Palestinian refugees who left the country which became Israel during its war of liberation has been a highly controversial issue since 1948. Most of them followed the request of the Great Mufti, high priest of the Moslems, to leave Israel and join the armies of the Arab states to destroy Israel. A small number fled because they felt endangered by Jewish resistance groups. They have organized a number of groups—Al Fatah, the Popular Front for the Liberation of

Palestine, and others—which dominate Lebanon and carry out terrorist raids in Israel. They are able to recruit many young Arabs among the refugees in Lebanon, Syria, and the Gaza Strip, mainly because the Arab countries, after the war of 1948, never really integrated the refugee masses into their economies, but kept them in camps so that the United Nations' special agency, the United Nations Work and Relief Agency for Palestine Refugees, would provide their food, clothing, and medical services. Unfortunately, the education of the refugee children and youth was entrusted from the beginning, first under the auspices of the International Red Cross and then of the American Friends Service Committee, to Arab zealots, who taught the students to hate Israel and who prepared them for war, instead of teaching peace, which would have been the aim of the United Nations. Their terrorist activities, including the bombing of airplanes in foreign countries, the hijacking of airplanes, and indiscriminate arson attacks, create serious danger of worldwide conflict; Russia and Red China support the terrorist movement with money and weapons, while the United States' policy is generally pro-Israel.

## An Assessment of the UNRRA

Unlike the League of Nations and the International Labor Organization, which also were active in the area of social policy and social welfare, the UNRRA did not recommend measures to its member governments, but was an action organization which carried out its operation on its own. Its executive functions were entrusted to a director-general (first former New York governor Herbert H. Lehman, then former New York mayor Fiorello LaGuardia, finally United States Army Major General Lowell W. Rocks) and to the UNRRA staff, which at its peak in 1946 numbered almost 25,000 persons. Some of the difficulties they encountered have been described above. The diseased, starving, and desperate populations of the liberated countries demanded immediate attention, but the UNRRA could not build its operations upon former experience and tradition. Its international staff worked in 42 countries throughout the world, making sacrifices with admirable devotion under trying circumstances. The executive branch, in New York, was able to delegate substantial authority to its local missions and welfare and health teams.

UNRRA financial operations were based on the principle that member countries which had not suffered enemy occupation should carry the financial burden for relief activities, but that all members should share the administrative cost, contributing 1 percent of their gross national product. In the receiving countries, UNRRA relief supplies should not create national indebtedness; instead, countries with sufficient national resources should pay for the relief actions. In fact, the United States, Great Britain, and Canada together contributed 94 percent of all the funds for relief. In many other countries the agency had difficulty collecting the promised contributions; only 13 of the 48 UNRRA nations made the second financial contribution approved by the UNRRA Council.

Although some members of the UNRRA staff felt that it was desirable to transfer the UNRRA from an emergency agency to a permanent organization of the United Nations, the political frictions among the Allied powers which had developed between 1945 and 1946 induced the representatives of Great Britain and the United States to request at the UNRRA Council meeting in Rome in the fall of 1946 that UNRRA operations should be terminated. This decision was taken, although there was consensus that in several countries, the problems of relief and rehabilitation had not been solved, particularly assistance to displaced persons. At the suggestion of the Soviet Union and Norway, the Council resolved that the remaining international activities in the area of relief and rehabilitation should be transferred to the United Nations and its specialized agencies, the World Health Organization (WHO), the International Labor Organization (ILO), the International Refugee Organization (IRO), and the Food and Agriculture Organization (FAO), as well as to the Children's Emergency Fund (UNICEF) and the United Nations Educational, Scientific, and Cultural Organization (UNESCO). These transfers were carried out at the UNRRA Council meeting at Washington, D.C., in December 1946. LaGuardia resigned as director-general, and Lowell W. Rocks was elected his successor to liquidate the agency.

The work of UNRRA initiated the important role of the United Nations in the area of health, economic progress, education, cultural achievement, and social welfare. It saved millions of people throughout the world from hunger, starvation, and death, and started the countries invaded by enemy forces during the Second World War on the road to agricultural and industrial recovery and normal living conditions. It helped repatriate millions of persons and resettled other refugees and displaced persons in new homes. But the UNRRA had to face severe difficulties in its work. Its goals and functions were never clearly defined: the exact tasks of "rehabilitation" were never clearly stated. Numerous labor strikes and civil wars in Greece, Yugoslavia, and China seriously impeded UNRRA operations, as did the different points of view and policies of the Allies after the defeat of the Axis nations.

A number of nations which received from the UNRRA assistance essential to their rehabilitation became reluctant to admit later how much they had benefited from the UNRRA's international support. Even its successor organizations within the framework of the United Nations have played down the value of UNRRA operations to gain approval for themselves.

No thoughtful historian expected UNRRA to restore all the damage caused to all nations involved in the war to the extent that further reconstruction would be unnecessary. But the UNRRA achieved the rebuilding of essential transportation systems and public utilities in the liberated countries, provided food to prevent wholesale starvation, sent medical supplies, and reestablished health services.

The experience of UNRRA as an international organization was highly significant. When its member nations could no longer agree on essential policies, it was dissolved. The size of its operations and of its staff and its dependence on the repeated granting of funds in the postwar period made disagreement unavoidable. Stresses among its administration and its staff were to be expected. The few cases of inefficiency, dishonesty, or corruption in UNRRA operations were soon discovered and did not result in serious losses.[24]

Despite its brief operation, the UNRRA proved that an international organization is able to work at least as well as a national one. Its experience is valuable in view of the dire need for further global cooperation in numerous essential areas of human progress. The UNRRA's success is also documented by the fact that after its termination, a number of international agencies were set up under the auspices of the United Nations to carry on its work.

## Notes

[1]Herbert Hoover, *Relief of Belgium and Northern France: American Epic* (New York: Henry Regnery, 1959); Clarence Pickett, *For More than Bread* (Boston: Little, Brown, 1953); Howard L. Brooks, *Prisoners of Hope* (New York: Fischer, 1942); Varian Fry, *Surrender on Demand* (New York: Random House, 1945).

For an interesting survey of the development of international health and social services, with special reference to the role of Switzerland, see Emma Steiger, "Internationale Beziehungen in der sozialen Arbeit" (International Relations in Social Welfare), *Gesundheit und Wohlfahrt, Revue Suisse d'Hyene* (Zurich), 30, no. 8 (Aug. 1950), 341–72.

[2]Martin Gumpert, *Dunant, The Story of the Red Cross* (New York: Oxford University Press, 1938); Ernest P. Bicknell, *With the Red Cross in Europe* (Washington: American National Red Cross, 1938); Percy H. Epler, *The Life of Clara Barton* (New York: Macmillan, 1917), and *Clara Barton: A Story of the Red Cross* (New York: Appleton, 1918); Jeanette C. Nolan, *The Story of Clara Barton* (New York: Messner, 1962); John Maloney, *Let There Be Mercy* (New York: Doubleday, 1944).

[3]Susan T. Pettis, "American Social Work Overseas," *Encyclopedia of Social Work* (1965), pp. 90–96.

[4]Harriet E. Davis, ed., *Pioneers in World Order* (New York: Columbia University Press, 1944); Martin Hill, *The Economic and Financial Organization of the League of Nations* (Washington: Carnegie Endowment, 1946); Arthur Sweetzer, "The Non-Political Achievements of the League," *Foreign Affairs* (Oct. 1940); Carlile A. Macartney, *Refugees, The Work of the League* (London: League of Nations Union, 1936); William J. Goode, "Illegitimacy, Anomie, and Cultural Penetration,"

*American Sociological Review* (Dec. 1961), 910–25; and Elenora Chutty, "For the World's Children," *Children* (March–April 1963), 79ff.

[5]George Woodbridge, *The History of UNRRA* (New York: Columbia University Press, 1950, 3 vols.); UNRRA, *The Story of UNRRA* (Washington, D.C., 1944); National Planning Association, *UNRRA: Gateway to Recovery* (Washington, D.C., 1944); Stephen Rauschenbush, *America's Great Hope: European Recovery* (Washington, D.C.: Public Affairs Institute, 1948), pp. 35–51.

[6]Woodbridge, *History of UNRRA*, p. 247, quoting a statement of the Director General, Herbert Lehman.

[7]Clifford E. Whitman and Ted Watkins, "Headquarter Recruitment of Non-United States Nationals for UNRRA" (New York: UNRRA, 1944), p. 135.

[8]Woodbridge, *History of UNRRA*, p. 434.

[9]Ibid., pp. 20–23.

[10]Fred K. Hoehler, *Europe's Homeless Millions* (New York: Foreign Policy Association, 1946), pp. 7–17, 19–21, 54–66, 78–92.

[11]Woodbridge, *History of the UNRRA*, pp. 72, 75–78.

[12]Walter Friedlander, *Introduction to Social Welfare*, 3rd ed. (Englewood Cliffs, N.J.: Prentice-Hall, 1968), p. 533.

[13]Woodbridge, *History of the UNRRA*, p. 228.

[14]Ibid., pp. 289, 294.

[15]Ibid., pp. 261–62; John Kenneth Galbraith, *Recovery of Europe* (New York: National Planning Association, 1946), pp. 9–25.

[16]Woodbridge, *History of the UNRRA*, pp. 356–58.

[17]Ibid., pp. 371–72.

[18]Ibid., pp. 378, 382.

[19]Ibid., pp. 443–47.

[20]Ibid., pp. 410ff.

[21]Friedlander, *Introduction to Social Welfare*, p. 535; Hoehler, *Europe's Homeless Millions,* and "Displaced Persons," in George de Huzar, *Persistent International Issues* (New York: Harper & Row, 1947), pp. 41–68; Norman Bentwich, *The Refugees from Germany: 1033–1935* (London: Allen & Unwin, 1936); National Planning Association, *Europe's Uprooted People* (Washington, D.C., 1944); Jane Perry and Clark Carey, *The Role of Uprooted People in European Recovery* (Washington, D.C.: National Planning Association, 1948); and Elfan Rees, *We Strangers and Afraid* (Geneva: United Nations, 1959), and "The Refugee Problem: Joint Responsibility," *The Annals,* 329 (May 1960), 15–22.

[22]Ira Hirshman, *The Embers Still Burn* (New York: Praeger, 1948); Friedlander, *Introduction to Social Welfare*, pp. 535–36.

[23]Woodbridge, *History of the UNRRA*, pp. 515–17; Hirshman, *The Embers Still Burn.*

[24]Ibid., pp. 546, 549; Julia Henderson, "The Challenge of World-Wide Social Conditions," *The Annals,* 329 (May 1960), 1–14.

### Selected References

Bosanquet, Helen. *Social Work in London, 1869 to 1912: A History of the London Charity Organization Society.* London: J. Murray, 1914.

CURTI, MERLE, *American Philanthropy Abroad: A History.* Brunswick, N.J.: Rutgers University Press, 1948.

DAVIS, ALLAN F., AND MARY LYNN McCREE, eds., *Eighty Years at Hull House.* Chicago: Quadrangle, 1969.

DAVIS, HARRIET E., ed., *Pioneers in World Order.* New York: Columbia University Press, 1944.

DE HUZAR, GEORGE, *Persistent International Issues.* New York: Harper & Row, 1947.

DE SCHWEINITZ, KARL, *England's Road to Social Security*, 2nd ed. Philadelphia: University of Pennsylvania Press, 1943.

FRIEDLANDER, WALTER A., "The History of Charities in France," pp. 1–26 in *Individualism and Social Welfare in France.* New York: Free Press, 1962.

FRY, VARIAN, *Surrender on Demand.* New York: Random House, 1945.

GALBRAITH, JOHN KENNETH, *Recovery in Europe.* New York: National Planning Association, 1946.

GERSON, WALTER M., *Social Problems in a Changing World.* New York: Crowell, 1969.

GRAHAM, JAMES J., *The Enemies of the Poor.* New York: Random House, 1970.

GUMPERT, MARTIN, *Dunant: The Story of the Red Cross.* New York: Oxford University Press, 1938.

HENDERSON, CHARLES R., *Modern Methods of Charity.* New York: Macmillan, 1914.

HEYWOOD, JEAN S., *Children in Care: The Development of the Service for the Deprived Child.* London: Routledge & Kegan Paul, 1959.

HIRSHMAN, IRA, *The Ambers Still Burn.* New York: Praeger, 1948.

HOEHLER, FRED K., *Europe's Homeless Millions.* New York: Foreign Policy Association, 1946.

HOOVER, HERBERT, *Relief for Belgium and Northern France: American Epic.* New York: Regnery, 1957.

HOROWITZ, IRVING L., *Three Worlds of Development: The Theory and Practice of International Stratification.* New York: Oxford University Press, 1966.

INDIA PLANNING COMMISSION, *Plans and Prospects of Social Welfare in India: 1951–1961.* Delhi: Ministry of Information, 1963.

ISENBERG, IRVIN, *The Developing Nations: Poverty and Progress.* New York: Wilson, 1969.

ISHIDA, TAKASHI, *Japanese Society.* New York: Random House, 1971.

KONOPKA, GISELA, *Eduard Lindeman and Social Work Philosophy.* Minneapolis: University of Minnesota Press, 1958.

KUEHL, WARREN F., *Seeking World Order: The United States and International Organization Until 1929.* Nashville, Tenn.: Vanderbilt University Press, 1969.

LEONARD, E. M., *The Early History of English Poor Relief.* Cambridge: Cambridge University Press, 1900.

LUBOVE, ROY, *The Progressives and the Slums.* Pittsburgh: University of Pittsburgh Press, 1962.

MARSHALL, DOROTHY, *The English Poor Law in the Eighteenth Century.* London: Routledge, 1926.

McCLOY, SHELBY T., *Government Assistance in Eighteenth Century France.* Durham, N.C.: Duke University Press, 1946.

NATARAJAN, SWAMINETH, *A Century of Social Reform in India,* 2nd ed. Bombay: Asia Publishing House, 1963.

OWEN, DAVID, *English Philanthropy, 1660–1960.* Cambridge, Mass.: Harvard University Press, 1964.

PUMPHREY, RALPH E., AND MURIEL W. PUMPHREY, *The Heritage of American Social Work: Readings in Its Philosophical and Institutional Development.* New York: Columbia University Press, 1961.

RAUSCHENBUSH, STEPHEN, *America's Greatest Hope: European Recovery.* Washington, D.C.: Public Affairs Institute, 1948.

REES, ELFON, *We Strangers and Afraid.* Geneva, Switzerland: United Nations, 1959.

RICH, MARGARET E., *A Belief in People: A History of Family Social Work.* New York: Family Service Society of America, 1956.

RIDENOUR, NINA, *Mental Health in the United States: A Fifty-Year History.* Cambridge, Mass.: Harvard University Press, 1961.

SAMUELSON, KURT, *From Great Power to Welfare State: 300 Years of Swedish Social Development.* London: Allen & Unwin, 1968.

TRATTNER, WALTER I., *Crusade for the Children: A History of the National Child Labor Committee and Child Labor Reform in America.* Chicago: Quadrangle, 1970.

WOODBRIDGE, GEORGE, *The History of UNRRA,* 3 vols. New York: Columbia University Press, 1950.

# Structure of international
# social welfare operations

*2*

International social welfare organizations can be classified in four groups:

1. *Agencies of international government,* such as the United Nations itself, the UN Economic and Social Council (ECOSOC), the International Labor Organization (ILO), the World Health Organization (WHO), the United Nations Educational, Scientific, and Cultural Organization (UNESCO), the United Nations Development Program, the United Nations International Children's Emergency Fund (UNICEF), the United Nations High Commissioner for Refugees (UNHCR), the Food and Agriculture Organization (FAO), the International Development Association (IDA), and the International Bank for Reconstruction and Development (IBRD).

2. *Private (nongovernment) organizations of international character,* such as the International Red Cross, the International League of Red Cross Societies, the International Council on Social Welfare, the International Association of Schools of Social Work, the International Federation of Social Workers, World Young Women's Christian Association (World YWCA), World Alliance of Young Men's Christian Associations, (World YMCA), International Conference of Catholic Charities, Catholic International Union for Social Service, World Federation for Mental Health, Boy Scouts World Bureau, World Association of Girl Guides and Girl Scouts, Union Internationale pour l'Etude Scientifique de la Population, World ORT Union, International Association for the Scientific Study of Mental Deficiency, and International League of Societies for the Mentally Handicapped. A pioneer voluntary foreign aid society was the Aide Suisse à des Régions extra-Européennes (Zurich), supported by the Swiss government. The International Council on Social Welfare (formerly the International Conference of Social Work), founded in 1928, not only arranges international conferences on social welfare every two years, but also serves as a consultant to the Economic and Social Council of the United Nations. In 1972, the Council included 63 national committees, among them 14 African countries. The Council has its European head-

quarters in Geneva, Switzerland. The best-known international voluntary agency is the League of Red Cross, Red Crescent, and Lion and Sun Societies, headquartered in Geneva, which coordinates the services of its 112 national societies in the areas of disaster relief, aid to war prisoners, and training institutes. Other international voluntary agencies are the International Union for Child Welfare, the International Union of Family Organizations, the International Social Security Association (closely related to the International Labor Organization), and relief programs of the World Council of Churches and the World Organization for Rehabilitation Through Training. In wartime, the International Committee of the Red Cross, a group of about 25 Swiss citizens, provides services for wounded soldiers and for prisoners of war and disaster relief for civilians, at the request of the combatants.[1]

The International Council of Voluntary Agencies, with headquarters in Geneva, was founded in 1962, combining three international nongovernment coordinating organizations which help people in need. It consists of about 100 agencies. Its General Conference serves as the parliament and its Governing Board as the executive organ of the council. At its general conferences—the next is scheduled to meet in 1976—not only voluntary, but also government agencies participate and exchange their experiences. Special concerns of the council are aid to refugees, emergency measures in natural disasters, social and economic aid to developing nations, and services for migrants. The International Council of Voluntary Agencies (ICVA) is active in almost all social fields discussed in this book.[2]

In several countries, groups of young volunteers have formed who go to other countries to help out in agricultural work, language teaching, community development, and other services, at the same time establishing friendly personal and international contacts. Examples of such organizations are the International Voluntary Services (New York), Terre des Hommes (Switzerland), and the Peace Corps (United States), set up under government auspices and combined in 1972 with the Job Corps, a domestic service organization. Groups of young Germans have been going to Israel under the auspices of the Aktion Sühnezeichen (symbol of atonement) to work in kibbutzim, as a means of trying to compensate for the mass murder of Jewish people under the Nazi regime. In England, the Oxfam group organizes important aid services in natural disasters and famines. A worldwide agency to administer such voluntary groups is the International Secretariat for Volunteer Service (ISVS), headquartered in Geneva, which has a Coordinating Committee for Volunteer Service.

3. *National public agencies which serve in the international area,* such as the United States Agency for International Development (AID) in the Department of State, the United States Department of Health, Education

and Welfare, the United States Office of Child Development, and the United States Children's Bureau. There are numerous similar government agencies in other countries. Most of these agencies are essentially independent, operating without force to further the common interests of mankind in an example of constructive international cooperation.[3]

4. *Private (nongovernment) organizations in many countries which extend their health and welfare services to foreign countries,* for instance, the Swedish and Danish Redda Barmen (Red Cross), the Swiss Aid to Europe, the Dutch Interchurch Aid, Unitarian Service Committee, British and American Friends Service Committee, Catholic Community Service Council, American Jewish Joint Distribution Committee, American ORT Federation, Church World Service, Cooperative for American Relief Everywhere (CARE), and Institutes of International Education.

### The United Nations System

The United Nations is composed of six major organs: the General Assembly as its parliament, the Security Council as its peacekeeping board of directors, the Economic and Social Council, the Trusteeship Council, the International Court of Justice, and the Secretariat. The General Assembly sets the budget, elects the nonpermanent members of the Security Council, and appoints the Secretary General.[4] (See Figures 1 and 2.)

When the United Nations was founded in 1945, 51 nations were represented in the General Assembly. Since then the United Nations has become a completely different organization, encompassing 132 nations of different nature than the members of 1945. With the end of colonial empires, 60 new countries obtained membership; from 1960 to 1967, 17 other nations, 16 of them African, joined the United Nations.[5] If, as now seems possible, West and East Germany, North and South Vietnam, and North and South Korea become members, and if Japan and India become permanent members of the Security Council, further changes in the structure and operations of the United Nations can be expected.[6] Suggested changes in the organization and operation of the United Nations include the formation of small committees of Security Council members to secure peaceful settlement of threatening conflicts; the selection of five of the ten nonpermanent members of the Security Council from the so-called "middle-powers;" the establishment of criteria for future membership in the United Nations to prevent its flooding by microstates; and the establishment of a United Nations Fact-Finding Center with a modern system of fact finding and data handling, to prevent the outbreak of hostilities and to secure cease-fire and truce agreements.[7]

The United Nations was founded to keep peace among nations and

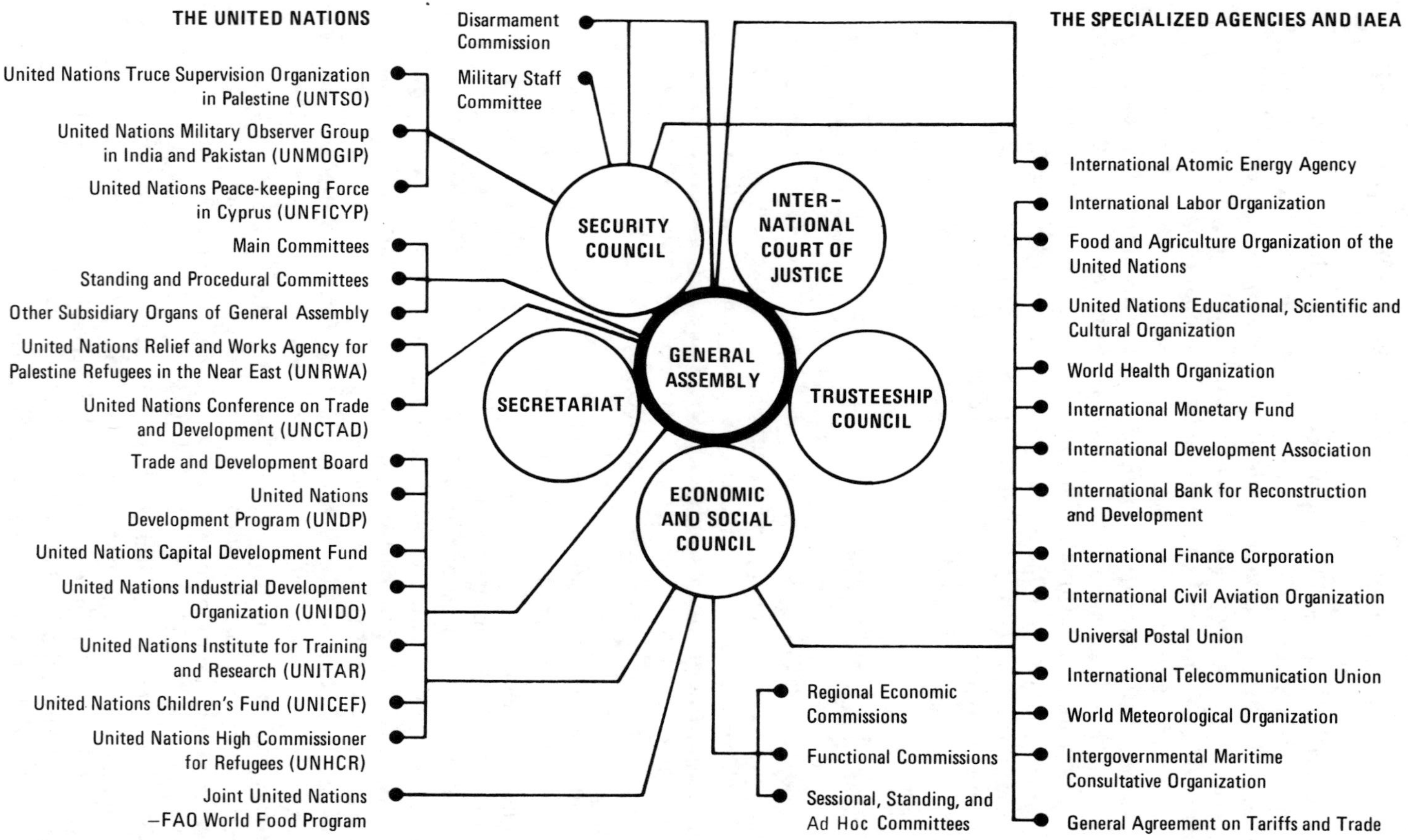

**Figure 1** The United Nations system

THE UNITED NATIONS

Disarmament Commission

Military Staff Committee

United Nations Truce Supervision Organization in Palestine (UNTSO)

United Nations Military Observer Group in India and Pakistan (UNMOGIP)

United Nations Peace-keeping Force in Cyprus (UNFICYP)

Main Committees

Standing and Procedural Committees

Other Subsidiary Organs of General Assembly

United Nations Relief and Works Agency for Palestine Refugees in the Near East (UNRWA)

United Nations Conference on Trade and Development (UNCTAD)

Trade and Development Board

United Nations Development Program (UNDP)

United Nations Capital Development Fund

United Nations Industrial Development Organization (UNIDO)

United Nations Institute for Training and Research (UNITAR)

United Nations Children's Fund (UNICEF)

United Nations High Commissioner for Refugees (UNHCR)

Joint United Nations —FAO World Food Program

SECURITY COUNCIL

INTER-NATIONAL COURT OF JUSTICE

GENERAL ASSEMBLY

TRUSTEESHIP COUNCIL

SECRETARIAT

ECONOMIC AND SOCIAL COUNCIL

Regional Economic Commissions

Functional Commissions

Sessional, Standing, and Ad Hoc Committees

THE SPECIALIZED AGENCIES AND IAEA

International Atomic Energy Agency

International Labor Organization

Food and Agriculture Organization of the United Nations

United Nations Educational, Scientific and Cultural Organization

World Health Organization

International Monetary Fund

International Development Association

International Bank for Reconstruction and Development

International Finance Corporation

International Civil Aviation Organization

Universal Postal Union

International Telecommunication Union

World Meteorological Organization

Intergovernmental Maritime Consultative Organization

General Agreement on Tariffs and Trade

32

UP BY GENERAL ASSEMBLY

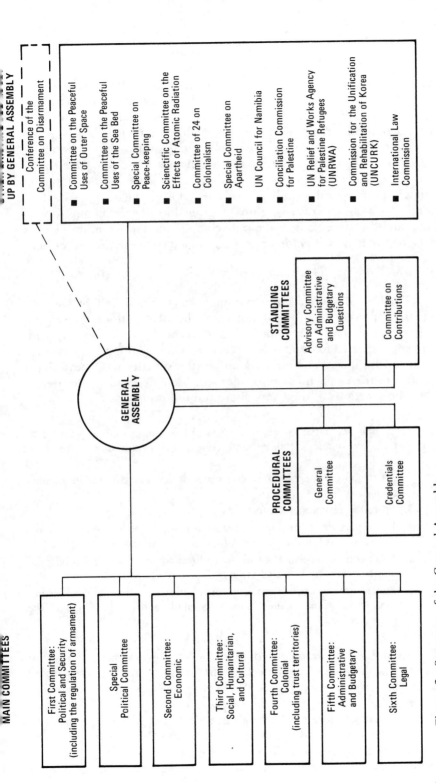

**Figure 2** Structure of the General Assembly

to foster economic and social progress for all mankind. It has been unable to fulfill these functions because the individual nations (particularly the superpowers) have denied the United Nations the resources necessary to implement its programs. Therefore, the United Nations so far has lacked the financial and legal means to prevent wars; to protect the environment against the dangers of pollution and population explosion, to curb the arms race, and to ensure peaceful social and economic development throughout the world. Another unsolved problem, the danger of a thermonuclear war, requires real global partnership.[8] Peace among the nations can be achieved only when public opinion in those nations decides that effective means of enforcement must be given to the United Nations.

*The Economic and Social Council*

The United Nations Economic and Social Council (ECOSOC) is the organization in charge of social welfare and health questions. (See Figure 3.) It is composed of 27 members elected by the General Assembly, with a president elected for a one-year term. The Council usually meets twice a year, in the spring in New York and in the summer in Geneva. Each member of the Council has one vote, and a simple majority decides.[9]

The functions of the Council are the following:

1. To make or initiate studies, reports, and recommendations on international economic, social, cultural, educational, health, and related matters
2. To promote respect for and observance of human rights and fundamental freedoms
3. To call international conferences
4. To prepare draft conventions for submission to the General Assembly on matters within the purview of the Economic and Social Council
5. To negotiate agreements with specialized agencies defining their relationship with the United Nations
6. To coordinate their activities by consultation with them and by further recommendations to the General Assembly and the members of the United Nations

Among the commissions of the Council, several have important influence in the field of social welfare: the Population Commission, the Social Commission, the Commission on Human Rights, the Commission on the Status of Women, and the Commission on Narcotic Drugs. As a rule, members of these commissions are elected after consultation with the Secretary-General and are confirmed by the Council, to guarantee that experts from essential disciplines, rather than merely political appointees, are elected. There are also various subcommissions, and an

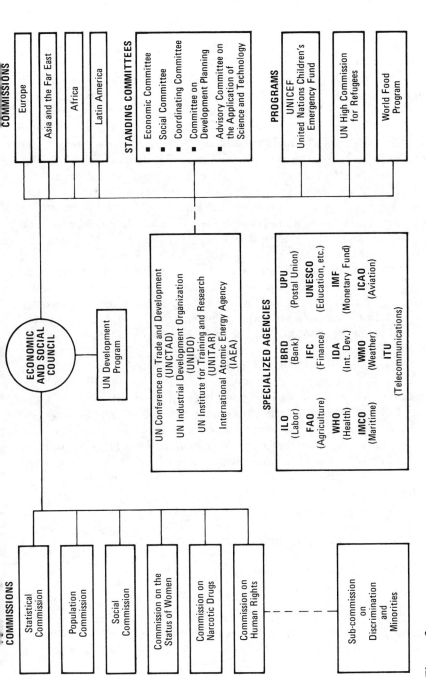

**COMMISSIONS**

Europe

Asia and the Far East

Africa

Latin America

**STANDING COMMITTEES**

- Economic Committee
- Social Committee
- Coordinating Committee
- Committee on Development Planning
- Advisory Committee on the Application of Science and Technology

**PROGRAMS**

UNICEF United Nations Children's Emergency Fund

UN High Commission for Refugees

World Food Program

**ECONOMIC AND SOCIAL COUNCIL**

UN Development Program

UN Conference on Trade and Development (UNCTAD)
UN Industrial Development Organization (UNIDO)
UN Institute for Training and Research (UNITAR)
International Atomic Energy Agency (IAEA)

**SPECIALIZED AGENCIES**

ILO (Labor)
FAO (Agriculture)
WHO (Health)
IMCO (Maritime)

IBRD (Bank)
IFC (Finance)
IDA (Int. Dev.)
WMO (Weather)
ITU (Telecommunications)

UPU (Postal Union)
UNESCO (Education, etc.)
IMF (Monetary Fund)
ICAO (Aviation)

**COMMISSIONS**

Statistical Commission

Population Commission

Social Commission

Commission on the Status of Women

Commission on Narcotic Drugs

Commission on Human Rights

Sub-commission on Discrimination and Minorities

**Figure 3**

35

important part of the Council's work is carried out by regional commissions in Europe (Geneva), in Asia and the Far East (Bangkok), in Latin America (Santiago), and in Africa (Addis Ababa).

The Economic and Social Council has several standing committees, some of which are immediately concerned with social welfare activities: the Committee for Development Planning and the Advisory Committee on the Application of Science and Technology to Development. Among the special committees, the International Narcotics Control Board inherited its functions from the League of Nations Permanent Central Opium Board and Drug Supervisory Body. Other important committees are the Governing Council of the United Nations Development Program, the Executive Board of the United Nations Children's Fund, the Executive Committee on the Program of the United Nations High Commissioner for Refugees, and the Industrial Development Board of the United Nations Industrial Development Organization.[10]

Two other influential committees of the Council are the Administrative Committee on Coordination and the Inter-Agency Consultative Board of the United Nations Development Program. Both are composed of international civil servants; their membership includes the Secretary-General of the UN and directors of the specialized social and economic agencies.

The Economic and Social Council has also established a Committee on Non-Governmental Organizations, representing over 220 private international organizations which have been granted consultative status with ECOSOC. In recent years this committee has been violently attacked for political reasons by Russia and some of the Arab countries. However, the Secretary-General of the United Nations has acknowledged that these private organizations have demonstrated at each critical point a unique ability to reach public opinion and to clarify issues involved in the interest of the United Nations.[11]

### The Specialized Agencies of the United Nations

*The International Labor Organization*

The oldest agency is the International Labor Organization (ILO). (See Fig. 4 for the ILO and other specialized agencies of the United Nations.) Founded in 1919 under the auspices of the League of Nations, it tries to encourage social legislation and economic progress. The ILO has helped in the improvement of labor–management relations, in the development of social security insurance laws, in the replacement of outdated poor relief by social assistance laws, in maternity and infant protection, in child labor legislation, and in the protection of women and

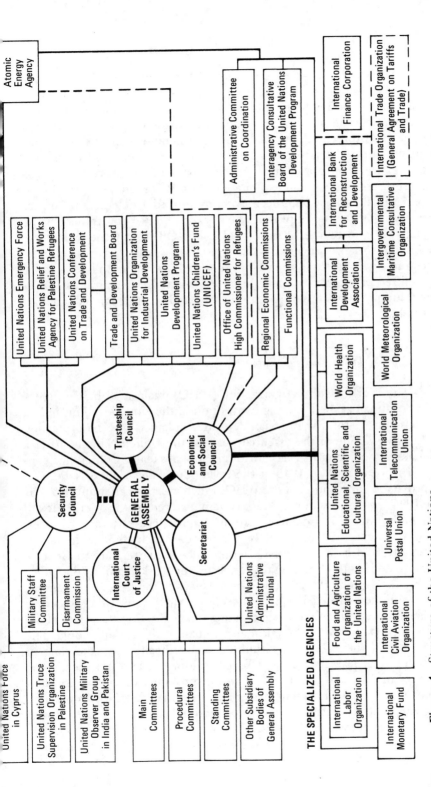

**Figure 4** Structure of the United Nations

37

illegitimate children. It tries to promote the improvement of labor conditions and to prevent human suffering and deprivation by recommending regulation of working hours, prevention of industrial injuries and unemployment, legislation to obtain an adequate living wage and sound labor supply, and protection of workers and their families against sickness and disablement. It also advocates the protection of women and young persons against damaging forms of employment, and foreign workers against discrimination and exploitation. The ILO is administered by the International Labor Conference, composed of four delegates from each member country (one employer, one worker, and two government representatives), and by the International Labor Office in Geneva. Material relating to social security and social legislation is collected from all countries and exchanged to promote progressive legislation. An international committee of experts is available for consultation; technical assistance and training fellowships can be applied for; and several regional seminars are held.[12]

## The World Health Organization

The World Health Organization (WHO) was established at the request of Brazil at the founding convention of the United Nations in San Francisco in 1945. The Brazilian delegate explained that the protection of health was one of the essential goals of the United Nations. After a preparatory meeting in Paris, an International Health Conference convened in New York in 1946 at the invitation of the United Nations to approve the constitution of the WHO, which was thereafter approved by the UN General Assembly. WHO is administered by the World Health Assembly, whose 135 member nations send delegates to annual meetings, by an executive board of 18 persons elected by the World Health Assembly, and by a Director-General. Its headquarters are in Geneva. The World Health Organization continues the work begun by the Office for Public Hygiene (Paris) under the auspices of the League of Nations, and continued during the Second World War by the United Nations Relief and Rehabilitation Administration. Its goal is the attainment of the highest possible level of physical and mental health for all people. The preamble of the WHO constitution defines "health" as "the state of complete physical, mental, and social well-being, and not merely the absence of disease or infirmity." Its major programs include the promotion of maternal and infant hygiene, nutritional diets, environmental hygiene, and campaigns against dangerous communicable diseases, mainly tuberculosis, malaria, venereal diseases, typhus, yaws, and trachoma. WHO attempts to prevent epidemics from crossing national boundaries, assists stricken countries in eradicating contagious diseases, acts as a clearinghouse for scientific information on health problems, and informs its members of the latest developments in the health sciences, such as nuclear radiation hazards and the use of new vaccines.[13] It publishes an international pharmacopoeia on drugs, medicines, and other health materials. It operates an epidemic disease warning system and recommends health regulations on international travel to prevent the spread of epidemics. WHO also advises its members on effective ways of organizing health services and dispatches on request, teams of physicians, sanitary engineers, nurses, teachers, and social workers to assist in setting up such health services. It provides funds for health workers to obtain advanced training abroad and helps various governments to improve and develop training facilities for their health personnel. WHO tries to break the infamous vicious circle, "disease breeds poverty and poverty breeds disease."

In addition to its headquarters in Rome, WHO has regional offices for Africa (Brazzaville, Congo), for South Asia (New Delhi), for the Western Mediterranean (Alexandria, Egypt), for the Western Pacific (Manila), for the Americas (the Pan American Sanitary Bureau, Washington, D.C.), and for Europe (Copenhagen). The delegates to the World Health Assembly are experts in public health. All member nations contribute to WHO's budget according to an agreed-upon scale of assessment. Beyond these contributions, WHO is assisted by the United Nations Technical Assistance Fund.[14]

Together with the World Meteorological Association, the WHO has launched atmospheric-pollution monitoring networks which are detecting background pollution in a number of countries, while the World Health Organization itself monitors urban areas with higher pollution levels.

*The Food and Agriculture Organization*

The United Nations Food and Agriculture Organization (FAO), headquartered in Rome, was established immediately after the foundation of the United Nations in 1945. Its aim is to abolish malnutrition and famine, a need which was particularly urgent at the end of World War II, by developing methods to increase food production and to better distribute agricultural and fishing products. Since progress in medical science and sanitary facilities has reduced mortality rates, it is critical that agricultural production be augmented by scientific methods. FAO furnishes technical information and instruction as well as experts for demonstration projects in crop and animal improvement, forest and fishery development, and modern methods of conservation and processing and marketing of foods. Medical research programs of FAO are coordinated under the aegis of WHO; for example, the program to control schistosomiasis in eight countries in Africa, Asia, and Latin America. In 1960 a special Freedom from Hunger Campaign under the auspices of FAO and supported by 71 national committees and over 100 private voluntary organizations raised over $221 million.

FAO encourages the conservation of soils, plants, animals, and marine life. Under the International Plant Protection Convention, it has set up a regional network of agencies which cooperate in controlling pests and diseases, and a computerized data bank to match fertilizer and herbicide application to soil properties for rational use and for the prevention of pollution. FAO furthermore promotes the establishment of regional gene banks to preserve seed and plant collections under the most favorable conditions.

The administration of FAO is directed by a biannual conference which meets in Rome and consists of delegates of all member nations, a council of 37 members elected by the conference as managing board, and a Director-General elected by the conference for a four-year term. Funds for FAO action programs are derived mainly from the United Nations Development Program; it has joint responsibility with the United Nations for the World Food Program.[15]

### The United Nations International Children's Fund

The United Nations International Children's Emergency Fund was the heir of UNRRA when its operations were ended by a decision of the UN Security Council in 1946; it received most of the remaining funds of UNRRA. It has since been funded by voluntary contributions from governments, foundations, and private resources and by its own fund-raising through sales of greeting cards and other publications. UNICEF headquarters are at the United Nations building in New York. Its executive board consists of 30 members and its executive director is appointed by the Secretary-General of the United Nations in consultation with the UNICEF executive board. The executive board reports annually to the UN General Assembly and to the Economic and Social Council. While UNICEF was founded as an emergency agency to help the devastated countries after the Second World War, in 1953 it was transformed into a permanent program by decision of the General Assembly. Its assignment is to conduct long-range projects of child health protection and training of child welfare personnel.

UNICEF operations are sponsored jointly by the host countries, by the United Nations itself, and by the World Health Organization and the

Food and Agriculture Organization. At the outset, UNICEF continued UNRRA's mass feeding programs for children in the countries which had suffered the most destruction during the war. Later it directed its efforts toward reducing diseases of children, such as tuberculosis, malaria, yaws, leprosy, and intestinal infections, as well as eliminating malnutrition through school feeding and special dietary programs. It also supported family and child welfare services and various vocational training programs for children and adolescents. In cases of natural disaster such as earthquakes, floods, and volcanic eruptions, UNICEF provides emergency relief—food, clothing, drugs, and shelter—to alleviate the burden on local welfare services.[16]

UNICEF supported the establishment of the International Children's Center (Paris) which, in cooperation with the Sorbonne University, provides training, research, and demonstration projects for physicians, nurses, physiotherapists, and social workers. It also maintains a postgraduate training center for doctors and nurses at the All-Indian Institute for Health and Public Hygiene (Calcutta).[17]

The work of UNICEF is reviewed annually by the Social and Economic Council and the UN General Assembly. Significant examples of the productive operations of UNICEF are described in a report by Dwight H. Ferguson on his experiences in Asia and South America during 1969 and 1970, observing UNICEF programs in India, Hong Kong, Taiwan, Manila, and in the Andes in South America. The main causes of the success of these programs were UNICEF's genuine concern for children and their families and the fact that the operations involved local participation and met the expressed, urgent needs of the people. At the celebration of the twenty-fifth anniversary of the United Nations, Secretary-General U Thant emphasized that UNICEF had helped over 100 developing countries to ensure for their children better health, nutrition, and education. Despite such successes, however, the need for further measures remains urgent. Half of the children in these countries never attend school, only two of twelve children complete elementary school, and there are now more sick, undernourished, and uneducated children in the world than there were in 1960.[18]

### High Commissioner for Refugees

When the UNRRA was forced to terminate its operations in 1946, millions of refugees and displaced persons still needed settlement or repatriation. Therefore, the UN General Assembly approved the establishment of an International Refugee Organization. This organization, along with the Economic and Social Council, succeeded despite serious difficulties and political obstacles in providing assistance to 1.6 million refugees, in resettling about 1 million displaced persons, and in repatriating many others. In 1951 the International Refugee Organization was liquidated, but the General Assembly of the United Nations had decided in 1949 to set up a High Commissioner for Refugees, whose office began operations in Geneva in 1951. The High Commissioner is nominated by the Secretary-General of the United Nations and elected by the General Assembly.

The office was originally established for a period of three years, but it has since been renewed for five-year periods. The High Commissioner is supported by an executive committee of 30 members. Its budget is financed by voluntary contributions from governments and private groups, and during the World Refugee Year (1959–60) intensified collections were made to assist in the settlement of numerous refugees. (The office of the High Commissioner for Refugees (UNHCR), as well as UNICEF and the United Nations Development Program, are direct sections of the United Nations, while the WHO, FAO, and ILO are independent specialized agencies.)

In addition to establishing the office of the High Commissioner for Refugees, the United Nations, after the 1948 war in Palestine, set up a relief fund for Palestinian refugees and in 1949 established a special organization, the United Nations Relief and Works Agency for Palestine Refugees (UNRWA). This agency was assigned the task of providing food, shelter, health services, and other basic rations to the Palestinian refugees who had fled from Israel during and immediately after the war. They were maintained in camps in the Gaza Strip under Egyptian auspices, and also in Jordan, Lebanon, and Syria. Preceding the setup of the UNRWA, the International Red Cross and the American and British Friends Service Committees had supported the refugees. However, there is substantial controversy over whether these services were given in the sense of the United Nations Charter—to maintain peaceful relations in the Middle East—since most of the administrative and teaching personnel were actually preparing the refugees for a revenge war, rather than for peace.[19] Later, vocational training programs were organized with the goal of making the refugees, whose number increased from 800,000 to nearly 2 million, self-supporting. However, no effective integration or settlement of the refugees in their Arab host countries was achieved.

The director of the UNRWA, called the Commissioner-General, is appointed by the Secretary-General of the United Nations. He is assisted by an advisory commission consisting of representatives from Arab governments in the Middle East and from Belgium, France, Turkey, the United Kingdom, and the United States. The agency's budget is voted by the UN General Assembly, which has recently been reluctant to approve it, particularly since the so-called "Six Day War" of 1967, which created many new refugees, mainly living in Jordan. These refugees have formed guerrilla terrorist groups which have bombed and hijacked planes in several countries, practices condemned by the United Nations.

Another short-term organization, set up in 1950 after the Korean War, was the United Nations Korean Reconstruction Agency (UNKRA), which provided emergency relief and reconstruction assistance to devastated areas of Korea from 1950 to 1959. Aid for the program was provided on a voluntary basis by 39 countries.[20]

The work of the High Commissioner for Refugees was increased when new masses of refugees fled from Hungary to Austria and Yugoslavia, masses of Chinese fled from North China to Hong Kong, and recently when refugees from several African nations fled to neighboring states.[21]

### The UN Educational, Scientific, and Cultural Organization

The United Nations Educational, Scientific, and Cultural Organization (UNESCO) was established in London in 1945 to promote collaboration between nations through education, science, and cultural activities as a contribution to peace and security. Members of the United Nations automatically become members of UNESCO; other nations can be elected to membership by a two-thirds vote of the General Conference of UNESCO upon the recommendation of its executive board and approval of the UN Economic and Social Council. The General Conference elects the Director-General and an executive board of 18 members. Headquarters are in Paris. (See Fig. 5.)

The functions of UNESCO include the collection, analysis, and dissemination of material in the areas of education, science, and culture. UNESCO invites numerous experts to conferences and seminars, promoting international cooperation and fostering education on all levels, literacy campaigns, and research in community development and social planning. It organizes studies to develop arid and semi-arid regions of the world, often in cooperation with the Food and Agriculture Organization and the United Nations Development Program. UNESCO promotes progress in education, human values, and social behavior. It works toward a world community by promoting special projects such as international schools, camps, youth conferences, children's villages, and music festivals. It makes use of constructive, peaceful technical achievements, as well as the findings of cultural anthropology, psychology, and sociology, to develop adult education and encourage creative arts and scientific

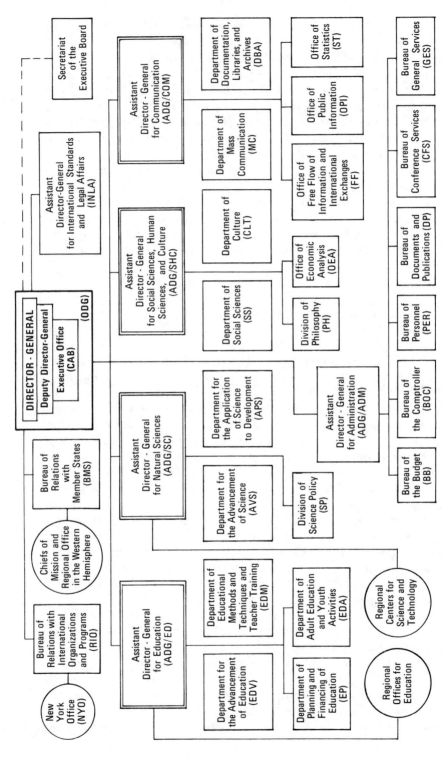

**Figure 5** Structure of the UNESCO Secretariat

44

research, always with strict objectivity toward the diverse indigenous cultural and religious values. The principles of UNESCO include a sincere belief in equal educational opportunities for all human beings, the unrestricted pursuit of truth, and free exchange of knowledge and ideas. UNESCO's international activities to promote education for justice, liberty, and mutual understanding; to spread cultural and scientific knowledge, and to overcome racial prejudice and political tensions are essential for world peace. Although UNESCO lacks the funds to establish separate research institutes, it supports such international institutions as the Zoological Station at Naples and the High Altitude Research Stations in Switzerland.[22]

As early as 1949 UNESCO sponsored the foundation of the International Union for the Conservation of Nature. Since 1961 UNESCO has had a special ecology and conservation section which has carried on extensive scientific research dealing with oceans, humid tropics, and arid zones. In 1968 UNESCO organized the International Conference on the Scientific Basis for Rational Use and Conservation of the Biosphere. The Inter-Governmental Maritime Consultation Organization is responsible for placing restraints on contamination of the oceans by ships and other equipment. The International Civil Aviation Organization is presently studying the problem of sonic boom caused by supersonic aircraft.

1970 was designated as International Education Year by the UN General Assembly. On that occasion, René Matheu, Director-General of UNESCO, reminded member nations that in many countries education is in crisis; that the elements of education are poorly integrated; that elementary schools, high schools, colleges, and universities are often isolated institutions; that one-third of the world's people are illiterate; and that the idea of lifelong education is still unrealized.[23] UNESCO has much work ahead.

### The United Nations Technical Assistance Program

Following the example of President Harry Truman's Point Four Program (now under the Agency for International Development [AID] in the Department of State), which promoted agriculture and natural resources, health, education, welfare, industry, and government services at the request of foreign nations, the Economic and Social Council of the United Nations suggested to the General Assembly in 1948 that it establish a similar international program under UN auspices. The program was set up with moderate funds and the stipulation that assistance should be rendered only to meet urgent needs at the request of the governments concerned. Host countries were expected to contribute substantially to

the operation. The first emergency relief under the program was given
to India and Pakistan, which had become independent. Projects were to
be carried out by the Food and Agriculture Organization, the World
Health Organization, the United Nations International Children's Emergency Fund, and other specialized agencies of the United Nations.[24] It
soon became evident that the need for such aid was much larger than
originally anticipated. As soon as 1949, the Economic and Social Council
with the approval of the General Assembly established the Expanded
Program of Technical Assistance (EPTA, now merged with the United
Nations Development Program), funded by voluntary extra-budgetary
contributions of UN members and of the specialized agencies. The goal
of EPTA is to provide to developing countries, in a cooperative program,
the technical knowledge of the United Nations and its specialized agencies as the basis for an attack on poverty, malnutrition, disease, igno-
rance, and economic backwardness. The program includes planning of
economic and technical development, organization of public services,
development of trade unions and cooperatives, vocational and management training, help in modern agricultural methods, fisheries and for-
estry, animal husbandry, education, public health services, disease
control, transportation and communication systems, and civil aviation.
Skills of the industrial nations were to be brought to the developing
nations by experts who would work with their opposite numbers in the
new nations. Fellowships were made available so that persons from developing nations could take advanced training in the industrial countries and
could learn from international experts.

Pledges for voluntary contributions for the EPTA program are collected during the annual session of the UN General Assembly. The Economic and Social Council set up a Technical Assistance Committee to
supervise the program, with a Technical Assistance Board composed of
the administrative heads of United Nations technical assistance programs
and specialized agencies. Since 1952, the UN Secretary-General has been
the executive chairman of the board. He appoints resident representatives of the EPTA in countries which have large-scale programs; they
coordinate the activities of the various organizations.

The objective of the EPTA is to strengthen the national economy
and the independence of those countries which apply for assistance.
EPTA programs must not interfere with the internal affairs of the host
country and must be allocated without consideration of the color, race,
and religion of its population. Countries requesting help from the Expanded Technical Assistance Program prepare data establishing their
needs and the type of measures requested for a solution of the problems.

During the operation of the program, it became evident that governments of developing nations needed to strengthen their administra-

tions because government functions had increased, and the public sector had to assume new obligations. Therefore, the UN General Assembly in 1958 established an experimental program called Operational, Executive and Administrative Personnel (OPEX) under which the United Nations sends senior administrators of developed countries on short-term assignments to developing countries, to assist in the organization of civil service systems and to strengthen administration in key areas such as economic planning. Their travel costs were paid from technical assistance funds which supplemented their low local salaries. Under the Expanded Technical Assistance Program, training grants were allocated to countries in Asia and Africa for the education of social workers in rural villages, to serve in public assistance, child welfare services, elementary and health education, nursing, home economic and sanitary services, and midwifery. In India, three-woman teams of social village workers were developed; one worker gave nursing and midwifery service, a second assisted in elementary education and taught crafts and adult literacy classes, and the third worked with children, primarily of toddler age, and set up a child care center. In village improvement work such as this, Peace Corps volunteers from the United States and other countries have also rendered valuable help.

The Economic and Social Council of the United Nations and its Social Commission have emphasized that the training of professional social workers and of auxiliary personnel for the social services and for community development is an essential element of the Technical Assistance Program. They encourage self-help activities and improve health and living standards, dietary standards, and public social services. International experiences have confirmed the value of this program.[25]

### Financial Aspects of Technical Assistance

During the period of preparation for the founding of the United Nations, a monetary and financial conference met at Breton Woods, New Hampshire, under the leadership of Lord John Meynard Keynes and Harry Dexter White. The conference led to the setting up of the International Monetary Fund and of the International Bank for Reconstruction and Development (IBRD), now called the World Bank. The aim of the Fund was to preserve the currencies of its members, with a pool of foreign exchange to avoid difficulties in maintaining a system of currency management. However, the Fund was unable to deal with the economic problems of the postwar world; in Europe, the Marshall Plan was needed to help restore the war-torn countries. The Fund was unable to establish sound economic conditions in the developing countries, also.

The International Bank for Reconstruction and Development, whose capital has grown from $10 billion to over $24 billion, has used only about 10 percent of its subscribed capital, selling bonds to underwrite its major operations. While in its first years the Bank used its funds for reconstruction in Europe, it now invests its capital for economic development in about 80 countries; the investments are guaranteed by the receiving governments. Applications are carefully studied with regard to the countries' economic conditions; political considerations are not important. The World Bank has established an Economic Development Institute, an advisory service to governments. The Bank succeeded in settling serious disputes between Pakistan and India over the waters of the Indus River.

An affiliate of the Bank is the International Finance Corporation, founded in 1956 at the suggestion of the United States to make loans to private enterprises. Another affiliate is the International Development Association (IDA), which is able to make loans to its members under less stringent conditions than those of the World Bank. Credits are given for five-year terms, with amortization after ten years. Loans are for the purpose of improving the economic infrastructure of the receiving countries. They are important because many developing countries cannot obtain loans on commercial terms.[26]

The International Development Association obtains its funds from the initial subscriptions of its members, from periodic replenishments from transfers of income from the World Bank, and from income accumulated by its own funds. The contributing membership consists of Australia, Austria, Belgium, Canada, Denmark, Finland, France, Germany, Italy, Japan, Kuwait, Luxembourg, the Netherlands, Norway, South Africa, Sweden, the United Kingdom, and the United States. However, 86 countries are on the receiving membership list. Its close connection with the World Bank is secured by the fact that its president serves also as president of the International Monetary Fund. IDA's board of governors is composed of one member from each member nation (usually the finance minister or the governor of its central bank). IDA has 20 executive directors, of whom 5 are appointed by the 5 largest shareholders and 15 are elected by the other shareholders for two-year terms. There is no veto power. The staff of IDA is chosen on the basis of professional competence, not political considerations; over 70 nations are represented. IDA loans are given, in general, to countries poorer than those aided by the World Bank. Nevertheless, the projects it supports still need to be economically and technically sound and of high priority for the economic development of the nation. Loans have been given to India, Pakistan, Taiwan, Ceylon, Sudan, and Turkey; to six other African countries; and to Papua and New Guinea. They were used for home construction and factories, harbor and railroad construction, and building of electric generators, water systems, 593 schools and 37 teachers' colleges, and 8 agricultural universities in Africa, Asia, and Latin America.[27]

In contrast to the interest-free loans of the International Development Association, the loans of the World Bank Group carry annual interest of 7 percent. Most of these loans have been granted for construction of railways, ports, power facilities, and highways. Recently, Robert McNamara, president of both organizations, has required that the World Bank Group give higher priority to projects which would substantially reduce unemployment and underemployment in the developing countries and which would serve the poorest groups in these countries rather than the elite and the wealthy classes. Among the policy changes devised are (1) the assumption of the risks of failure of projects receiving IDA loans, especially of rural improvement projects; (2) the financing of small-scale industries; (3) the support of government water and soil conservation projects; (4) the building of roads to connect rural areas with markets in the cities; (5) the teaching of labor-intensive techniques; and (6) the granting of agricultural credit to the poorest third of the farmers. Such projects frequently oppose the will of the ruling elites of the developing countries.[28] For the benefit of the social welfare and health of the underprivileged groups in the developing countries, one may hope that the World Bank Group approves this change of policy.

The need to find the resources for the economic development of new nations led in 1952 to the establishment of a Special United Nations Fund for Economic Development (SUNFED), but this measure was opposed by most of the industrial countries, which objected to such decisions of the General Assembly because a majority of its membership was composed of developing countries. Thus, SUNFED never became a major force in economic development of the Third World.

However, the United Nations Special Fund, requested by the General Assembly in 1957 and in operation from 1959 until 1966, was an active multilateral organization whose governing board was composed of equal numbers of donor nations and receiving countries, recommended by the Economic and Social Council and approved by the General Assembly. Its function was to provide systematic, sustained assistance for the integrated technical, economic, and social development of the less-developed countries. It was to concentrate on large projects of high priority with the prospect of early results, integrated with national or international development programs. Project support was to include surveys, research, training, and pilot and demonstration schemes. It could involve expert services and fellowships for training abroad. The Special Fund was directed by a governing council of 18 members, with a Managing Director appointed by the UN Secretary-General after consultation with the governing council and confirmation by the General Assembly. Paul G. Hoffman, former chief administrator of the Marshall Plan, was appointed first managing director, and Sir Arthur Lewis (of Great Britain) deputy of the Special Fund.

In countries receiving international technical assistance, the resident representatives of the Technical Assistance Board were simultaneously Special Fund agents who assisted developing countries to identify and implement projects suitable for Special Fund support. Projects proposals were reviewed by the consultative board and submitted to the governing council of the Special Fund. After approval by the council, either the United Nations or one of its specialized agencies prepared an operational plan which had to be signed by the host country, the Special Fund, and the executing agency before the project was carried out. Its progress was reviewed regularly. For training projects, only specially prepared trainers, not just teachers or social workers or engineers, were appointed if the government asking for such assistance guaranteed the maintenance of the institution. No pure research was supported; applied research was funded only under the condition that it promise early results for the entire economic development of the region.[29]

In 1966 the UN Expanded Technical Assistance Program and the Special Fund were merged into the United Nations Development Program to ensure an integrated attack on development problems. The United Nations Development Program governing council of 37 members replaced the Technical Assistance Committee of the Economic and Social Council and the governing council of the Special Fund. An Inter-Agency Consultative Board replaced the Technical Assistance Board and the consultative board of the Special Fund. The staffs of both organizations were combined, and the former managing director of the Special Fund is now the administrator and executive chairman of the UN Development Program.

In regard to the impact of foreign aid given by industrial countries to developing countries, Gunnar Myrdal says that such measures are urgently needed in the near future, and that not only the United States but *all* wealthy industrial countries should feel obliged to contribute. A fair division of the aid burden among all wealthy industrial countries can best be made under the auspices of the United Nations and its specialized international organizations.[30]

### The World Food Program

Following the practice of the United States and Canada of shipping surplus food to hungry people in other countries, in 1962 the United

Nations General Assembly and the Food and Agriculture Conference jointly created a World Food Program. The program was initially set up for a three-year experimental period, but in 1965 it was given permanent status. The World Food Program is administered by an intergovernmental committee and an executive director, A. H. Boerma. Over 70 governments voluntarily sponsor this program, sending food in emergencies such as earthquakes, hurricanes, floods, and droughts, as well as to help countries which have had to house numerous refugees. Food is also supplied for school nutrition programs, for large-scale settlement activities, and to support industrial development in countries which have difficulty raising funds for adequate wages for industrial workers. The World Food Program makes it possible to promote economic and social development in large-scale settlement projects, by supplying commodity surpluses that enable farmers to continue their work without having to depend on the harvest. Because some developing countries find it difficult to raise matching funds, the World Food Program has developed a flexible policy of financial requirements.[31] Despite the efforts of the United Nations and the Food and Agriculture Organization, most developing countries have so far not increased their food supply in relation to their industrialization to an extent that they do not have to import food any longer. This is especially true in India, Pakistan, and Bangladesh.

Although the 1960s were designated by the United Nations as the Development Decade, during which 1 percent of the national income of each industrial nation was to be contributed to underdeveloped nations, the goal of a 5 percent annual economic growth rate in the latter was not achieved. The acceleration of industrialization in developing countries faced serious obstacles. Still, recent trends are hopeful. The recently created United Nations Advisory Committee on the Application of Science and Technology may be able to provide developing countries with suggestions on how obstacles to economic and social progress can be overcome.[32]

### Voluntary International Organizations

Article 70 of the United Nations Charter provides that

the Economic and Social Council may make arrangements for representatives of the specialized agencies to participate, without vote, in its deliberations and in those of the commissions established by it, and for its representatives to participate in the deliberations of the specialized agencies.

Article 71 provides that

> the Economic and Social Council may make arrangements for consultation
> with *non-governmental organizations* which are concerned with matters within
> its competence. Such arrangements may be made with international orga-
> nizations and, where appropriate, with national organizations after consul-
> tation with the Member of the United Nations concerned. [Italics added.]

Voluntary or nongovernmental organizations now play a very important
role in international social welfare. The excerpts from the United Nations
Charter confirm this important role, which actually precedes the creation
of the United Nations, dating back to the period of the First World War
and the League of Nations.[33] The first voluntary international organization in the field of social welfare, the International Red Cross (described
in Chapter 1), remains one of the most effective such organizations, both
in war and in natural disasters. National governments and international
government agencies assume the responsibility for far-reaching operations only if there is no other way out, preferring to use voluntary organizations, sometimes with government financial support.[34]

A characteristic example of government–voluntary agency cooperation, mentioned in Chapter 1, is the large-scale relief operation undertaken after the 1948 war of liberation of Israel. Israel defended itself
successfully against the aggression of neighboring Arab nations. About
800,000 Palestinians fled Israel. At this point the United Nations asked
the International Committee of the Red Cross and the International
Committee of the League of Red Cross Societies, together with the
American and British Friends Service Committees, to care for the refugees. The expenses for the operation of refugee camps, health services,
and food provision were assumed by the United Nations and the UN
International Refugee Commission. Another example of cooperation occurred at the end of the Korean War, when nongovernment (voluntary)
organizations set up a relief and rehabilitation program, raising the necessary funds for relief supplies and personnel under the direction of the
United Nations and its specialized agencies.[35]

The Yearbook of the Union of International Associations (Brussels)
lists over a thousand such international voluntary organizations.[36] They
are classified in 19 categories according to their objectives; the three
largest groups are concerned with labor, employers, trade unions, and
professionals; commerce and industry; and science and research. Although in this context we obviously cannot list all such organizations, we
shall mention briefly some of the most important ones.

Protestant and Orthodox churches have organized the World Council of Churches, which supports ecumenism with a substantial number of
international organizations devoted to health and welfare pursuits. The

International Conference of Catholic Charities coordinates international Catholic social services under the spiritual guidance of the Vatican. It includes more than 30 Catholic agencies, such as the Catholic International Union for Social Service (Brussels), the International Conference of Catholic Organizations (Geneva), and a special Information Center; all aim to contribute to the betterment of international life under the inspiration of Christian principles.[37] The Society of Friends religious philosophy, a spirit of international cooperation and peace, is an essential contribution to the basic aims of the United Nations and to supranational understanding. Some of their activities in international welfare operations have been discussed in Chapter 1. The Society of Friends has a delegation at UN headquarters. The World Jewish Congress represents a number of Jewish international organizations, as well as many Jewish agencies devoted to health and welfare activities on a national level frequently not limited to persons of the Jewish faith. Chapter 1 discussed the operations of the American Joint Distribution Committee, the World ORT Union, and the United Hebrew Immigrant Aid Service. Other Jewish agencies in the United States, Israel, Great Britain, and France are also active in international health and welfare services.[38] Other major religions—Buddhists, Bahai, Seventh Day Adventists, and so on—so far have not set up special international federations for health and welfare services, although in Mohammedan countries the Red Crescent Societies parallel the Red Cross Societies in Christian nations and are members of the International Red Cross and of the International League of Red Cross Societies.[39]

In the communist countries, federations of workers, teachers, women, youth, journalists, writers, and other groups operate under the leadership and direction of the national communist parties. However, since the Cominform was dissolved in 1956, no formal communist international organization has been established which could be classified as an international agency in the field of health and welfare.[40]

The Conference of Consultative Non-Governmental Organizations, founded in Geneva in 1948 with a second bureau in New York, coordinates the experience and knowledge of all consultative organizations to the United Nations. The Standing Conference of Voluntary Agencies Working for Refugees consults with the UN High Commissioner for Refugees, his executive committee, and the UN Economic and Social Council. The Union of International Associations in Brussels, mentioned earlier in this chapter, has served since its reorganization in 1949 as a service center for all international organizations, publishing yearbooks which explain their activities.

Other voluntary international organizations are active in the prevention of crime and delinquency, in the treatment of offenders and juvenile delinquents, in migration and rehabilitation, and in public and mental health. Some have been founded at the suggestion of UNESCO, UNICEF, and the Economic and Social Council itself.[41]

In most cases there is a close interrelationship between voluntary international organizations in the areas of social welfare, health services, and economic development, and official (public) government international organizations. This is true particularly in technological fields such as international transportation, air traffic, meteorology, and postal services, but also in welfare, education, and health activities.[42] Sometimes voluntary international federations are transformed into government agencies, and vice versa. The similarity of expertise and the common interests often lead to both organizational liaison and individual cooperation.

The need for broad public support for international organizations, both official and private, is evident, not only for moral reasons, but for organizational and economic ones as well. But the difficulties of mobilizing world opinion, demonstrated by the political division of the world into several opposing camps, make it unlikely that a common public opinion could easily be established. However, better international understanding and cooperation are necessary in a world which is able to destroy itself with modern nuclear weapons. To promote such progress, the World Federation of United Nations Associations has been created, with the goal of supporting the United Nations Department of Public Information. National chapters of the Federation seek to convince the public in their countries that the maintenance of peace and disarmament, particularly of nuclear weapons, is needed now more than ever before.[43] It would seem to be the obligation of all international voluntary agencies to give strong support to this educational task in the spirit of the United Nations—not to applaud every action of the United Nations or to deny its weaknesses and faults, but to strengthen peaceful cooperation in solving the tremendous problems of health, education, welfare, famine, overpopulation, and disease.

Despite the attempts of the United Nations and its affiliated organizations to improve health and living conditions and the economic status of the developing nations, recent experience is that the gap in living standards and productivity between the rich and the poor nations has widened. This must be of major concern to all human beings interested in social justice and peace. Recommendations on how to close this gap were presented at a 1969 conference under the chairmanship of Lester Pearson, foreign secretary of Canada.[44] The conference report emphasized the necessity for all nations to remain deeply concerned with the fate of the developing, poorer countries and not to give this concern lower priority than their internal political and financial problems. In their participation the United Nations and other international bodies the powerful nations should avoid arrogance, sharing the desire for improved living standards and prosperity for poorer peoples on the basis of international ethics and social justice. They should recognize that the abolition of famine, poverty, and disease is in the interest of all peoples on the earth. To reach this goal, waste should be avoided in all aid operations, productive development should be supported, and foreign aid should be considered a moral responsibility.

In contrast to earlier centuries, in our time a global conscience is now slowly developing, created by religion, ethics, and the humanities and strongly supported by social work. This movement recognizes that fundamental changes must be effected by eliminating the inequality between rich and poor nations and by preventing crime, delinquency, immorality, and injustice within all countries. Education in the social sciences is needed to release the inner reserves of initiative and energy which will be able to achieve these goals.

In international as well as in domestic social work, social workers must respect their clients as human beings, listening to their ideas and plans for overcoming problems of poverty and suffering. Social workers with a knowledge of the social sciences and social hygiene will be able to help persons in need to control their fate and improve their living conditions. Of course, material needs must not be neglected, but all such efforts must be made with full respect for the clients' dignity and deep compassion for their suffering.[45]

While rapid progress has been made in technology, human beings have not achieved similar control over their own lives. Although there is much talk of the individual's right to self-determination, in reality he is more and more lost in the confusion of urban centers. The technological revolution has reinforced man's muscle and brain, but his heart and his emotions have not been enlarged. Only with the inner growth of human beings can we hope for real progress in the external world. All humanity, especially social workers, have still to learn not just to love our own family and friends, but also to have compassion for the suffering of people of other countries, religions, and races. The destructive powers of atomic energy no longer permit hostility toward strangers or other nations.

The urgent demand for social change requires a higher degree of maturity and tolerance than in earlier, simpler periods of human history. Present problems in many countries are racial and political, but also mental and intellectual; social workers must be equipped to solve such problems,[46] particularly in international social work. They must understand the culture and social values of foreign countries if they are to establish effective personal relationships in those nations.

## Notes

[1]Dorothy Lally, "International Social Welfare Services," in *Encyclopedia of Social Work, 1971,* pp. 684–86 (New York: National Association of Social Workers, 1971).

[2]*International Council of Voluntary Agencies News,* No. 63 (December 1973), p. 2.

[3]Eugen Pusíc, *Social Welfare and Social Development* (Paris: Mouton, 1972), pp. 71–75.

[4]Ralph Townley, *The United Nations* (New York: Scribner's, 1968), pp. 30–31.

[5]David A. Kay, *The New Nations in the United Nations* (New York: Columbia University Press, 1970), pp. 182–84.

[6]National Policy Panel of the United Nations Association of the United States of America, *The United Nations in the 1970s* (New York, 1971), pp. 15–25.

[7]Ernst B. Haas, *Beyond the Nation-State* (Stanford, Ca.: Stanford University Press, 1964), pp. 29–32.

[8]Charles W. Yost, "Views from the U.S. Mission," *Vista,* 5, no. 6 (May 1970), 32–56; U Thant, "From the Secretary-General," *Vista,* 5, no. 6, 23; Richard N. Gardner, "New Tasks for the 70s," *Vista,* 5, no. 6, 39–50, 171; Joseph Frankel, *International Relations* (New York: Oxford University Press, 1964), pp. 182–89.

[9]Townley, *The United Nations,* pp. 36–37.

[10]Townley, *The United Nations,* pp. 37–39; Robert A. Asher, "International Agencies and Economic Development," in *International Organization,* 22, no. 7 (1968), 441–45; Julia J. Henderson, "The United Nations Program of Regional Development," in *Urban Development* (New York: Columbia University Press, 1967), pp. 338–47; A. M. Rosenthal, *The United Nations, Its Record and Prospects* (New York: Manhattan Publishers, 1953), pp. 9–13; Hertha Kraus, ed., "International Cooperation for Social Welfare," *The Annals,* 329 (May 1960).

[11]William Korey, "We—The Peoples," *Vista,* 5, no. 6 (May 1970), 25–31, 154.

[12]James T. Shotwell, ed., *The Origins of the International Labor Organization* (New York: Columbia University Press, 1934); Walter Friedlander, *Introduction to Social Welfare,* 3rd ed. (Englewood Cliffs, N.J.: Prentice-Hall, 1968), pp. 543–44; E. B. Sheldon and W. E. Moore, eds., *Indicators of Social Change* (New York: Russell Sage Foundation, 1968).

[13]C. E. A. Winslow, "International Cooperation in the Service of Health, *The Annals,* 232 (Jan. 1951); Friedlander, *Introduction to Social Welfare,* 3rd ed., pp. 545–46.

[14]Walter R. Sharp, *International Technical Assistance* (Chicago: Public Administration Service, 1952), pp. 73–77; Friedlander, *Introduction to Social Welfare,* 3rd ed., pp. 544–46; Rosenthal, *The United Nations,* pp. 44–46.

[15]Townley, *The United Nations* pp. 280–84; Friedlander, *Introduction to Social Welfare,* 3rd ed., p. 546; Patricia H. Durston, "The Sea Farm," *Vista,* 1, no. 6 (May/June 1966), 31–41.

[16]Townley, *The United Nations,* pp. 242–43; Friedlander, *Introduction to Social Welfare,* 3rd ed., pp. 537–40; Alice C. Shafer, "UNICEF in Central America," in Kraus, "International Cooperation for Social Welfare," 69–77; Michael N. Scelsi, "UNICEF at Work Around the World," *Children Today,* 1, no. 1 (Mar.–Apr. 1972), 19–23.

[17]Georges Sicault, *The Needs of Children* (New York: Free Press, 1963), pp. 52–55; Yul Brynner, *Bring Forth the Children* (New York: McGraw-Hill, 1960).

[18]Dwight H. Ferguson, "The 25th Anniversary of UNICEF," in *Social Service Review* (Chicago), 46, no. 2 (June 1972), 170–92.

[19]Sibylla G. Thickness, *Arab Refugees: A Survey of Resettlement Possibilities* (London: Royal Institute of International Affairs, 1949); Joseph B. Schechtman, *The Arab Refugee Problem* (New York: Philosophical Library, 1952), and *The Refugee in the World: Displacement and Integration* (New York: Barnes & Noble, 1963); Friedlander, *Introduction to Social Welfare*, 3rd ed., pp. 541–42; Townley, *The United Nations*, pp. 241–42.

[20]Townley, *The United Nations*, p. 242; Rosenthal, *The United Nations*, pp. 17–25.

[21]Marie Dresden Lane, "The Resettlement of Unwanted Refugees by the International Refugee Organization," *The Social Service Review*, 26, no. 3 (Sept. 1952), 270–83; Townley, *The United Nations*, pp. 240–42; Friedlander, *Introduction to Social Welfare*, 3rd ed., pp. 540–42; Elfan Rees, *We Strangers and Afraid* (New York: Carnegie Endowment, 1959), pp. 5–29, 38–48, 59–72.

[22]Townley, *The United Nations*, pp. 252–53; Kenneth Soddy, *Mental Health and Infant Development* (New York: Basic Books, 1953); Friedlander, *Introduction to Social Welfare*, 3rd ed., pp. 546–53; Howard A. Rusk and Donald V. Wilson, "New Resources for Rehabilitation and Health," *The Annals*, 329 (May 1960), 97–106.

[23]René Matheu, *UNESCO Courier* (Paris, February 1970); Paul Lengrand, *An Introduction to Lifelong Education* (Paris: UNESCO, 1971).

[24]Pierre Laroque, "Social Implications of Technical Assistance Programmes," in *Social Service and the Standard of Living* (Madras, 1952), pp. 207–14.

[25]Eugene Staley, *The Future of Underdeveloped Countries* (New York: Harper & Row, 1954); Townley, *The United Nations*, pp. 267–73; Friedlander, *Introduction to Social Welfare*, 3rd ed., pp. 548–52; Philip M. Glick, *The Administration of Technical Assistance* (Chicago: University of Chicago Press, 1957); Margaret Mead, *Cultural Pattern and Technical Change* (Geneva: UNESCO, 1957); Walter R. Sharp, *International Technical Assistance* (Chicago: Public Administration Service, 1952), pp. 1–23, 73–77; Rosenthal, *The United Nations*, pp. 40–50; Victor D. Carlson, "Pakistan: Cooperative Ventures in Social Welfare," *The Annals*, 329 (May 1960), 88–96; Charles L. Robertson, "The Creation of UNCTAD," in Arthur M. Cox, *Prospects for Peacekeeping* (Washington, D.C.: Brookings Institution, 1967), pp. 258–74.

[26]Townley, *The United Nations*, pp. 255–61; Walter H. C. Laves, "Political Development Assistance by United Nations Organizations," in Robert Kox, ed., *The Politics of International Organizations* (New York: Praeger, 1970), pp. 117–27; Susan Strange, "The Meaning of Multilateral Surveillance," ibid., pp. 231–47.

[27]International Development Association, *Fifty Questions and Answers* (New York: United Nations, 1970); Leon Gordener, "Multilateral Aid and Influence on Government Policies," in Cox, *Prospects for Peacekeeping*, 128–52. It is regrettable that the United States Congress in January 1974 refused to contribute $1.5 billion to the Fund.

[28]Escott Reid, "McNamara's World Bank," *Foreign Affairs*, 51, no. 4 (July 1973), 794–810.

[29]Townley, *The United Nations,* pp. 272–82; Paul G. Hoffman, "Multilateral Aid," *Vista,* 6, no. 5 (May–June 1971), 15–19; Edward Rice, "Management—Indian Style," *Vista,* 5, no. 3 (Nov.–Dec. 1969), 53–58.

[30]Gunnar Myrdal, *Challenge to Affluence* (New York: Macmillan, 1963), pp. 138–41.

[31]Townley, *The United Nations,* pp. 283–87.

[32]Ibid., pp. 285–86; A. W. Samets, "Production of Goods and Services," in Sheldon and Moore, eds., *Indicators of Social Change;* Michael Crozier, "The Present Convergence of Public Administration and Private Enterprises," *International Social Science Journal,* 20, no. 1 (Jan. 1968), 9–16.

[33]Charlotte E. Owen, "International Voluntary Social Work," *Social Work Yearbook* (1949), 252–60; Bertram Pickard, *The Greater United Nations* (New York: Carnegie Endowment for International Peace, 1950); Friedlander, *Introduction to Social Welfare,* 3rd ed., pp. 556–57; Dorothy Lally, "International Voluntary Agencies," *Encyclopedia of Social Work,* pp. 415–17.

[34]Pickard, *The Greater United Nations,* p. 56; Lewis M. Hostein, "Voluntary Agencies and Foundations in International Aid," *The Annals,* 329 (May 1960), 57–68; Susan T. Pettis, "American Social Work Overseas," *Encyclopedia of Social Work 1965,* pp. 90–97; Lally, "International Social Welfare Agencies."

[35]Friedlander, *Introduction to Social Welfare,* 3rd ed., p. 542; Pickard, *The Greater United Nations,* p. 57; Thickness, *Arab Refugees;* Schechtman, *The Arab Refugee Problem* and *The Refugee in the World;* James M. Reael, "The United Nations and Refugees," *International Conciliation,* 137 (Mar. 1962); Don Peretz, "Israel's Administration and Arab Refugees," *Foreign Affairs* (Jan. 1968), 336–46.

[36](Brussels: Union des Associations Internationales); Pickard, *The Greater United Nations,* pp. 9–14.

[37]Pickard, *The Greater United Nations,* pp. 35–37; Msgr. Raymond J. Gallagher, "Catholic Social Services," *Encyclopedia of Social Work 1965,* pp. 133–35; Lewis M. Hopkins, "Voluntary Agencies and Foundations in International Aid," in Kraus, "International Cooperation for Social Welfare," 57–68; Elizabeth Shirley Enochs, "A Mass Attack on a Basic Problem: A Child Nutrition Project in Latin America," in Kraus, "International Cooperation for Social Welfare," 115–22.

[38]Philip Bernstein, "Jewish Social Services," *Encyclopedia of Social Work 1965,* pp. 418–28; Pickard, *The Greater United Nations,* pp. 35–36; Boris Bogen, *Jewish Philanthropy* (New York: Macmillan, 1917).

[39]Pickard, *The Greater United Nations,* p. 39.

[40]Pickard, *The Greater United Nations,* pp. 38–39; Bernice Q. Madison, *Social Welfare in the Soviet Union* (Stanford, Ca.: Stanford University Press, 1968), pp. 210–40.

[41]Pickard, *The Greater United Nations,* pp. 70–79.

[42]Paul S. Reinsch, *Public International Unions,* 2nd ed. (Boston: World Peace Foundation, 1916); Pickard, *The Greater United Nations,* pp. 39–41.

[43]Brock Chisholm, "Growing Up in a Changing World," *International Social Work,* 1, no. 3 (July 1958), 25–29; Pickard, *The Greater United Nations,* pp. 43–49.

[44]*Partners in Development: Report of the Commission on International Development* (New York: Praeger, 1969).

[45]Eileen Younghusband, *Social Work and Social Change* (London: Allen & Unwin, 1964), pp. 104–8.
[46]Ibid., pp. 112–20.

## Selected References

*Books*

ALMOND, GABRIEL A., AND JAMES S. COLEMAN, *The Politics of the Developing Areas.* Princeton, N.J.: Princeton University Press, 1960.

ASHER, ROBERT E., *Development Assistance in the Seventies: Alternatives for the United States.* Washington, D.C.: Brookings Institution, 1970.

BOZEMAN, ADDA B., *The Future of Law in a Multi-Cultural World.* Princeton, N.J.: Princeton University Press, 1971.

BROWN, JOAN L., *Poverty vs. Not-a-Crime: Social Services in Tasmania.* Hobart, Tasmania: Tasmanian Research Association, 1972.

CASTANEDA, JORGE, *Legal Effects of United Nations Resolutions.* New York: Columbia University Press, 1969.

COSGROVE, CAROL ANN, AND KENNETH J. TWITCHETT, eds., *The International Actors: The United Nations and the European Economic Community.* New York: St. Martin's Press, 1970.

COX, ARTHUR M., *Prospects for Peacekeeping.* Washington, D.C.: Brookings Institution, 1967.

DAHRENDORFF, RALF, *Konflikt und Freiheit—Auf dem Wege zur Dienstklassengesellschaft* (Conflict and Freedom: On the Way to a Service-Class Society). Munich: Piper, 1972.

FRANK, CHARLES R., JR; JAGDISH N. BRAGSWATT; ROBERT D'A. SHAW; AND HARALD B. MALJREN, *Assisting Developing Countries: Problems of Debt-Sharing, Jobs, and Trade.* New York: Praeger, 1972.

FRANKEL, JOSEPH, *International Relations.* New York: Oxford University Press, 1969.

FRIEDLANDER, WALTER A., "International Social Welfare," chap. 17 in *Introduction to Social Welfare,* 3rd ed. Englewood Cliffs, N.J.: Prentice-Hall, 1968.

GORDENER, LEON, *The United Nations Secretary-General and the Maintenance of Peace.* New York: Columbia University Press, 1967.

GOSOVIC, BRANISLAV, *UNCTAD* (United Nations Conference on Trade and Development): *Conflict and Compromise.* Leyden: Sijthoff, 1972.

JAMES, ALAN, *The Bases of International Order.* New York: Oxford University Press, 1973.

KHINDUKA, S. K., "Social Planning and Community Organization," pp. 1346–51 in *Encyclopedia of Social Work 1971.* New York: National Association of Social Workers, 1971.

KIMCHE, DAVID, *The Afro-Asian Movement: Ideology and Foreign Policy in the Third World.* New York: Halsted, 1973.

LALLY, DOROTHY, "International Social Welfare Services," pp. 676–86 in *Encyclo-*

*pedia of Social Work 1971.* New York: National Association of Social Workers, 1971.

LILLICH, RICHARD B., ed., *Humanitarian Intervention and the United Nations.* Charlottesville, Va.: University of Virginia Press, 1973.

MARTIN, ERNEST W., *Comparative Development in Social Welfare.* London: Allen & Unwin, 1972.

MENDE, URSULA, *Internationale Sozialarbeit* (International Social Work). Neuwied, Germany: Luchterhand, 1972.

MILLER, LINDA B., *World Order and Local Disorder: The United Nations and Internal Conflicts.* Princeton, N.J.: Princeton University Press, 1967.

MYRDAL, GUNNAR, *Beyond the Welfare State: Economic Planning and Its International Implications.* New Haven, Conn.: Yale University Press, 1967.

RIMLINGER, GASTON V., *Welfare Policy and Industrialization in Europe, America, and Russia.* New York: John Wiley, 1971.

ROSENBAUM, NAOMI, and ROBERT A. DAHL, *Readings in the International Political System.* Englewood Cliffs, N.J.: Prentice-Hall, 1970.

ROSENTHAL, A. M., *The United Nations: Its Record and Prospects.* New York: Carnegie Endowment for International Peace, 1953.

ROSTOW, WALTER W., *The Stages of Economic Growth: A Non-Communist Manifesto.* Cambridge: Cambrige University Press, 1960.

SCHOECK, HELMUTH, *Entwicklungshilfe: Politische Humanität* (Development Aid: Humanistic Policy). Vienna: Langen-Müller, 1972.

SHARP, WALTER R., *The United Nations Economic and Social Council.* New York: Columbia University Press, 1969.

SMITH, CONSTANCE, AND ANNE FRIEDMAN, *Voluntary Associations: Perspectives on the Literature.* Cambridge, Mass.: Harvard University Press, 1972.

SPROUT, H., AND M. SPROUT, *Foundations of International Policies.* New York: Macmillan, 1963.

TOWNLEY, RALPH, *The United Nations: A View from Within.* New York: Scribner's, 1968.

TUITE, MATTHEW, ROGER CHRISHOLM, AND MICHAEL RADNOW, *Interorganizational Decision Making.* Chicago: Aldine-Atherton, 1972.

UNITED NATIONS, *How People Work Together: The United Nations and the Specialized Agencies.* New York: Manhattan, 1953.

WALTERS, FRANCIS P., *History of the League of Nations.* New York: Oxford University Press, 1960.

WARWICK, DONALD P., AND SAMUEL OSHERSON, *Comparative Research Methods.* Englewood Cliffs, N.J.: Prentice-Hall, 1973.

WHITE, JOHN, *Regional Development Banks.* New York: Praeger, 1972.

*Articles*

CANAT, PIERRE, "The Anti-Education of Children and Adolescents," *International Child Welfare Review,* 14 (Aug. 1972), 48–53.

CASSIERER, HENRY R., "Television and the Education of the Family," *International Child Welfare Review*, 14 ( Aug. 1972), 22–42.

COHEN, WILBUR J., AND DOROTHY LALLY, "International Social Welfare: A Report on the First United Nations Conference of Social Welfare," *Welfare in Review*, 7 (Jan.–Feb. 1969), 1–8.

COSER, LEWIS, "Peaceful Settlements and the Disfunctions of Secrecy," *American Political Science Review*, 53 (Mar. 1959), 177–86.

DELCOURT, JACQUES, "Le Futur du Service Social" (The Future of the Social Services), *Service Social dans le Monde*, no. 5 (1972), 267–75.

DUMÉE, JEAN-PIERRE DUBOS, "Television of the Future," *International Child Welfare Review*, 14 (Aug. 1972), 5–21.

GUIGUI, ALBERT, "Workers' Education and the International Labor Office," *ILO Panorama*, 44 (Oct. 1970), 10–15.

HAAS, ERNST B., "System and Process in the International Labor Organization," *World Politics*, 14 (Jan. 1962), 322–52.

LIPSET, SEYMOUR MARTIN, "Some Social Requisites of Democracy: Economic Development and Political Legitimacy," *American Political Science Review*, 53 (Mar. 1959), 69–105.

POITRAS, G. E., "Welfare Bureaucracy and Clientele Policies in Mexico," *Administrative Science Quarterly*, 18 (1973), 18–26.

RICKENBACH, WALTHER, "Zehn Jahre Europäische Sozialcharta" (Ten Years of European Social Charters), *Schweizerische Zeitschrift für Gemeinnützigkeit*, 111 (Feb. 1972), 36–45.

STEIGER, EMMA, "Internationale Beziehungen in der sozialen Arbeit" (International Relations in the Social Services), *Gesundheit und Wohlfahrt*, 8 ( Aug. 1950), 1–25.

SZALAI, ALEXANDER, "The Future of International Organizations," *Associations Internationales*, 5 (1972), 267–75.

ZUMBACH, PIERRE, "Les activitées de l'Union Internationale de protection de l'enfance," *Les Carnets de l'enfance*, 14 (1971), 10–113.

# International community development

## 3

Community development in developing nations is the most relevant activity in the area of welfare, health, and education. It is defined by the United Nations as "the policy and process of creating conditions of economic and social progress for the whole community with its active participation and the fullest reliance upon the community's own initiative." It integrates a country's ability to adapt to new ways of living with a fund of social and economic techniques and tools drawn from worldwide experience.[1]

The need for a policy of community development was occasioned by foundation of the United Nations, which made abolition of colonialism and recognition of legal equality among the countries of the world a new basic concept of international relations.[2]

## The Purpose of Community Development

Community development is one of the essential ways of bridging the deep chasm between the standard of living of the industrial countries and that of the developing countries. This is necessary in order to overcome the envy of the developing world, which aspires to equal economic and health conditions but which cannot reach this goal without adequate help. The idea of community development is implied in the Preamble of the Charter of the United Nations:

> To establish conditions under which justice and respect for the obligations arising from treaties and other sources of international law can be maintained, and to promote social progress and better standards of living in larger freedom, [and] to employ international machinery for the promotion of the economic and social advancement of all people.

Principles of community development incorporate the idea that people in developing countries need not only the will to help themselves to improve conditions, but also the supporting services of regional or state governments, training for the necessary economic and social changes, research and experiments in social policies, land tenure, legislative reforms, and local and regional planning.[3]

To be efficient, increases in agricultural or industrial production and income must be supplemented by improvements in living and housing conditions and in environmental sanitation, by the control of diseases, by educational progress, and by social and child welfare services. There must also be improved methods of communication between rural communities and regional or state governments and cooperation from voluntary private social agencies. Community development projects should be designed to meet the basic needs of the community and carried out in response to the expressed needs of the people, not on the whim of an elite or of ambitious officials. They need concerted action, the enthusiasm of the participants, and a multipurpose program. In most rural underdeveloped regions the people are interested mainly in obtaining more land for better agriculture and production; employment for workers who aren't needed for farm work; water for drinking and irrigation; roads to bring products to market; health services; and schools.[4]

Changing the attitudes of the people in a community is as important as achieving material improvements, because only then is there a realistic chance that technical progress will be maintained after external assistance has started such progress. Therefore in any development project it is important to secure real participation of the local population and to establish an efficient local government administration based on a representative participation of the people. Local instruments for such community development may be a school, a village council, a youth club, a community center, a water and sewage system, a literary club. No training for the project, however necessary, should interfere with agricultural labor in a rural village, and any such training must consider cultural patterns, use simple skills, and be based on people's ability for self-help. Modern technical methods should be introduced with caution, and teamwork and initiative should be stressed. The participation of women and youth is usually essential. Sometimes people need only material assistance, such as tools and funds, in order to stimulate initiative and the proper use of local natural resources.

There is general agreement that an effective community development program must consider the needs of youth, but because the aim of community development is to meet the social, health, and economic needs of all age groups, youth should not be treated as a separate element in the population. However, since the needs of the young generation are one of the essential considerations, and since youth predominates among all age groups in all developing countries, it is important to obtain the cooperation and participation of youth in the formulation of the program. Young people frequently are more able to accept change than the older generation, are more interested in innovations, and are more able to become efficient agents of social and economic change.[5] Youth has made important contributions to community development projects in Cuba, Tanzania, Ceylon, Nigeria, Kenya, Chile, Thailand, Indonesia, Jamaica, Iran, and Argentina.[6]

Community development projects on a regional or national scale require careful planning, recruiting and training of personnel, experiments with their mobilization, reliable administration, research, and natural resources. National religious and cultural traditions must be considered in order to enlist effective participation of local leadership and broad popular support. The timing of the projects should aim at the achievement of first results within three to five years. Resources of voluntary agencies should be used whenever possible. Support from regional or national transportation resources, schools, hospitals and health centers, and planned coordination are often necessary to make a project successful.[7]

A broad range of community development activities in Hong Kong were developed with the cooperation of the public authorities, the universities, and religious and humanitarian social agencies, and have been carried on under the auspices of the Hong Kong Council of Social Service. They include sanitary improvements in resettlement estates, reduction of pollution and juvenile delinquency, housing projects for fishermen living in sampans and wooden stilt houses, consumer credit cooperatives, child and youth services, recreation activities, cooperation between hospitals and schools, training courses for community workers and volunteers, and community surveys on land use and transportation.[8]

International assistance for community development projects in many parts of the world whose problems are basically the same is rendered by numerous public and private agencies, as discussed in Chapter 2. Each project, in spite of similarities, is still a unique challenge. National and international voluntary agencies such as the Agency for International Development, the U.S. Foreign Operations Administration, the Asia Foundation, the Colombo Plan, and the United Nations South Pacific Commission promote conferences, seminars, and exchanges of information in the area of community development. Specialized agencies of the United Nations hold frequent regional seminars, conferences, and study tours to improve methods of community development.

Community development has become one of the significant movements of our time. It may well result in substantial economic and social progress in a number of developing countries which might not be able to avoid famine, undernourishment, or starvation because of increasing population and insufficient resources. In some developing countries, people are much more concerned with economic and social improvements than is the population in the rich, industrial nations.[9]

### The Need for Patience

In order to achieve an essential improvement of living conditions, community development needs to change a number of vital conditions in a country. Some of the important changes are: limit population growth; upgrade general education and vocational training; transfer to a mobile social structure; recognize the individual personality; increase industrial production; establish a modern system of transportation; change from the extended family structure to the "nuclear family"; provide the wife with a more independent position; shift from natural exchange to a money society; and introduce division of labor into the economy of production.[10] No country can expect rapid achievement of the goals of community development and at the same time desire more material goods and higher incomes, but not many are willing to accept slow progress. The usual consequence is that expectations of the poverty-stricken for a higher standard of living are not met, which increases their inclination to use violent means against ruling groups that are unwilling to give up any of their advantages.

Most developing countries have until recently been dominated by old traditions, which contended that poverty, disease, and death were part of a fate against which man could not protect himself. The ruling casts exercised all political power, controlled the land and all material wealth, and monopolized education, science, and technical knowledge. The masses, mostly rural peasants, were satisfied with minimal income and no political influence. But now, through the influence of radio and television and reductions in the illiteracy rates, the poor are beginning to revolt against the ruling elites, the owners of the estates, the chieftains of the tribes, and the priests.[11]

The new leadership in the developing countries consists of the following groups: (1) the leaders of the independence movements who liberated the countries from the colonial powers; (2) the intellectuals, who studied in the industrial countries (or recently in the universities of their own nations) and blame their governments for the dearth of academic positions; (3) leaders of the trade unions (who often come from intellectual rather than from worker backgrounds), who are gaining influence with the growth of industrialization, find support from the international trade union movement, and are often political allies of their own governments; (4) skilled workers, foremen, and master artisans (this group is still small in most developing countries, but the support of trade unions may enable it to organize and strengthen this middle class); and (5) the army and the officer corps (in most developing countries the military dominates politics, and has frequently overthrown civilian governments and set up military dictatorships).[12]

In planning the educational and vocational training facilities of community development programs, a country must consider the needs of its labor market and situation, and estimate the employment opportunities of its agricultural and industrial production, so as to avoid education and training for nonexistent positions. Unemployment and dissatisfaction among the newly educated are already serious obstacles to successful community development in several countries.[13]

### Community Welfare Centers

Community welfare centers play an important role in developing countries, by trying to improve the cultural as well as the economic resources of the local communities, and by trying to stimulate the population to use their initiative for cultural progress and economic planning and production more effectively. In Hong Kong there are "village clans halls," which now serve for village council meetings, classes, athletic courses, and recreation (before they were used only for ancestor worship and clan meetings). In Thailand a community welfare center, called a *wat*, is used by teams from the World Health Organization and UNICEF as a clinic for treating patients suffering from yaws, for literacy classes, and for dramatic arts courses with the support of the national government. In most community welfare centers the training of local leadership has priority attention. A center must have the whole-hearted participation of the people in order to be effective.[14]

Public schools have been used as community welfare centers in rural areas of the Philippines, India, Latin America, the Middle East, and the South Pacific. The interest of most rural populations is in economic improvement, health services, infant and maternity care, family and youth services, better housing and gardening, better schools and nutrition, religious services, and recreation. If such centers are organized by voluntary organizations, government subsidies often support their efforts.[15] For example, in Ceylon, village centers in over 700 villages with 400,000 members engage in adult education, which includes folk singing, handicraft courses, and cinema shows. In Ruanda-Urundi about 30 welfare centers train African women in child care, hygiene, and family life education. Similar courses are offered in Arabic countries and in Asia under the auspices of the Near-East Foundation and the Ford Foundation, with emphasis on recruiting and training local village workers. In India, Ceylon, and in several islands of the South Pacific special indigenous community centers were necessary because of the cultural and language differences which could not be served by general institutions. On the island of Celebes in Indonesia migrants from Sumatra and Java organized self-help community centers and cooperative societies because no local facilities were acceptable to them.

One of the earliest community development projects in India was the Etawah Pilot Project in the Utter Pradesh. This project used the methods of modern cooperatives in 96 villages with 90,000 people, and the results were better food production, revitalization of local government, and improved social, health, and welfare services.[16] In Eastern Nigeria the Udi Development Center set up dispensaries, schools, village halls, and maternity homes through voluntary labor of the villagers, and improved crops, roads, and sanitation facilities. One notable feature of this project was that educated Africans were willing to perform manual labor; in most developing countries, academically trained persons refuse to do manual labor.[17]

After the Second World War national community development projects were used in Yugoslavia, Greece, Korea, and Burma to repair war damages. In Egypt, Pakistan, Ceylon, and Burma national community development projects were used either for economic progress or as demonstrations of government political power. Such national projects in Greece, South Korea, Gold Coast, Eastern Nigeria, Pakistan, Malaya, Burma, Zaire, Ceylon, Jamaica, Peru, Mexico, Bolivia, Indonesia, India, and Swaziland were supported by international organizations, especially the United Nations and its specialized agencies—UNICEF, the World Health Organization, Food and Agriculture Organization, and UNESCO.[18]

Administrators of many community development projects had serious difficulty securing cooperation among the conventional national government agencies, the newly established coordinating community development councils, and regional or local agencies organized to implement the process. Mayer concluded that the following administrative procedures seem necessary: (1) to assign a clear responsibility to each agency involved; (2) to coordinate the activities of all departments and organizations and to define their specific responsibilities in the community development precisely; and (3) to see to it that the new coordinating council does not try to override existing agencies, but acts as an adjunct of the organizational structure and stimulates local committees to use governmental and voluntary services for the benefit of the development project.[19]

In community development, economic and material needs are essential, but because community development is a human as well as an economic undertaking, it requires understanding the cultural, religious, and social conditions of the community as well as of its economic needs, based on a thorough research of the people's attitudes and values and their readiness and motives for participating in the project. People need recognition of their dignity, status, prestige, and honor so that they can receive the satisfaction of group accomplishment through participation in planning and execution.[20]

Many community development projects have benefited from technical assistance rendered by regional or national government resources or from international aid, which provides experts and material help. In the rural regions of countries like India, local participation is frequently stimulated by discussion groups, which determine the most relevant social and economic needs and engage self-help and cooperative efforts for progress. In some developing countries, pamphlets, film demonstrations, puppet shows, pageants, and theater performances have also been used very successfully to call attention to community development projects.[21]

United Nations policy in recent years has emphasized the necessity of multipurpose programs in community development, orienting the projects to regional and national planning and to the training of local leaders for community development. Furthermore, community development projects in regional or national settings must be coordinated with local conditions.[22]

The goal of training projects for local personnel in community development is to secure more efficient cooperation between the local village staff and regional or national administrations of the entire community development program. This requires an active, intelligent interest among the villagers to complete their work and so raise the standards of living for the entire community. It is no easy task to overcome the spirit of narrow self-interest and to encourage a sense of community responsibility that is absent from many cultures. Inertia and apathy have to be replaced by a new spirit of mutual help and self-help. Women can play an essential part here, because formerly only the men made decisions in such projects. Women workers who cannot attend training courses in distant training centers because of responsibility to family and for small children sometimes can be trained in their own homes.[23] Village workers need supervised field experiences and realistic conditions to prepare them for community development service.

## The Early Role of the UN

During its first decade the United Nations and its specialized agencies concentrated their community development efforts on rural development, but in the middle of the 1950s this policy shifted to a more balanced consideration of both rural and urban aspects of development. There was a series of seminars on problems of urbanization in connection with industrialization in the developing nations. Some of the subjects discussed were the movement of poverty-stricken masses from rural regions into cities, the deterioration of housing and employment conditions, the lack of adequate health care, proper nutrition of newcomers, and the prevalence of severe social disorganization.

During the decade from the middle 1950s to the middle 1960s rapid urban growth in many developing countries made solutions for these problems more urgent. Programs of concerted international action were prepared, particularly by UNESCO: they recommended cooperative measures, specific urban development projects, the inclusion of urban planning in basic research and in city and regional planning, and the expansion of community services and special assistance for new immigrants to the cities. The two main measures were technical assistance in constructing housing for low-income populations, and plans for industrial development and new employment facilities. The products of these concerns were the creation in 1965 of the United Nations Industrial Development Organization (UNIDO) and of the United Nations Center of Housing, Building, and Planning. Since this time, the trend of United Nations activities has been toward a more comprehensive approach to the problems of urbanization in the developing countries. This approach requires an integration of the social, economic, and physical aspects of development and full consideration in national and regional programs of urban needs.[24]

In most industrial nations, particularly in the United States, it will be necessary to change the economy slowly from rapid growth, the expansion of industrial establishments, and urbanization so as to improve the standards of living and the opportunities for all classes of society by providing more material and spiritual goods for the poor, the minority groups, the aged, and the disabled and by providing equal education for all children and equal health care and better employment opportunities for all. Worldwide, the industrial nations are islands of wealth in an ocean of poverty and suffering.[25]

One of the main obstacles to a more equal distribution of wealth, economic opportunities, and living standards is that we don't know how to modernize and change a peasant agriculture (such as India's and many of those in Asia and Africa) to a healthy mixture of agriculture and industry without disturbing the balance and environment of the native culture. United Nations agencies such as the Economic and Social Council, the Food and Agriculture Organization, the World Health Organization, and the United Nations Educational and Cultural Organization and many voluntary agencies like the Quaker Overseas Volunteers for Service, which is administered by the Friends Service Council in England, have attempted to alleviate discrepancies and to help in a change for progress.[26]

The trend of these UN and UNESCO policies is from a preoccupation with rapid urban growth and the shift from the rural regions to the cities to a comprehensive consideration of all—including the positive aspects of urbanization policy. While questions of urban congestion, lack of health and welfare services, and the distribution of social services between the urban and rural population remain important and require remedial action, the crucial need of the new countries is for effective national planning for the entire economic, social, and political development. The specific cultural, political, and economic conditions of each country demand careful special consideration. Some difficulties are the danger of overcentralization of population and industries in some metropolitan centers, a lack of personnel trained in planning for efficient development projects, the lack of administrative machinery to cope with urbanization problems, the complexity of this planning process, the difficulty of transferring methods and experiences from one country to another, and the high cost of planning.[27] Planning is particularly relevant in the fields of urban housing, social services for children and juveniles, health facilities, and treatment of shantytowns and squatter settlements. There is a lack of communication among developing countries; consequently, theoretical studies and practical experiences in dealing with problems of urbanization are not well known, and a communications system for these questions through the United Nations seems desirable.[28]

### Planned Communities

An important aspect of international concern about urbanization is how to distribute the growing conglomeration of metropolitan and largely industrial and commercial cities, and at the same time to prevent or control air, water, noise, and soil pollution and aesthetic abominations. One answer that has been employed by several countries is the planned development of new cities. In England this movement was started in 1902 by the well-known book by Sir Ebenezer Howard, *Garden Cities of the Future,*[29] but after the Second World War action was based on the New Towns Act of 1946 and the Town and Country Planning Act of

1968.[30] To date there has not been strong and effective participation of the residents among new communities in England and Scotland in planning for further development because of the obvious needs for government planning and the set-up of authorities under the local and the national New Town Authority.

An interesting version of the well-planned new city is under way in France, in the small city of Le Vaudreuil on the Seine River near Rouen, about 60 miles west of Paris. It is the product of a rare international cooperation between the French government and the United States Department of Housing and Urban Development.[31] The aim of this new experiment is to reduce the pollution of the Seine and to stabilize the population of the industrial city of Rouen, and at the same time to keep development flexible enough to allow for further growth according to the population influx, the demands of industry, and transportation needs. Other interesting experiments in new cities in Germany and Israel are discussed by Shimon Gottschalk.[32]

In Brazil there is an unusual type of community development program for commercial employees called the Social Service of Commerce (*Serviço Social do Comércio*), with 21 regional divisions and headquarters in Rio de Janeiro. Its services for commercial employees and their families in 150 Brazilian cities include educational and cultural activities (libraries, artistic courses, conferences, training seminars); leisure and recreation activities (sports, holiday centers, vacation camps, excursions, weekend facilities); health services (sanitary education, services for babies and mothers, clinics, laboratories, nursing and therapy services, preventive medical care); housing (construction of modern housing units and apartments that are sold under easy terms to commercial employees); individual assistance via consultation with social workers (legal service, emergency relief credits); and inexpensive meals.[33]

### Squatter Settlements and Shantytowns

An especially serious urban problem for developing countries is that of squatter settlements and shantytowns. About one-third of the people of Mexico City, one-half of Ankara, and more than one-half of Leopoldville in Zaire live in such squatter settlements. In many Latin American, African, and Asian countries such settlements are uncontrolled and are changing the cultural and political climate of cities that used to be the residences of the countries' elites.[34] The growing size of modern metropolises makes it difficult for the poverty-stricken, who are the bulk of the people in squatter settlements, to live far away from the city center where they may be able to find work. In contrast to the squatter settings of the previous centuries, present squatter cities and shantytowns often are interspersed with sections of the central city and so are a particular problem of the new urbanization. If the settlement is established through an organized invasion, it usually faces legal suits and police action. Dwellers in such settlements differ widely in social and economic status. Often they are the very poorest, but sometimes, as in Lima, Peru, and Hong Kong, they are people of the working-class level. Many of the "temporary settlements" in Latin America, North Africa and Asia have developed into "incipient squatter settings," but they still show a high density and a lack of proper street alignment and open space. In many places the inhabitants have established a district municipal administration of their own, but usually there is only a very limited capacity to control sanitation, health conditions, housing, and transportation. There are exceptions to this: some squatter settlements in Latin America are the result of planning and orderly administration.[35] "Semisquatter settlements" are often used by middle-income families in suburban settings, even though they lack adequate public utilities, sanitation, and paved roads. Their population is of a wide range, usually including a good portion of middle-class and working-class persons.

Many of the people who live in "provisional squatter settlements" and shantytowns are unemployed and have little or no income. The basic motivation for living in a squatter settlement is not having to pay rent, since most of the rural poor who migrate to the cities can't begin to afford contemporary urban housing.[36] Improvement of the health and housing conditions of these settlements can be obtained only if the poor themselves mobilize their initiative and cooperation. Most settlements on land of high value will be wiped out.[37]

### The Goals of Community Development

The process of community development was almost unknown to the developing countries 25 years ago, but it is now a universally accepted and endorsed objective of international action. It includes elements of social and economic growth and change; improving standards of living, if possible for the entire population; increasing the national income; adopting new technology, skills, and capacities; reforming the socio-economic structure; and changing occupations and basic economic philosophy. Community development is not simply organic growth, nor a mechanical production process, but it involves different elements of both physical and human changes. It is a system of human relationships that leads to the desired objectives.[38]

The goals of community development—raising the standards of living, health, education, and welfare—are clear, but often they are not based on popular preferences, since not all strata of the population always recognize their general value. Changes in the environment, in the employment structure, in the agricultural labor force, and in the birth rate are often not readily accepted by a population.

Certain changes that accompany technical and economic development, such as air and water pollution, and increases in noise, congestion, juvenile delinquency, crime, and social pathology, are highly undesirable correlates of development that thoughtful measures within the development plan should prevent. If we compare results of the community development process in a series of countries we find that progress in social and structural change is greater than in purely economic change, especially in industrial development.[39] One very essential influence of technological change is its effect on employment opportunities. It means a sizable reduction in the demand for manual labor, particularly for agricultural work, but also for unskilled labor in urban settings. Formerly certain simple skills assured a relatively stable employment and social status, but with industrialization and technological progress there is a rapid decline in such work opportunities. Employment requires more education, training, and technical skills that still are rare in numerous developing countries. Therefore unemployment tends to be high among those workers who because of their origin, the locality of their home, and their family background have the least education and training. The developing countries have to strengthen vocational education and technical training so that education does not lead to dead ends and unemployment. In most countries there also is a need to retrain older workers, to prevent widespread casual work and unemployment.[40] Under these circumstances every country needs more teachers, instructors, and vocational counselors and fewer manual laborers. Many trade unions are in danger of becoming little more than protection organizations for their members' jobs, of ceasing to represent the working class as such and the common interest.[41]

As we mentioned earlier, community development operations are particularly necessary in slums, shantytowns, and squatter settlements. These places are evidence of the failure of a society to meet the employment, housing, and health needs of the poorer parts of its population. Millions of families continue to move from rural villages and small towns to larger cities without having means to purchase or rent decent housing or to pay their living expenses. The absorption of these new urban populations has international implications, since they appear in numerous developing countries, but so far the only action that international public and private organizations have taken has been some modest financial assistance measures.[42] In ten years the Special Fund of the United Nations Development Program has financed nearly one thousand projects, and of these only 15 have been in the field of housing, building, and planning. Urban problems such as slums and squatter settlements require responsible changes in the present policies of land control and utilization, and new approaches, in which human factors, manpower needs, and resources find primary consideration. Different countries need different changes, but interprofessional activities will be required, wherein the social reformer, the architect, the city planner, the social anthropologist, the social worker, the lawyer, members of the health professions, the finance and housing expert, the cooperatives, the community developer, and the systems analyst all play their roles.

The United Nations has been involved in pilot projects for dealing with the problems of slums and squatter settlements in India, the Philippines, Puerto Rico, Africa, Thailand, and Latin America. These projects show that at present government resources must be supplemented by international loans; citizens' group activities; self-help and neighborhood actions; and assistance through credits from savings and loan associations, cooperative societies, and land reform measures. Until there is comprehensive national and international action, a cooperative program will be required, combining legislation for land reform, government measures for regulation of land tenure and basic community facilities, rehabilitation of slum areas, public and private credit facilities, and technical assistance for slum clearance and aid to the people.[43]

Valuable illustrations of the importance of the active participation of the population in community development were offered in 1966 at the International Conference of Social Work in Washington, D.C., from southern Italy and Pakistan.[44] After the Second World War and the fall of the Fascist regime in Italy, the *Cassa per il Mezzogiorno* (Southern Italy Development Fund) enabled the poor population to overcome their economic and social depression and the paucity of local resources through public employment on roads, port facilities, school and hospital construction, and new industrial enterprises. Following this initial phase, the population was encouraged to develop its own industrial and agricultural enterprises. Social services played an important role in this process of developing self-help activities in southern Italy and in Sardinia by, among other things, stimulating cooperatives and getting greater participation among women.

In East Pakistan economic and social development is the concern of the government, but citizen participation was encouraged by two five-year plans that strongly emphasized the engagement of the people to make their own contribution to community development. The measures included educating the masses to accept social change and new ideas, "democratic decentralization," and getting people to contribute to local and national development projects. New towns had to be built for the numerous refugees from India and for the substantial masses that were to be resettled in rural regions. This program was supported by "improvement trusts," in both cities and villages, which assumed responsibility for planning the necessary development of streets, drainage, public utilities, land acquisition, and sanitary systems. Citizen participation proved difficult in rural regions, because of the many refugees, migrants, ricket pullers, and beggars, but it was more successful in urban projects where voluntary agencies assisted in the establishment of "project councils" which organized health services, recreation facilities, adult literacy classes, vocational training centers, and other educational facilities. These, however, are but modest beginnings; development of genuine readiness for citizen participation in the larger aspect of social and economic development in underdeveloped countries will require patience and time.[45]

### The Peace Corps and Similar Groups

Some impact on international social welfare development has been made by organizations such as the U.S. Peace Corps, the German *Entwicklungsdienst,* and similar Canadian, Dutch, and Scandinavian groups of mostly young persons and students who have volunteered to serve in the developing countries in education, health services, and economic development operations. They receive no real salary, only a nominal allowance and maintenance, so they gain satisfaction for their sacrifice in serving under trying circumstances through the knowledge that they are helping people who badly need it.[46] There are serious questions about the impact of these activities, but the positive results—progress in education and in the self-reliance of the people, especially of the youth and women—are more important than certain misgivings and the misunderstandings that are inevitable when young and often rather poorly informed men and women arrive in primitive countries to try to teach or at least to encourage persons of completely different cultures to attempt social change and new forms of economy and living. In contrast to the highly paid officials of most governments and international organizations that send missions to the developing countries, Peace Corps members and similar volunteers of other Western countries live under simple conditions with the natives, share their primitive food and housing, and are able to establish trust and cooperation, which rarely exist between the delegates from industrial nations and the populations of developing countries. Communist propaganda has tried to portray the Peace Corps as an instrument of capitalistic oppression that supports the "establishment" in the developing countries by teaching western methods in schools. This portrait is not accurate. The vast majority of Peace Corps volunteers and similar young volunteers from Switzerland, the Netherlands, the Scandinavian countries, Germany, Australia, Canada, and New Zealand have worked sincerely in schools, kindergartens, children's centers, health services, hospitals, clinics, agricultural experiments, and related activities without any intention of supporting capitalism or neocolonialism. The final story of the impact of such volunteers will not be known for several years, but a realistic understanding of conditions in the developing countries by numerous idealistic people in many nations will contribute insight into the need for mutual cooperation and international concepts and so will support the global ideas so necessary for the world of today and tomorrow.[47]

### Social Planning

An important element in the process of community development is social planning. It was the main topic discussed at the International Conference of Social Work in Athens in 1964. Representatives agreed that the concept of social progress included not only economic considerations but also value judgments, peace in freedom, the extension of human rights, the elimination of poverty, preservation of health, and the promotion of education.[48]

The need for planning was included in reports to this conference submitted by delegates from the United States, Great Britain, Denmark, Finland, the Netherlands, Austria, Belgium, Brazil, Yugoslavia, Pakistan, India, Sweden, Norway, Israel, Germany, the Philippines, Venezuela, Greece, Canada, Jamaica, Italy, and Japan. Social planning for community development must take account of cultural, social, and economic conditions and of existing laws and customs, and it must tend to coordinate the efforts of all public and voluntary organizations at the local, regional, and national levels to achieve its goals.[49]

Mexico, in 1933, was the first nation to initiate planning for "national" economic and social development; Turkey followed in 1934, the Philippines in 1935, Chile in 1939. Many recently independent nations continued projects started by the former colonial governments. The United Nations and its affiliated agencies help many developing nations in this planning, with expert advice and financial assistance.[50]

Economic, social, and political development in the Western industrial countries occurred slowly, over several centuries, but the developing nations are attempting with the aid of foreign assistance to achieve such a dynamic change in a short span of time, without the necessary cultural, technical, and spiritual preparation of the population. This lack of basic requirements leads necessarily to failures and disappointments, particularly since few agricultural and industrial workers are willing or able to accept the work habits of a technical society, and since trade unions in the new countries are easily used by the authorities to serve as their allies, not as representatives of the working masses.[51]

The urgent need for an effective program of international community development was dramatically shown in September 1972 at the board meeting of the World Bank, when bank President Robert McNamara reported that development in the poorer nations has not yet reached the lower income strata of these countries, has not yet contended with the inhuman deprivations in hundreds of millions of lives in the developing world. The rich countries, with their immense incomes and technical capacity, provide only half of the assistance to the poor nations which was set as a target by the United Nations for the "Second Development Decade." Mr. McNamara proposed the establishment of specific targets to improve the incomes of the poorest 40 percent of the population in each country: an attack on unemployment and underemployment; land and tax reforms; public measures to ensure aid to disadvantaged groups; and the elimination of discriminatory policies in prices of land, labor, and capital.[52]

## Notes

[1]United Nations, *Social Progress Through Community Development* (New York, 1955, pp. 5–13); Ernest B. Harper and Arthur Dunham, eds., *Community Organization in Action* (New York: Association Press, 1959), pp. 524–26.

[2]Richard F. Behrendt, *Soziale Strategie für Entwicklungsländer*, 2nd ed. (Frankfurt a/M.:S. Fischer, 1968), pp. 11–20; Wilbur J. Cohen, "Social Planning and Urban Development," in Eugen Pusíc, ed., *Urban Development: Its Implications for Social Welfare* (New York: Columbia University Press, 1967), pp. 237–45; Gunnar Myrdal, *Beyond the Welfare State* (New Haven: Yale University Press, 1960), pp. 226–64; Arthur Dunham, *The New Community Organization* (New York: Crowell, 1971).

[3]"Social Service in Community Development," *International Social Service Review*, No. 6 (March 1960), 2–5; Behrendt, *Soziale Strategie*, pp. 90–94; Wilfred H. Chinn, "Social Development in the United Kingdom African Territories," *Annals*, 329 (May 1960), 78–87; Morris Ginsberg, "Toward a Theory of Social Development: The Growth of Rationality," in Raymond Aron and Bert F. Hoselitz, eds., *Le Développement social* (Paris: Mouton, 1965), pp. 27–66; Eugen Pusíc, *Social Welfare and Social Development* (Paris: Mouton, 1972), p. 28.

[4]United Nations, Bureau of Social Affairs, *Social Progress through Community Development* (New York, 1955), pp. 7–9; Maurice Dobb, *Economic Growth and Under-*

*developed Countries* (New York: International Publishers, 1963), pp. 45–59; Stanley A. Hetzler, *Technical Growth and Social Change* (New York: Praeger, 1969); Gunnar Myrdal, *The Challenge of World Poverty: A World Anti-Poverty Program in Outline* (New York: Pantheon, 1970).

[5]Peter Kuenstler, "Youth and Community Development," *Les Carnets de l'enfance* (Geneva), 22 (Apr.–June 1973), 81–93; W. J. H. Kouwenhoven, "Volunteer-Aided Community Development: An Introductory Study" (Washington, D.C.: International Secretariat for Volunteer Service, 1966).

[6]Kuenstler, "Youth and Community Development," p. 89.

[7]Ibid., pp.. 11–13; Arnold M. Rose, "Sociological Factors Affecting Economic Development in India," *Studies in Comparative International Developments*, 3, No. 9 (Beverly Hills, Ca., 1967–68), 169–81; Behrendt, *Soziale Strategie*, pp. 310–15.

[8]Hong Kong Council of Social Service, *Community Development Resource Book 1972* (Hong Kong, 1973).

[9]United Nations, *Social Progress Through Community Development*, pp. 14–17; Henry de Decker, *Nation et développement communautaire en Guinea et en Sénégal* (Paris: Mouton, 1967); Paul Herbert Guinault, *Community Development Programs in Greece with Special Consideration of Welfare Through Employment* (New York: United Nations, 1953); Erbaki Hermasi, *Leadership and National Development in North Africa* (Berkeley: University of California Press, 1972).

[10]Arnold J. Toynbee, *A Study of History* (London: Oxford University Press, 1950), pp. 260–72; Behrendt, *Soziale Strategie*, pp. 124–32; Gabriele Wülker, "Strukturprobleme asiatischer und afrikanischer Entwicklungslander," in Hermann Ziock, ed., *Die Internationale Politik* (Munich: R. Oldenburg, 1968), pp. 38–41.

[11]Bert F. Hoselitz, "Stratification and Economic Development," *International Science Journal*, 16, No. 2 (1964), 237–51.

[12]Wülker, *Strukturprobleme*, 43–46; Herman Ziock, ed., *Entwicklungshilfe* (Frankfurt a/M.: Ullstein, 1966), 101–9; International Social Science Council, Shigeto Tswio, ed., *Environmental Disruption* (Tokyo, 1970); Luz A. Einsiedel, *Success and Failure in Selected Community Development Projects in Batanga* (Manila: University of Philippines Press, 1968); Frances Violich, *Community Development and the Urban Planning Process in Latin America* (Los Angeles: University of California Press, 1967).

[13]Erhard Eppler, "Beschäftigung und Erziehung in Entwicklungsländern" (Employment and Education in the Developing Countries), *Zur zweiten Entwicklungsdekade* (Bonn: Friedrich-Ebert Stiftung, 1970), pp. 21–27; Lewis Coser, *Social Functions of Conflict* (New York: Free Press, 1963); United Nations, Regional and Community Development Section, "Methods of Community Development," *Community Development Journal*, 6, No. 3 (Autumn 1971), 148–55; Lee J. Cary, ed., *Community Development As a Process* (Columbia, Mo.: University of Missouri Press, 1970). The importance of self-determination in community development is emphasized in Helmuth Heisler, "A Reconsideration of the Theory of Community Development," *International Social Work*, 14, No. 2 (1971), 24–33.

[14]Heisler, "A Reconsideration of the Theory of Community Development," pp. 18–23.

[15]Heisler, "A Reconsideration of the Theory of Community Development," pp. 28–30; Behrendt, *Soziale Strategie*, pp. 106–8, 125, 130–33, and 177–78; Gerhard

Colm and Theodore Geiger, *Development of the Emerging Countries* (Washington, D.C.: Smithsonian Institution, 1962), pp. 49–52; Eugene Staley, *The Future of Underdeveloped Countries* (New York: McGraw-Hill, 1954), pp. 20–21.

[16]Albert Mayer, *Social Progress Through Local Action* (Berkeley: University of California Press, 1953); Rose, "Sociological Factors," pp. 171–74; Bertram G. Gross, *Action Under Planning: Essays in Guided Economic Development* (New York: McGraw-Hill, 1966); Everett M. Rogers, *Modernization Among Peasants: The Impact of Communication* (New York: Holt, 1969); Kusum Nair, *Blossoms in the Dust* (New York: Praeger, 1961), pp. 29–31; 75–87.

[17]Mayer, *Social Progress Through Community Development*, pp. 39–40.

[18]Mayer, *Social Progress Through Community Development*, pp. 45–73; Doreen Warriner, *Land Reform in Principle and Practice*, (Oxford: Oxford University Press, 1969); Laurence I. Hewes, Jr., "Land Reform in South Vietnam," *Center Magazine*, (June 1972), 18–19; Christian P. Pothelm, *The Dynamics of Political Modernization* (Berkeley: University of California Press, 1972).

[19]Mayer, *Social Progress Through Community Development*, pp. 73–74.

[20]Mayer, *Social Progress Through Community Development*, pp. 75–78; Herbert Marcuse, "The Problem of Social Change in the Technological Society," in Aron and Hoselitz, eds., *Le Développement social*, 139–60; Bertrand de Jouvenel, "Orientation de l'efficience," ibid., pp. 161–73; V. K. R. V. Rao, "Some Problems Confronting Traditional Societies in the Process of Development," ibid., pp. 199–221.

[21]Mayer, *Social Progress Through Community Development*, pp. 84–85.

[22]Ibid., pp. 94–97; A. Waterston, *Development Planning: Lessons of Experience* (Baltimore: Johns Hopkins Press, 1965); Kurt G. Kiesinger, "Unsere Kulturpolitischen Autgaben in der Entwicklungshilfe," in Hermann Ziock, ed., *Entwicklungshilfe*, pp. 77–100; Gabriele Wülker, "Sociologische Probleme der Entwicklungshilfe," ibid., pp. 101–20.

[23]Mayer, *Social Progress Through Local Action*, pp. 99–105; Eileen Younghusband, "Intercultural Aspects of Social Work," in Robert W. Klenk and Robert M. Ryan, eds., *The Practice of Social Work* (Belmont, Ca.: Wadsworth, 1970), pp. 43–45.

[24]United Nations, "An Urbanization Policy for Economic and Social Development," *International Social Development Review*, No. 1 (New York, 1968), 3–4; Arthur F. Raper, *Rural Development in Action: The Comprehensive Experiment of Comilla, East Pakistan* (Ithaca, N.Y.: Cornell University Press, 1970); Barbara Ward, "Urbanization: International Perspectives," *The Social Welfare Forum 1967*, pp. 159–71.

[25]Gunnar Myrdal, *Challenge to Affluence* (New York: Random House, 1963), pp. 7–8; Francine R. Frankl, *India's Green Revolution: Economic Gains and Political Costs* (Princeton, N.J.: Princeton University Press, 1971).

[26]Chris Lawson, "Quaker Volunteers—What Use?" *Friends World News*, No. 96 (Spring 1972), 451–52; Peter Kapenga, "Changes Essential to Close Gap Between Rich, Poor Nations," Friends Committee on Legislation of California *Newsletter*, 21, No. 7 (July 1972), 5–6.

[27]*International Social Development Review*, No. 1, 3–6.

[28]Ibid., p. 6; Lucien Mehl, "Problems of Future Urban Development," in *Urban Development*, pp. 78–99; Michel de Chalendar, "Social Implications of Advanced Urban Planning and Development," ibid., pp. 147–51; J. B. Langlot, "The Impact of Urbanization on Rural Areas," ibid., pp. 163–88; Ali Akbar, "New Trends in

Client Participation," ibid., pp. 227–36; Asoka Mehta, "The Social Impact of Urbanization as a Universal Process," ibid., pp. 25–34; André Vincent, "La Politique du développement proposé par le rapport Pearson," *Les Carnets de l'enfance*, No. 13 (Jan.–March 1971), 7–20.

[29]Ebenezer Howard, *Garden Cities of the Future* (London: Farber & Farber, 1902).

[30]J. B. Cullingworth, *Town and Country Planning in England and Wales* (Toronto: University of Toronto Press, 1964); Great Britain, Ministry of Housing and Local Government, *The Needs of New Communities* (London: H.M.S.O., 1967); Maurice Broady, *Planning for People* (London: Bedford Square Press, 1968); British Councils of Social Service, *Participation and All That* (London, 1969); J. H. Nicholson, *New Communities in Britain* (London: Councils of Social Service, 1961); United Nations Department of Economic and Social Affairs, "Urbanization: Development Policies and Planning," *International Social Development Review*, No. 1 (1968), 1–130.

[31]"Le Vaudreuil: French Experiment in Urbanism Without Tears," *Science*, 174, No. 4004 (Oct. 1, 1971), 39–41.

[32]Shimon Gottschalk, "Citizen Participation in the Development of New Towns: A Cross-National View," *The Social Service Review*, 45, No. 2 (June 1971), 194–204; Bruno Merk, "Public Subsidized Housing in the State of Bavaria," in Erika Spiegel, ed., *Entlastungsstadt Perlach in Munich* (Hamburg: Neue Heimat, May 1967); M. Goldman, *Legal Aspects of Town Planning in Israel* (Jerusalem: Institute for Legal Research and Corporative Law, 1966).

[33]Social Service of Commerce, "Educational Work for Trades People's Welfare" (Rio de Janeiro, 1973).

[34]John B. Turner, "Uncontrolled Urban Settlement: Problems and Policies," *International Social Development Review*, No. 2 (1968), 107–30; Gideon Sjoberg, *The Pre-Industrial City* (New York: Free Press, 1960); Bertram G. Gross, "The Administration of Economic Planning: Principles and Fallacies," *Studies in Comparative International Developments*, 3, No. 5 (1967–68); Hans W. Singer, "International Aid to Development," *Les Carnets de l'enfance*, 14 (Apr.–June 1971), 27–39.

[35]Turner, "Uncontrolled Urban Settlement," pp. 115–17; Charles Abrams, *Man's Struggle for Shelter in an Urbanizing World* (Cambridge: MIT Press, 1964); G. H. Sewell, *Squatter Settlements in Turkey: Analysis of Social, Political and Economic Problems* (Cambridge: MIT Press, 1964); M. Juppenlatz, *Urban Squatter Resettlement* (New York: Sapang Palay, 1965); P. Descloitres, *L'Algérie des bidonvilles* (Paris); Paul Sebag, *Un Faubourg du Tunis* (Paris: Presses Universitaires de France, 1960).

[36]Ruben Utria, "The Housing Problem in Latin America in Relation to Structural Development Factors," *Economic Bulletin for Latin America* (New York, 1964).

[37]Turner, "Uncontrolled Urban Settlement," pp. 118–21.

[38]United Nations Research Institute for Social Development, "The Concept of Development and Its Measurement," *International Social Development Review*, No. 2 (New York, 1970), 1–6; United Nations Department of Economic and Social Affairs, *1967 Report on the World Social Situation* (New York, 1969), pp. 96–97 (hereafter referred to as the *1967 Report*).

[39]Ibid., pp. 3–6.

[40]Myrdal, *Challenge to Affluence*, pp. 15–52.

[41]Myrdal, *Challenge to Affluence,* p. 39; United Nations, "Community Planning in Marginal Urban Settlements," *International Social Development Review* (New York), No. 2 (1970), 7–12; John C. Turner, "Uncontrolled Urban Settlement: Problems and Policies," *ibid.,* 107–30.

[42]"Community Planning in Marginal Urban Settlements," in *International Social Development Review,* pp. 7–12; Elmer C. Bratt, "Economic Growth and Fluctuation," *The Annals,* 393 (Jan. 1971), 122–31; Simon Kutzets, *Economic Development and Cultural Change* (Chicago: University of Chicago Press, 1963), pp. 13, 68; Inga Thorsson, "The Social Aspects of Development," *Les Carnets de l'enfance,* 13 (March 1971), 23–35.

[43]Charles A. Frankenhoff, "Elements of an Economic Model for Slums in a Developing Economy," *Economic Development and Cultural Change* (Chicago: University of Chicago Press, 1967); Maria Luiza Moniz de Arago, "The Special Needs of Young Children in Shantytowns," *Urban Development: Its Implications for Social Welfare* (New York: Columbia University Press, 1967), pp. 348–58.

[44]Albino Sakko, "New Trends in Clients' Participation," in Eugen Pusíc, ed., *Urban Development,* pp. 217–26; Ali Akbar, "A View from a Developing Country," ibid., pp. 227–36.

[45]Nair, *Blossoms in the Dust,* pp. 46–57.

[46]David Hapgood and Meridan Bennet, *Agents of Change* (New York: Little, Brown, 1968); Hermann Ziock, *Entwicklungshilfe-Baustein für die Welt von Morgen* (Frankfurt a/M.: Ullstein, 1966); Charles Creesy, "Politics and the Peace Corps," *The New Leader* (Nov. 30, 1970), 11–15; Stanley Meisler, "Isolated Success," in P. Chatterjee, ed., *The Nation in India* (Philadelphia: Liveright, 1972).

[47]Gabriele Wülker, "Soziologische Probleme der Entwicklungsländer," in H. Ziock, ed., *Entwicklungshilfe-Baustein,* pp. 101–20; Werner Lamby, "Entwicklungspolitik im internationalen Feld," ibid., pp. 141–47; Gunnar Myrdal, *An International Economy: Problems and Prospects* (New York: Free Press, 1956), pp. 180ff.; Myrdal, *Beyond the Welfare State,* pp. 200–25; Helmuth Heisler, "A Reconsideration of the Theory of Community Development," *International Social Work,* 14, No. 2 (1971), 26–33; James J. Shields, *Education in Community Development* (New York: Praeger, 1967); Bruno Knall, *Grundsätze und Methoden der Entwicklungsprogrammierung* (Wiesbaden: Harassowitz, 1969).

[48]Charles I. Schottland, "Issues in Social Planning for the Future of the Conference" (Athens, 1964), pp. 4–9; "Children and Youth in Development Planning," UNICEF (New York, 1964).

[49]Roger Marier, "Planning and Coordination of Services," *Social Progress Through Social Planning, The Role of Social Work: Proceedings of the XIIth International Conference of Social Work in Athens* (New York: ICSW, 1964), pp. 311–12; S. K. Khainduka, "Social Planning and Community Organization: Community Development," *Encyclopedia of Social Work, 1971,* pp. 1343–51.

[50]Alfred Jacobs and Ernst Hickmann, *Entwicklungspolitik* (Darmstadt: Hoppenstedt, 1960), pp. 649ff; Gabriele Wülker, "Strukturprobleme," pp. 84–86; Behrendt, *Soziale Strategie,* pp. 47–54.

[51]Behrendt, *Soziale Strategie,* pp. 465–68; Myrdal, *Beyond the Welfare State,* pp. 159–76.

[52]Robert McNamara, "Report to Board of Directors," *International Newsletter* (World Bank), No. 10 (Dec. 1972), p. 15.

82    *International community development*

## Selected References

*Books*

ALLEN, FRANCIS R., *Technology and Social Change.* New York: Appleton-Century-Crofts, 1957.

ANDERSON, NELS, *The Urban Community: A World Perspective.* New York: Holt, 1959.

ARENSBERG, CONRAD M., AND ARTHUR H. MINKOFF, *Introducing Social Change.* Chicago: Aldine, 1964.

ARON, RAYMOND, AND BERT F. HOSELITZ, *Le Développement social.* Paris: Mouton, 1965.

BATAN, JORGE, HARLEIGH L. BROWNING, AND ELIZABETH JELIN, *Men in a Developing Society* (Mexico). Austin: University of Texas Press, 1973.

BATTEN, T. R., *The Human Factor in Community Work.* London: Oxford University Press, 1965.

———, *Training for Community Development.* London: Oxford University Press, 1965.

BEHRENDT, RICHARD F., *Soziale Strategie für Entwicklungsländer,* 2nd ed. (Social Strategy for Developing Countries). Frankfurt a/M.: Fischer, 1968.

———, *Zwischen Anarchie und neuen Ordnungen* (Between Anarchy and New Arrangements). Freiburg: Rombach, 1967.

BENNETT, AUSTIN E., *Reflections on Community Development Education.* Orono: University of Maine Press, 1969.

BHATTACHARYYA, S. N., *Community Development in Developing Countries.* Calcutta: Academic Publishers, 1972.

BIDDLE, WILLIAM W., *The Community Development Process.* New York: Holt, 1965.

BOEHM, E. A., *Twentieth-Century Economic Development in Australia.* New York: Barnes & Noble, 1972.

BOSERUP, ESTER, *Women's Role in Economic Development.* New York: St. Martin's, 1970.

BROKENSHA, DAVID, AND PETER HODGE, *Community Development: An Interpretation.* San Francisco: Chandler, 1969.

BROWNELL, BAKER, *The Human Community: Its Philosophy and Practice for a Time of Crisis.* New York: Harper & Row, 1950.

CARY, LEE J., ed., *Community Development as a Process.* New York: Columbia University Press, 1970.

CHOWDRY, D. PAUL, *Voluntary Social Welfare in India.* New Delhi: Sterling, 1971.

CLINARD, MARSHALL B., *Slums and Community Development: Experiments in Self-Help.* New York: Free Press, 1966.

COHN, BERNARD S., *India: The Social Anthropology of a Civilization.* Englewood Cliffs, N.J.: Prentice-Hall, 1971.

COSER, LEWIS A., *Social Functions of Conflict.* New York: Free Press, 1963.

DENTON, GEOFFREY, et al., *Economic Planning and Policies in Britain, France and Germany.* London: Allen & Unwin, 1968.

DU SAUTOY, PETER, *The Organization of a Community Development Programme.* London: Oxford University Press, 1962.

ETZIONI, AMITAI, AND EVA ETZIONI, eds., *Social Change: Sources, Patterns, and Consequences.* New York: Harper & Row, 1965.

FARLEY, RAWLE, *The Economic Development of Latin America: Development Problems in Perspective.* New York: Harper & Row, 1973.

FIELD, ARTHUR J., ed., *Urbanization and Work in Modernizing Societies.* St. Thomas, Virgin Islands: Caribbean Research Institute, 1967.

FOSTER, GEORGE M., *Traditional Cultures and the Impact of Technological Change.* New York: Harper & Row, 1962.

FRY, JOHN R., ed., *The Church and Community Organization.* New York: National Council of Churches, 1965.

GALBRAITH, JOHN KENNETH, *Economic Development.* Cambridge: Harvard University Press, 1964.

————, *Economics, Peace and Laughter.* Boston: Houghton Mifflin, 1971.

HÄFELIN, ULRICH, *Möglichkeiten der Verwirklichung der Demokratie in den neuen Staaten Afrikas und Asiens* (Opportunities of Realization of Democracy in the New Nations of Africa and Asia). Basel: Helbing & Lichtenhahn, 1962.

HAGEN, EVERETT E., *On the Theory of Social Change: How Economic Growth Begins.* Homewood, Ill.: Dorsey, 1962.

HAMBRIDGE, GOVE, ed., *Dynamics of Development: An International Development Reader.* New York: Praeger, 1964.

HAYES, SAMUEL P., JR., *Measuring the Results of Development Projects.* Paris: UNESCO, 1959.

HEATH, DWIGHT B., CHARLES J. ERAMUS, AND HANS C. BUECHLER, *Land Reform and Social Revolution in Bolivia.* New York: Praeger, 1969.

HEILBRONER, ROBERT L., *The Great Ascent: The Struggle for Economic Development in Our Time.* New York: Harper & Row, 1963.

HILL, POLLY, *Rural Hausa: A Village and a Setting.* Cambridge: Cambridge University Press, 1972.

HIRSCHMAN, ALBERT O., *The Strategy of Economic Growth.* New Haven, Conn.: Yale University Press, 1958.

HONEY, JOHN C., *Planning and the Private Sector: The Experience in Developing Countries.* New York: Dunellen, 1970.

HOROWITZ, IRVING LOUIS, *Three Worlds of Development,* 2nd ed. New York: Oxford University Press, 1972.

HYMAN, HERBERT H., et al., *Inducing Social Change in Developing Countries.* New York: United Nations Research Institute for Social Development, 1967.

INTERNATIONAL COUNCIL ON SOCIAL WELFARE, *New Strategies for Social Development —Role of Social Welfare* (Proceedings of the 15th International Conference of Social Welfare, Manila, 1971). New York, 1971.

JAKOBSON LEO, AND VED PRAKESH, eds., *Urbanization and National Development,* Vol. I: *South and Southeast Asia Urban Affairs Annuals.* Beverly Hills, Ca.: Sage, 1971.

JAYASENA, H., *Voluntary Action to Advance Economic and Social Development.* New York: International Society for Community Development, 1968.

KUNKEL, JOHN H., *Society and Economic Change: A Behavioral Perspective of Social Change.* New York: Oxford University Press, 1970.

KURODA, YASAMASA, *Reed Town, Japan: A Study in Community Power Structure and Social Change.* Honolulu: University of Hawaii Press, 1974.

LIPPIT, RONALD, JEANNE WATSON, AND BRUCE WESTLEY, *The Dynamics of Planned Change.* New York: Harcourt Brace Jovanovich, 1958.

LIPSET, SEYMOUR M., AND NEIL F. SMELSER, *Social Structure and Mobility in Economic Development.* Chicago: Aldine, 1966.

LOWIS, W. ARTHUR, *The Theory of Economic Growth.* London: Allen & Unwin, 1956.

McCORD, WILLIAM, *The Springtime of Freedom: The Evolution of Developing Societies.* New York: Oxford University Press, 1965.

McKINNON, RONALD I., *Money and Capital in Economic Development.* Washington, D.C.: Brookings Institution, 1973.

MALENBAUM, WILFRED, *Modern India's Economy: Two Decades of Planned Growth.* Columbus, Ohio: Merrill, 1971.

MAPARA, G. ed., *International Confederation of Trade Unions—Views on the Economic and Social Situation in Asia.* New Delhi: A. Solomon, 1962.

MARTIN, E. W., ed., *Comparative Development in Social Welfare.* London: Allen & Unwin, 1972.

MAYER, ALBERT, *Pilot Project India.* Berkeley: University of California Press, 1958.

MERLIN, PIERRE, *New Towns: Regional Planning and Development.* New York: Barnes & Noble, 1973.

MEYER, C. H., et al., *Community Work and Social Change.* London: Longmans, 1968.

MEZIROW, JACK D., *Dynamics of Community Development.* New York: Scarecrow, 1963.

MOORE, WILBERT E., *Industrialization and Labor: Social Aspects of Economic Development.* Baltimore: Johns Hopkins Press, 1965.

MYRDAL, GUNNAR, *Challenge to Affluence.* New York: Pantheon, 1963.

NAIR, KUSIM, *Blossoms in the Dust: The Human Factor in Indian Development.* New York: Praeger, 1961.

NATIONAL ASSOCIATION OF SOCIAL WORKERS, *Community Development and Community Organization: An International Workshop.* New York, 1968.

NAVAR, BALDEV RAJ, *The Modernization Imperative and Indian Planning.* Delhi: Vicas, 1972.

OTTENBERG, SIMON, *Leadership and Authority in an African Society: The Afkipo Village Group.* Seattle: University of Washington Press, 1971.

PAJESTKA, JOSEPH, *Social Dimensions of Development.* New York: United Nations, 1970.

POWELSON, JOHN, *Institutions of Economic Growth: A Theory of Conflict Management in Developing Countries.* Princeton, N.J.: Princeton University Press, 1972.

PUSÍC, EUGEN, *Social Welfare and Social Development.* Paris: Mouton, 1972.

ROBERTS, PAUL CRAIG, *Alienation and Soviet Economy.* Albuquerque: University of New Mexico Press, 1971.

ROY, PRODYTO, et al., *The Impact of Communication on Rural Development.* Paris: UNESCO, 1969.

SHAW, EDWARD S., *Financial Deepening in Economic Development.* New York: Oxford University Press, 1973.

SHERMAN, HOWARD, *Radical Political Economy.* New York: Basic Books, 1972.

SHIELDS, JAMES J., JR., *Education in Community Development: Its Function in Technical Assistance.* New York: Praeger, 1967.

SIRSIKAR, V. M., *The Rural Elite in a Developing Society: A Study in Political Sociology.* New Delhi: Orient Longman, 1970.

SPIEGELGLAS, STEPHEN, AND CHARLES J. WELSH, eds., *Economic Development: Challenge and Promise.* Englewood Cliffs, N.J.: Prentice-Hall, 1970.

STALEY, EUGENE, *The Future of Underdeveloped Countries.* New York: McGraw-Hill, 1954.

SWAMY, SUPRAMANIAN, *Indian Economic Planning: An Alternative Approach.* New York: Barnes & Noble, 1972.

SWERDLOW, IRVING, ed., *Development Administration.* Syracuse, N.Y.: Syracuse University Press, 1963.

UNITED NATIONS, *Decentralization for National and Local Development.* New York, 1962.

———, *Integrated Approach to Rural Development in Africa.* New York, 1971.

———, *Multinational Corporations in World Development.* New York, 1973.

———, *Planning for Balanced Social and Economic Development.* New York, 1964.

VIOLICH, FRANCES, *Community Development and the Urban Planning Process in Latin America.* Los Angeles: University of California Press, 1967.

VON DER MEHRDEN, FRED R., *Politics of the Developing Nations,* 2nd ed. Englewood Cliffs, N.J.: Prentice-Hall, 1970.

WALLACE, LUTHER T., et al., *Selected Perspectives for Community Resources Development.* Raleigh: North Carolina State University Press, 1969.

WARD, RICHARD J., *Development Issues for the 1970s.* New York: Dunellen, 1973.

WATANABE, TSUNEHIKO, "National Planning and Economic Development: A Critical Review of the Japanese Experience," *Economics of Planning,* 1970.

WATERSTON, ALBERT, *Development Planning: Lessons of Experience.* Baltimore: Johns Hopkins Press, 1965.

WEINTRAUB, D., M. LISSAK, AND Y. AZMON, *Moshava, Kibbutz and Moshov: Patterns of Jewish Rural Settlement and Development in Palestine.* Ithaca, N.Y.: Cornell University Press, 1969.

YOUNGHUSBAND, EILEEN, *Community Work and Social Change.* London: Longmans, 1969.

ZWANIKKEN, WILLEM A. C., *Report on the Situation of Community Work in the Netherlands.* The Hague: Clearing House, 1972.

*Articles*

ALEXANDER, CHAUNCY A., AND CHARLES McCANN, "The Concept of Representativeness in Community Organization," *Social Work,* 1 (Jan. 1956), 48–52.

AUSTIN, DAVID M., "Social Work's Relations to National Development in Developing Nations," *Social Work,* 15 (Jan. 1970), 97–106.

BELSHAW, H., "Some Social Aspects of Economic Development in Underdeveloped Countries in Asia," pp. 190–95 in Lyle W. Shannon, ed., *Underdeveloped Areas.* New York: Harper & Row, 1957.

BRIDGEHEAD, KATHRYN, "Mobile Creches in India: A New Basis for Community Development in Delhi," *Community Development Journal,* 7 (Apr. 1972), 136–41.

BROWN, MALCOLM J., "Social Work Values in a Developing Country," *Social Work,* 15 (Jan. 1970), 107–12.

BULSARA, JAL F., "Which Way for Social Welfare in the Developing World," *Community Development Journal,* 8 (Jan. 1973), 6–13.

CLINARD, MARSHALL B., "Evaluation and Research in Urban Community Development," *International Revue of Community Development,* 12 (1963), 187–98.

COLLINS, DOREEN, "First Thoughts on Social Policy in the Common Market," pp. 204–21 in Kathleen Jones, ed., *The Year Book of Social Policy in Britain 1971.* London: Routledge & Kegan Paul, 1972.

DAHLGAARD, LANGE, "Experiences and Problems in Long-Range Socioeconomic Planning in Denmark," *International Social Development Revue,* 3 (1971), 56–61.

DRUCKER, PETER F., "A Warning to the White Rich World," *Harpers Magazine,* 237, no. 1423 (Dec. 1968), 67–75.

DUBEY, S. N., "Tribal Welfare Programmes," *Indian Journal of Social Work,* 32, No. 3 (1971), 207–20.

DUNHAM, ARTHUR, "The Outlook for Community Development: An International Symposium," *International Revue of Community Development,* 5 (1960), 33–55.

DUTTON, EDWARD P., "A Bimodal Approach to Social Planning and Community Development Programmes and Their Evaluation," *Community Development Journal,* 7, No. 2 (1972), 91–98.

EPSTEIN, IRWIN, TONI TRIPODI, and PHILIP FELLIN, "Community Development Programmes and Their Evaluation," *Community Development Journal,* 8, No. 1 (Jan. 1973), 28–36.

FARAH, ABDULRAHIM ABBY, "Problems of African Social Development," *Social Welfare Forum 1972* (New York), pp. 135–172.

GOULET, DENIS, "The Disappointing Decade of Development," *The Center Magazine,* 2 No. 5 (Sept. 1969), 12–68.

HARRINGTON, MICHAEL, "Crises of Affluence," *The Center Magazine,* 2, No. 5 (Sept. 1969), 47–52.

HAUSSMAN, FAY, "Brazil's Domestic Peace Corps," *Saturday Review—World* (Oct. 9, 1973), 50–57.

HERMANSEN, OLE F., "Report on the Situation of Community Work in Field and Training in Denmark," *Report on Community Work* (Feb. 1972), 26–34.

HERSKOWITZ, M. J., "Motivation and Cultural-Change Patterns in Technological Change," pp. 41–52 in Jean Meynaud, ed., *Social Change and Economic Development.* Paris: UNESCO, 1963.

HERTZ-GOLDEN, HILDE, "Literacy and Social Change in Underdeveloped Countries," pp. 108–13 in Lyle W. Shannon, ed., *Underdeveloped Areas.* New York: Harper & Row, 1957.

HILL, ELLEN B., "Reflections on Assistance to Developing Countries," *International Revue of Community Development,* 15/16 (1966), 43–54.

HODGE, PETER, "Urban Community Development in Hong Kong," *Community Development Journal*, 7, No. 3 (Oct. 1972), 154–64.

HOSELITZ, BERT, "Problems of Adapting and Communicating Modern Techniques to Less Developed Areas," pp. 400–407 in Lyle W. Shannon, ed., *Underdeveloped Areas*. New York: Harper & Row, 1957.

————, "Stratification and Economic Development," *International Science Journal*, 16, No. 2 (1964), 237–51.

ILIOVICE, JEAN, "L'Apport européen au Service Social du tiers-monde," *Les Carnets de l'enfance*, 19 (1972), 103–11.

JAMES, ROBERT W., "Measures of Effective Community Development," *International Review of Community Development*, 8 (1961), 5–13.

KAITENBRONNER, JOOST, "The Concept of Development and Underdevelopment," *Les Carnets de l'enfance*, 17 (1972), 23–36.

KHINDUKA, SHANTI K., "Community Development: Potentials and Limitations," pp. 15–28 in *Social Work Practice*. New York: Columbia University Press, 1969.

————, "Social Planning and Community Organization: Community Development," *Encyclopedia of Social Work, 1971*, pp. 1345–57.

LONGMORE, WILSON, AND CHARLES P. LOOMIS, "Health Needs and Potential Colonialization: Areas of Peru," pp. 174–80 in Lyle W. Shannon, ed., *Underdeveloped Areas*. New York: Harper & Row, 1957.

MEAD, MARGARET, "Professional Problems of Education in Dependent Countries," pp. 340–50 in Lyle W. Shannon, ed., *Underdeveloped Areas*. New York: Harper & Row, 1957.

MINICLIER, LOUIS M., "Community Development in the World Today," *Community Development Revue*, 7 (June 1962), 69–72.

MORRIS, ROBERT, "The Social Dimension of Urban and Regional Planning," *International Revue of Community Development*, 15/16 (1966), 201–12.

NAGPAUL, HANS, "Conformity and Community Development," *International Revue of Community Development*, 11 (1963), 105–18.

PERNELL, RUBY, "Perspectives of Social Development at Home and Abroad," pp. 126–40 in *Social Welfare Forum 1968*. New York: Columbia University Press, 1968.

PETERSON, GUSTAVE H., "Latin America: Benign Neglect Is Not Enough," *Foreign Affairs*, 51, No. 3 (April 1973), 598–607.

POLSON, ROBERT A., "Theory and Training for Community Development," *Rural Sociology*, 23 (March 1958), 34–42.

ROSS, MURRAY G., "Community Participation," *International Revue of Community Development*, 5 (1960), 107–19.

SHERRARD, THOMAS, "Community Organization and Community Development," *Community Development Revue*, 7 (June 1962), 11–20.

SINGER, HANS W., "A New Approach to the Problem of the Dual Society in Developing Countries," *International Social Development Revue*, 3 (1971), 23–31.

TANNENBAUM, FRANK, "Technology and Race in Mexico," pp. 160–66 in Lyle W. Shannon, ed., *Underdeveloped Areas*. New York: Harper & Row, 1957.

TUMIN, MELVIN M., "Some Social Requirements for Effective Community Development," *Community Development Revue,* 11 (1968), 1–39.

TURNER, JOHN B., "Relation of Health and Welfare Planning to Social Change and Development," pp. 11–13 in *Social Work and Social Planning.* New York: National Association of Social Workers, 1964.

UNITED NATIONS COMMISSION FOR SOCIAL DEVELOPMENT, "Social Policy and Planning in National Development," *International Social Development Revue,* 3 (1971), 4–15.

YOUNG, FRANK W., AND RUTH C. YOUNG, "The Sequence and Direction of Community Growth: A Cross-Cultural Generalization," *Rural Sociology,* 27 (Dec. 1962), 374–86.

# *Family and child welfare services*

*4*

## Today's Families

Throughout this world the family is the kinship group that forms the basic unit of society. Social services for the family and its children are the fundamental means of social welfare. Families differ; in Western societies there is the conjugal or nuclear family, consisting of parents and children. Elsewhere there are extended family groups, such as the tribe, the clan, or some other, broader relationship group like the tribes and aboriginal groups among African nations and in some other developing countries.[1] In many societies the role of the family is changing, because of the influence of technology and industrialization; new mores and customs; new roles for women; different types of education in rural and urban surroundings; new forms of labor and employment; different forms of leadership and interrelationships between communities of rural and urban character; and new forms of nutrition, housing, and work. There is a general trend toward higher levels of living and better protection of family life against breakdowns, desertion, child marriages, and certain forms of polygamy. Despite differences in the functions of the family in different political and cultural societies, the consensus is that the basic needs of human beings, particularly of small children, are best met in the family unit. This includes nutrition, shelter, clothing, water, health care, and the fulfillment of religious or ethical needs. Family units are different in different countries, and there is a marked difference between family life in rural areas and family life in urban sections.

The family is still recognized as the cornerstone of human society in all nations, even in some that attempted to replace the family by state institutions. Within most societies family life differs according to region, class, nationality, religion, property, and customs, but there are important common elements and needs in family life everywhere.[2] Since the family as a social institution is highly responsive to social, political, and economic change, present world conditions require that social services for the family and children be adjusted to the changing needs of the families in the various countries of the world. These needs may be economic (income to produce or purchase food, clothing, medical service, or housing). They may be caused by lack of work, unemployment, or underemployment, or by poor health, illness, disabilities of a physical or mental nature, or accidents. There may be emotional problems—a lack of harmony between husband and wife and children, desertion by the father, adolescent delinquency or maladjustment. Social services must try to alleviate the stresses and sufferings from such conditions according to the customs of the different countries. Social work and social welfare assume different functions in various cultures, but the need for some type of social services for families and children is universal.[3]

In Asia and Africa the extended family comprises the families of brothers, cousins, sons, nephews, and their wives and children (in South Africa and the Islamic countries several wives). Beyond the extended family, the clan includes additional families that carry the same family name or that are descended from a common ancestor. The members of the clan feel stronger obligations to the clan's members than to the local community or to a religious society. In times of need, famine, old age, illness, or unemployment this solidarity is an important element of security for the family or clan members. In the frequent cases of unemployment in most developing countries this solidarity is an important economic protection for the unemployed, because these countries have no insurance legislation, but it is also a severe burden for those who are obliged to assist.[4] In these countries the extended famiiy supports the education and vocational training of its adolescents, and their higher incomes in later life will be an advantage for the entire family group. Notwithstanding such assets, in a period of growing industrialization and urbanization the extended family retards the process of social and economic progress, individual development and self-reliance, and the mobility and initiative that are desirable in modern life. This explains the growing trend in many new countries of leaving the rural communities and moving to the cities.

Social workers in family and children services have to help the families to learn how they can help themselves by good homekeeping and health and nutrition practices. They must also alert parents and children to use those institutions of society that can assist them in education, health care, economic welfare, legal protection, and emotional well-being, and thus strengthen family life.

The needs of families and children for social services exist independent of the varieties of cultures. In Africa these services have to support the traditional family pattern, the tribal extended family, with its support of sick family members in clinics and hospitals, and will have to protect family life against the dangers of disorganization in overcrowded slums of the cities. This may include insuring the legal status of marriages and of polygamy; health care; providing safeguards for mothers and children in case of divorce or desertion; helping in the education of the children, in preparing them for a vocation; preventing maladjustment and delinquency through health services and recreation; and generally improving family life. It may also require support in attempts to alleviate poverty and improve living conditions, in rural as well as in urban areas. It may lead to the development of systems of social security and children's allowances according to the facilities and economic conditions of the country.[5]

Some countries, such as the U.S.S.R., deny the need for professional social workers. In such countries, social services for families and children are performed by members of other professions or by workers' councils and factory stewards (though one may question whether those persons are well qualified to serve those in difficult emotional and personal circumstances that require professional knowledge and skills).[6] Even communist societies preserve the family and recognize the duty of parents to educate their children, and render essential support for these duties through children's allowances and social security benefits.

### The Family in China

There is much misunderstanding of family life in China among Western nations, but a great deal can be learned from the experiences of Professor C. K. Yang of the University of Pittsburgh, a sociologist who left north China a generation ago and who was able to visit China from October to November 1971. Yang found family life there greatly improved in comparison with the period before the Communist Revolution. Sanitation, public health facilities, and medical services are better than before, the severe hunger epidemics that used to occur repeatedly have been eliminated, workers in urban settings now have one rest day a week, and aged persons receive retirement allowances in state enterprises. Illiteracy has been reduced, and education is being transformed into production training and pragmatism. Physical culture is extremely popular and contributes to strength and health. Crime and banditry, formerly widespread, have mostly disappeared because of citizen's control. Family unity and tradition are still largely maintained; the three-generation family remains widespread in the country, but is also common in the cities. Functionally, however, the family in China is now less influential than in old times.[7] Families consume fewer luxury items, more basic necessities. Small towns develop industries. The communist regime has made old and young people politically conscious, well organized, and disciplined. Women are treated equally, but do not yet hold leadership positions in great numbers.

Madison emphasizes that social work does not exist as a profession in the Soviet Union, but that "welfare functions" are performed by persons with different backgrounds, mainly social insurance delegates of labor unions, physicians, nurses, teachers, and children inspectors, none of them trained in professional social work.[8] In contrast to Russia, social workers in France and most Latin American countries perform not only the social services for families and children, including special services for the aged and handicapped, but also personal services for the beneficiaries of the different social insurance programs.[9]

## Voluntary Agencies

Many social services for families and children are performed by social workers of voluntary agencies that are sectarian or humanitarian in character. This is true both of social agencies in many countries and of the international agencies we discussed in Chapter 2, but the main such international organization is UNICEF, the United Nations International Children's Fund. UNICEF performs social services for families and children in developing countries by training family and children's workers who work in cooperation with WHO, the World Health Organization. This includes support of graduate and postgraduate studies in connection with universities and institutes, of undergraduate departments of social work, and even of the training of auxiliary workers without academic background.[10] Such training projects have been assisted by voluntary agencies such as the Red Cross, the International YWCA, the British and American Friends Service Committees (Quakers), and by several Peace Corps volunteer associations.

## Child Care and Social Welfare Agencies

People in industrialized countries prefer that children be brought up in their own families, supported if necessary by advice and guidance from social workers and child guidance clinics. Until the end of the nineteenth century children who could not be brought up in their own families were usually placed in orphanages and other children's institutions, but now adoption or placement in a foster family is preferred. But in numerous Asian and African countries orphanages and children's schools still play a very important role in child care, and foster placement is less developed.[11] In Africa, remand homes, children's hostels, probation homes, industrial or "approved" schools, and rehabilitation centers still care for a substantial number of children in need of care and supervision. However even the developing countries are beginning to avoid institutionalization of children if possible and to secure education in their own families or in foster families.

An essential factor in family welfare services is the social and economic role of the wife and mother in the family. This role is determined by the religious and social traditions of the country's culture, and these differ from country to country. After the end of the colonial period, it was evident that women had often played important roles in the liberation of the new nations and had shown the capacity for political and economic leadership. These factors facilitated their emancipation and the recognition of their right to vote and to occupy higher political and economic functions. Women now have important social and political functions in India, Ceylon, Pakistan, Indonesia, Thailand, the Philippines, and several African countries, and their own organizations extend their influence to international women's federations and to the United Nations.[12]

After the Second World War intercountry adoptions became an important aspect of international child welfare policies. American parents were the first to adopt children from foreign countries, but Europeans also began to do so after the recovery of their nations from the economic destructions of the war. Parents in Switzerland, Denmark, Sweden, Germany, and Austria have adopted children from Italy, Greece, Poland, and Czechoslovakia, and also from Syria, India, Vietnam, the Philippines, Korea, and South America.

There is no uniformity in the adoption laws among nations. The "European Convention on Adoption of Children" in 1967 led several countries to improve their adoption laws. In 1971 the "World Congress on Adoption and Foster Placement" in Milan (Italy) asked the United Nations to invite an international conference in order to establish world conventions on adoption. The developing countries face serious psychological problems in allowing the industrial world to adopt their children. In giving up their children, their most valuable goods, they risk admitting that they cannot provide them with adequate lives and educations. There is another hazard in the practice of intercountry adoptions: families that adopt children from developing countries might consider this a substitute for such international aid as contributions for health services, agricultural and economic assistance, and services by agencies under the auspices of the United Nations that are essential for the further equalization of living standards and world peace. Fortunately this danger has not been realized in the adoption of Korean orphans and abandoned children by the Holt Adoption Program in Crosswell, Oregon.[13]

It is almost universally recognized that the family is the best environment for the nurture of children, especially young children, so that it is logical that all countries need social services that help the family fulfill its functions of educating their children. Some developing countries are still without such services. The United Nations and UNICEF are attempting to suggest an integration of social services for families and children in those countries that will include a preventive approach in health and social services with cooperation in economic and social measures for a healthy development of the entire rural and urban population. Toward this goal, comprehensive surveys of present needs and the development of a national plan for meeting these needs are necessary and should be supported on an international level by intergovernmental and voluntary organizations concerned with the welfare of families and children.[14]

*Adoption*

Most countries provide legal protection for children who have lost their parents through death, desertion, divorce, or incarceration, through guardianship, custodianship, or adoption. After the death of the father the mother usually assumes the role of guardian, but in different cultures there are various approaches to such a situation. For instance, in France there is no general guardianship for illegitimate children, but there are guardianships for such children in the Scandinavian and central European countries under the child welfare laws. These guardianships are often carried out by child welfare departments or by persons appointed by guardianship or juvenile courts.[15]

Adoption by relatives or by other persons usually is considered the best way to secure a normal life for orphans. Laws in most nations require a careful examination of the personality and fitness of the adopting parents in the interest of the adopted child, particularly if he or she is still a baby. The adoption of babies needs to be arranged quickly in order to avoid the damage that might result if the child is placed in an orphanage or nursing home where several different people might care for him instead of the care of one single deeply interested human being who is substituting for the mother.[16]

A number of international seminars and congresses on adoption have been held under the auspices of the United Nations, specialized agencies, and private social agencies and have contributed valuable knowledge on experience of adoption procedures and related social services for adopting parents and adopted children.

## The Families of Foreign Workers

Special problems exist for the families and especially the children of foreign workers, most of whom are in European countries—the Netherlands, Switzerland, Germany, Belgium, and France—from Italy, Spain, Greece, Yugoslavia, Turkey, Portugal, Algeria, Morocco, Tunisia, Czechoslovakia, Poland, and Hungary. (These foreign workers have been invited because of the serious manpower shortage in unskilled labor, especially in the construction trades, the hotel and restaurant business, textile factories, mining, and scavenger work.) Differences in language, culture, habits, and values make adjustment to the new countries of employment difficult, particularly for children of beginning school age and adolescence, unless special classes and social services are offered them (as is done in West Germany).[17] In Switzerland, where the proportion of foreign workers to the native labor force ranges from between 1 and 8 percent in the different cantons, child welfare agencies do not offer special priorities to foreign-born children. In West Germany several social agencies have offered special guidance, schooling, and social services to the families of different groups of foreign workers' families—that is, Catholic social agencies to Greek, Italian, Spanish, and Portuguese nationals, the *Arbeiterwohlfahrt* (Workers' Welfare Organization) for Turkish and Yugoslav workers, the *Innere Mission* for workers from the Scandinavian countries. In most reception countries special language classes have been established to assist foreign families. These have been more successful with younger children and adolescents than with older workers. In several countries of western and central Europe, the families of foreign workers have chosen to congregate in special regional or inner-city areas. Most such families prefer to accept social services from voluntary social agencies than from public welfare agencies, partly because of the fear of being expelled. In most European nations there is a smaller percentage of neglect, child abuse, or behavior problems among the children of foreign workers. Italian and Spanish workers have shown the highest amount of family affinity and compassion. The delinquency rate among foreign-born children has usually not been greater than that of the native population, but in France during recent years the rate among foreign adolescents has amounted to 6 percent of the total number of delinquent children.[18]

In the Renault automobile factories in France, there are 95,000 workers, 21,000 of whom are foreign immigrants from Algeria, Tunisia, Morocco, Portugal, and Spain. They are living in inadequate housing, frequently in slums and *bidonvilles* built of cardboard, corrugated iron, old car doors, and wood. In 1970 several of these slum areas were destroyed by fire, and the government promised to remove these danger zones, but as of 1973 nothing had been changed.

In England only those people in this new proletariat who came from Commonwealth countries have the right to vote. In France the same condition prevails (only those immigrants can vote who are natives of the French Antilles); in Holland it is those who are from the few remaining Dutch colonies. Some European countries discourage foreign workers from sending for their families and thus putting down roots. Such racism threatens the kind of turbulence and riots that occurred in 1973 in Rotterdam. Albert Coppe, former commissioner of the European Economic Council for social affairs, suggested that the European community should treat the foreign workers as a tenth partner so as to prevent disaster. Charles Barbeau, director of the Office of Immigration in France, warned that it is morally wrong to build wealth on the backs of foreign manpower. The danger is that black and brown workers from the developing countries will build the labor force that Europe needs to maintain modern industries and then be excluded from the fruits of their efforts.[19]

Drug abuse, mainly in hashish, generally exists among the families of foreign workers in the same proportion as among the native population. Two sticky matters are the question of intercountry adoption of foreign-born children when the father is unknown, and the question of financial support for foreign-born illegitimate children when the father does not reside in the native country of the mother.[20]

Aside from the human needs to be loved, educated, respected, and to participate in the native culture, there are the material needs of children to be sheltered, fed, and clothed, and there are also the needs to be protected against illness and disease. We shall discuss these in the next chapter. The young child is especially dependent upon the care he receives from his family or its substitute. It is generally recognized that infants in the developing countries are particularly endangered by poverty in rural villages, in newly established urban regions, and in slums and shantytowns where in a marginal economy unemployment often produces stark poverty, hunger, malnutrition, and diseases. As we discussed in Chapter 3, one of the functions of community development is to try to eliminate this vicious circle.

The infant mortality rate is highest in the poorest countries because of the high incidence of infectious diseases and poor nutrition. The degree of protection a child needs against the elements varies according to climate and social customs, but his health is still dependent upon his environment. In developing countries many families are too poor to afford decent clothes, so children are often clad in rags and go barefoot, which exposes them to disease-infested grounds or rivers. Nutrition in poor families is often low in milk and protein, so that children go hungry even if a large proportion of the income of the family is spent for food. When poultry and vegetables are raised, they often cannot be used for the family nutrition because they must be sold at the market to raise urgently needed cash for the family budget.

In the poorer developing countries the educational facilities for lower-income groups are extremely limited. The economic needs of the family frequently dictate that the child work to increase the family income, watching the flocks or in the city working for an artisan or shopkeeper. With increasing industrialization and urbanization, the stability of the family is threatened. The men leave the villages for the cities, hoping to earn more money, which speeds the transition from a traditional subsistence economy to a money economy. Men in the cities often spend money unwisely. If women decide to work, and if there are no other family members to care for them, their children are often exposed to maladjustment and predelinquency. Few developing countries have social services for the family and the children in rural areas to prevent these dangers. More than half of the world's population lives under unhygienic conditions, large numbers of them without sanitary facilities or safe drinking water. We shall discuss the health dangers arising from such conditions in the next chapter, but their impact on the lives of family and children is evident, as is the widespread breakdown of traditional values and the rapid change from a rural to an urban society and from a static to a dynamic way of life.[21]

There is hope that recent changes in social policy and social service orientation toward a strong emphasis on the need for social change and participation of the recipients of services in the decisions about the structure and goals of social services will help to overcome the dangers present in the transition of many developing countries into a new type of society that also involves the activities of the organizations in the field of international social welfare discussed in Chapter 2 and influences the life of families and children throughout the world.[22]

### The Home-Help Service

A service for families, children, and particularly old people that has recently become important on an international level is the home-help service (in Sweden it is called family aid). Great Britain had introduced a home-help service in 1946 under the National Health Service Act for families during times of illness or the mother's confinement, implemented through the local authorities. In 1952 Britain invited representatives from other European countries with similar services to a conference in London. After further conventions in Paris and Oxford, the International Council of Home-Help Services was founded in 1959 in Woudschoten (Ziest, Holland).[23] The need for home-helpers has been created by changes in family life and composition in modern industrialized societies. In the modern nuclear family in urban settings several generations no longer live together. There was scarcely need for outside help, but in industrial societies today the "conjugal family," involving only parents and children, is an isolated unit. If the mother is ill or has to go to the hospital or to a mental institution and the father has to go to work, a home-help worker is needed to take care of the children and to maintain the family household. She is paid by the father if he earns enough; otherwise she is paid by the public or private welfare agency that provides her.

Of particular importance are home-help services for elderly persons. In most Western countries old people receive social security benefits or pensions, and sometimes private annuities, which enable them to manage their own affairs economically. In the Scandinavian countries apartments are available for older people or widows and widowers, but many of them need home-helpers to take care of household tasks to enable elderly persons to live without being a burden to their families and to the community. In Sweden home-helpers are trained in special courses of from three to fifteen months to care for the whole family. Home-helpers in England are trained for a shorter time to care for the aged.[24] In order to perform their function properly, home-helpers in the United States, Great Britain, the Scandinavian countries, Germany, the Netherlands, Austria, and Switzerland receive professional supervision from trained social workers.

Social agencies provide home-help services on the basis of the responsibility and difficulty of the situation—whether the house has a husband and children or only one or two elderly persons. Some agencies consider the services for older people just as demanding and responsible as those for children, and think that additional centers for laundry, ironing, and mending of clothes and linen are needed.[25]

The International Council on Home-Help Services was established in 1959 as an international organization in the field of home-help services to make the work of home-help aides known to countries with little or no such services and to organize and sponsor international congresses on home-help services. By 1971, 15 countries were members of the International Council.[26]

In the area of values in family and child welfare services there are strong differences of opinion between most Western nations and the communist countries and Israel on the other side. In Western countries the superiority of family education, not just for infants but for all children and adolescents, is scarcely questioned, except for seriously mentally disturbed or handicapped children. (This also applies to the nuclear family in Asia and Africa.) The family is considered the basic social unit, the place of personal satisfaction, and the decisive factor in forming the personalities of children.[27] In contrast, the U.S.S.R., the east European countries, and the kibbutzim in Israel consider a collective upbringing, in children's institutions or colonies, to be superior for socialization.[28]

### Children's Villages

A special type of children's collective called children's villages was developed in the 1960s. One of the first of these was the Pestalozzi Children's Village in Switzerland, where war orphans from many countries constitute an international children's community. Another group are the so-called SOS Children's Villages, founded by Hermann Gmeiner in the village of Imst, Austria, in 1949. Gmeiner's concept was to offer a substitute home to orphaned and abandoned children, most of them victims of wars. They consist of "families" of a woman, called mother, and eight or nine boys and girls of about the same age. The selection of the children by the agency which administers the villages is made on the basis of the need of the children for admission to the village. The villages also have children who have proved very difficult or unmanageable in foster families. At admission most children are about six years old, because by that age enough serious difficulties have shown up that foster parents want to give up those children. When a children's village is about 12 to 15 family houses, a community center is built to house the office of the village manager (the only male in the village except a security guard); a large room for lectures, film performances, or athletics; a conference room; a library; a music room; a laundry; a sick station; some workshops; a kindergarten; a tailor and repair shop; and a grocery shop.[29]

The most problematic aspect of the child education in the SOS-children's villages is their refusal, on principle, to employ married couples as parents in the family houses, their insistence on assigning the task of family exclusively to the "mother." (At first they refused any kind of professional leadership or guidance, but later they established psychiatric and medical advisers in Vienna.) The connection with the child's natural family (mother or father) is not encouraged; in fact it is limited to one visit every three months, and then only after written application and with special permission of the village. During the vacations in school, the children have to remain in the village; they cannot visit their own parents. The separation is aggravated by the provision that once a child reaches the age of 14 (the end of compulsory school attendance in Austria), he or she is placed in an apprentice or domestic service job in the same village until he or she is of age, and the natural parents or guardians have to sign an obligation not to exercise any educational or other influence upon the child until this time. In defense of this one-sided principle of child education, Gmeiner states that few married couples are willing to assume the difficult role of educating orphans and difficult children. He also assumes that a married couple would not be willing to assume this function for unselfish reasons, would make severe demands upon apartment and salary, might consist of persons dissatisfied with their previous lives and work, that men would find it difficult to find work in or near the village and might quarrel among themselves, and that they might neglect the "foreign children" in preference to their own.[30]

One very critical point is the selection and training of the "house mothers." The official guidelines emphasize that these women are carefully selected and trained. The principle of selection is that these women must incorporate the ideal characteristics of the mother, must be willing to renounce for life the function of real motherhood, and to carry all duties and burdens of house mother without outside recognition and rewards. These women are between 25 and 40 years of age, unmarried or widows. Their training is in a course of three months in a children's village and two three-week field practices in another village, preferably during the vacation of the regular house mothers. No professional background, as kindergarten teacher, nurse, or social worker, is required, or even desired. The danger of exploitation of these nonprofessional village mothers is considerable.

The villages are nicely built, pleasant looking, and clean. They have acquired over 250,000 benefactors and contributors, and via an efficient advertising system they have established villages in Austria, Belgium, West Germany, Italy, France, Ecuador, Argentina, Uruguay, India, Iran, Japan, Korea, the Philippines, the United States, Brazil, Luxembourg, Switzerland, Lichtenstein, and Finland.[31]

Child welfare practices in Western nations require the selection of a suitable foster family, that is, a well-integrated couple capable of offering a child a stable experience in family and community living, capable of loving and fully accepting a child not their own, and of sharing responsibility for the child with the placing agency and the child's natural family.[32] The same principles should be recognized by the SOS-children's villages.

In Germany there is another group of children's villages, the Albert Schweitzer Children's Villages, (the first was in Gatow near Berlin), that prove it is not necessary to exclude married couples from caring for orphaned or deprived children. The first of these villages was financed by donations collected by school children, from the Berlin students' parliament, the Lions Club, the Berlin *Zahlenlotto,* and many individual contributions. In these children's villages the house mothers are trained as kindergarten teachers, social workers, psychologists, or teachers; their husbands work in their professions in the city and return home in the evening like normal family fathers and care for the children as they would for their own.

## The Aged

The international community has given much less attention to the aged in the world than to children. In an address to the United Nations Assembly in December 1970, Ambassador Arvid Pardo of Malta called this a severe neglect. A meeting of international scientists at the Center for the Study of Democratic Institutions in Santa Barbara, California, confirmed the need to develop new international methods to change prejudicial attitudes toward the elderly in the various cultures. The conference recommended postponement of retirement policies, improvement of measures of care of lonely aged persons, creation of new careers for elderly people that will allow them to use their life experiences and skills for the benefit of the communities, and acceptance of a "more flexible life style" in the form of sabbaticals during a person's entire lifespan for an enrichment of human life.[33] Arvid Pardo has suggested that the United Nations study present methods of care for the aged in different countries, especially those based on new medical advances in geriatrics. He has also called for a more efficient use of the knowledge and skills of the elderly in the different social systems and international cooperation in caring for the elderly; unfortunately, the United Nations General Assembly has yet to take any action on these recommendations.

## Care of Homeless Persons

Within the framework of family and child social services, care for homeless families presents a special problem. In France, where their number is estimated at more than 3 million people, they are called *quart monde* (fourth world). They consist of French families who have no homes, (about 5 percent of the population) and who live in slums called *bidonvilles, cités d'urgence,* and *quartiers dégradés;* of homeless foreigners (about 100,000), Africans, Spaniards, Italians, Yugoslavs, who came to France to find work; and of gypsies and similar tribes (about 120,000). The social service for these groups is provided by an agency called *Aide à Toute Détresse* (Assistance in Every Need), founded in 1957 by Abbé

Pierre and Abbé Joseph Wresinski. Their workers approach the homeless under religious charitable principles and house them in several camps in France and other countries. They attempt to integrate the homeless into the communities near the camps, and to educate and care for them with volunteer teachers, physicians, sociologists, and artists. In 1961 the organization established a research institute called the *Institut de Recherches et de Formation aux Relations Humaines,* which develops methods of rehabilitation and help for these clients. Teams of volunteers (scientists, priests, sociologists, librarians) who live in the camps among the homeless under the same conditions and who earn the minimum wage of a manual worker encourage their clients to join labor unions, try to find work for the unemployed, provide medical services and try to improve the self-respect among the homeless. Kindergartens and child centers assist in the education of the children, and special centers for difficult and disturbed youngsters attempt to prepare them for vocational training. There are also recreational facilities and clubs of various interests are organized.

In the Netherlands special settlements for homeless families have been established under the auspices of the National Department for Culture, Recreation, and Social Service. There also are some small institutions for homeless families with single-family houses, a kindergarten, a day care center for children, a youth club, and a recreation hall. The placement of homeless families in settlements and institutions is planned by the caseworker of the family service in cooperation with the manager of the settlement or institution. After a period of adjustment, an apartment or a house in another city is provided with social services for the family to assist in the final adjustment in the new community. Such projects have been conducted in Eindhoven, Overijessel, and Maastricht with the help of caseworkers and group workers who work with the surrounding population in order to facilitate the acceptance of homeless families without serious friction. Social planning for the operation is financially supported by the Dutch Department of Housing and the Department of Education. The success of these measures is secured by the effective cooperation between government agencies, the local public and private social agencies that prepare and support the homeless family and encourage involvement of the local population in helping the disadvantaged families.[34]

In Great Britain, according to the official 1969 statistics, there were only 3,594 homeless families (with 18,689 persons) placed in emergency shelters, but a private social agency called Shelter estimated at the time that there were about a million persons without a home. In numerous cities houses have been declared unfit for human habitation, and in 1970 the national government appropriated funds to enable local communities to establish renovation zones for the repair of inadequate housing in slum areas. Shelter, whose staff consists mainly of university students under 30 years of age, conducts social action programs to inform the public of the need to improve housing conditions and the plight of the homeless.

Clinical services for family planning based upon the 1967 law on family planning have been set up through the Family Planning Association, a private organization supported by local public services, private philanthropic and religious organizations, and individuals. This association works in about 1,000 advisory services, providing contraceptives and locating housing facilities.

A few private rehabilitation centers for homeless families have been organized, the Frimhurst Recuperative Home in Camberley (Surrey) and the Crowley House and the Middlemore Center in Birmingham, which operate with the subvention and assistance of the communal social services. Casework and social group work services are used to help rehabilitate families in these rehabilitation centers.

In Italy the problem of homeless families is caused in the northern provinces by the influx of rural workers from the south looking for employment in industry and from the middle of Italy where industrial development has been slowing down and numerous unemployed are not able to pay the high rents. In southern Italy and Sicily most people are barely able to gain sustenance from agricultural work or fishing and are often forced to move to the north to find work or to serve as sharecroppers or unskilled laborers exploited by the Mafia. Father Borelli, who lives in the slums of Naples, estimates the number of homeless families in Naples alone at nearly 5,500, over 24,000 persons. He conducted a research (assisted by students from the school of social work in Naples) that revealed serious overcrowding in the slums, severe poverty, illiteracy, unhealthy child labor, poor schools, and a lack of social services and medical aid. His findings made people aware of the neglect of numerous families, of the lack of housing and of financial resources, and of the inadequacy of the social policies of the city and province. As a result seven neighborhood social centers were established in Naples, three libraries, two kindergartens, five recreation clubs, two boy scout groups, a sport club, and some renter's clubs were organized, and improvements were made in the pavement of streets, the street lighting, sanitation, public transportation, and the schools.

In Sicily, there has been the work of Danilo Dolci for the peasants and fishermen of Partenico and Trappeto (near Palermo). Committees in England, the United States, Switzerland, Norway, Sweden, Austria, Germany, and Senegal (Africa) have been formed to support his innovative social action work. Construction of houses for homeless families was particularly important because a severe earthquake had destroyed numerous homes in Partenico and several nearby villages. Dolci's work was made difficult by the hostility of the Mafia, from bureaucrats sympathetic to the Mafia who feared that their mistakes might become known through Dolci's activities.

In Belgium the program for homeless families is combined with a broader community organization program conducted by *Action Nationale pour la Sécurité Vitale,* a private agency composed of 21 social societies of child and youth welfare, services for the aged and disabled. In the agency there are former prisoners, gypsies, foreign workers, and about 700,000 inhabitants of slum areas in various cities. In 1970 they were able to stop a large redevelopment project in Brussels that threatened to deprive 26,000 slum inhabitants of their homes.[35]

In Denmark an interesting research project on homeless families was conducted in Copenhagen under the auspices of the National Institute for Social Research during 1961 and 1962. A local family center in a slum region was compared to a control group living under the same conditions that did not receive counseling and casework service. Those families receiving social services from the family center improved more in their housing condition and especially in their familiar relations than the control group which had no such services.[36]

## Notes

[1]Charles I. Schottland, "The Changing Role of Government and Family," in Paul Weinberger, ed., *Perspectives on Social Welfare* (Toronto: Macmillan, 1968), 132–47; Rose L. Coser, *The Family: Its Structure and Functions* (New York: St. Martin's, 1964); United Nations, Economic Commission for Africa, *Report of the Workshop on Extension of Family and Child Welfare Services in Addis Ababa, Ethiopia* (1960), pp. 9–18; Tarlok Singh, "Unifying Approaches in Planning for Children," *Les Carnets de l'enfance,* 14 (Apr.–June 1971), 17–26; K. Roberts and G. White, "The Impact of Character Training Courses upon Young People," *British Journal of Social Work,* 2 (March 1972), 337–54.

[2]Herman D. Stein, "Family Welfare," *Self-Help in Social Welfare,* Proceedings of the Seventh International Conference of Social Work, (Toronto, 1954), pp. 104–7; A. R. Wadia, "Fundamental Education and Family Life," *Mobilizing Resources for Social Needs,* Proceedings of the Ninth International Conference of Social Work (Tokyo, 1958), pp. 236–38; "Services for Family Life," *Social Services and the Standard of Living,* Proceedings of the Sixth International Conference of Social Work (Madras, 1952), pp. 231–34; Eugen Pusíc, "A New Concept of Responsibility in Social Relations," in Katherine A. Kendall, ed., *Social Work Values in an Age of Discontent* (New York: Council on Social Work Education, 1970), pp. 62–75; Nina and George O'Neill, *Open Marriage: A New Life Style for Couples* (New York: Avon, 1973).

[3]Herbert H. Aptekar, "The Values, Functions and Methods of Social Work," in Katherine A. Kendall, ed., *An Intercultural Exploration* (New York: Council on Social Work Education, 1967), p. 3–59; Stein, "Family Welfare," pp. 105–7; Kenneth E. Boulding, "The Concept of World Interest," in Bert F. Hoselitz, ed., *Economics and the Idea of Mankind* (New York: Columbia University Press, 1965),

pp. 41–62; Alva Myrdal, "Education and the Standard of Living," in Gulestan Billimoria and Shirin F. Dastur, eds., *Social Services and the Standard of Living* (Madras: ICSW, 1952), pp. 159–74; William J. Goode, *The Family* (Englewood Cliffs, N.J.: Prentice-Hall, 1965), pp. 108–10; Nathalie P. Masse, "Un enseignement international pour les responsables de l'enfance dans le monde" (International Instruction for Those Responsible for Childhood in the World), *Les Carnets de l'enfance*, No. 12 (June 1970), pp. 17–26.

⁴Wülker, "Strukturprobleme," pp. 47–50.

⁵United Nations, *Workshop on Family and Child Welfare Services* (in Africa) (1969), pp. 12–15; United Nations, *1967 Report on the World Social Situation*, 58, 63–64; J. D. Souza, "Significant Projects in Fundamental Education," in *Social Services and the Standard of Living*, pp. 175–81; Mildred Arnold, "Worldwide Frontiers in Child Welfare" (Child Welfare Report #11), (Washington, D.C.: U.S. Department of Health, Education, and Welfare, 1962); Hada Badran, "Social Work Programmes in Egypt," *International Social Work*, 14, No. 1 (Jan. 1971), 25–33; Paul Halmos, ed., *The Canford Families: A Study in Social Casework and Group Work* (Keele, Staffordshire: University of Keele Press, 1962).

⁶Bernice Z. Madison, *Social Welfare in the Soviet Union* (Stanford, Ca.: Stanford University Press, 1968), pp. 147–76; Nina V. Orlova, "Schutz und Förderung der Kinder in der Sovietunion" (Protection and Development of Children in the Soviet Union), Nachrichtendienst (Frankfurt a/M., April 1970), 96–100; Anna Pollender, "Erziehungs- und Berufsberatungsstellen in der Volksrepublik Polen" (Child Guidance and Vocational Information in Poland), *Theorie und Praxis der sozialen Arbeit*, 24 (Aug. 1973), 307–13.

⁷C. K. Yang, "First U.S. Sociologist to Visit China," *American Sociologist*, 7, No. 5 (May 1972), 1, 19; Ruth Sidel, "Social Services in China," *Social Work*, 17, No. 6, (Nov. 1972), 5–13; Ruth Sidel, *Women and Child Care in China* (New York: Hill & Wang, 1972).

⁸Madison, *Social Welfare in the Soviet Union*, pp. 90–94.

⁹Walter Friedlander, *Individualism and Social Welfare* (New York: Free Press, 1962), pp. 36–40, 43–48; Alvin L. Schorr, *Social Security and Social Services in France* (Washington, D.C.: U.S. Department of Health, Education, and Welfare, 1965), pp. 33, 40.

¹⁰Dorothy Lally, "International Social Welfare," *Encyclopedia of Social Work* (1965), pp. 411–12, 417; *The Role of Voluntary Agencies in Technical Assistance* (New York: American Council of Voluntary Agencies for Foreign Service, 1953), pp. 28–39, 51–59, 60–77; Charles G. Chakerian, *From Rescue to Child Welfare* (New York: Church World Service, 1968), pp. 14–35.

¹¹Chakerian, *From Rescue to Child Welfare*, pp. 40–44; United Nations, *Workshop on Family and Child Welfare Services*, p. 26; Madison, *Social Welfare in the Soviet Union*, pp. 74–75; J. S. Kleinfeld, "Characteristics of Successful Boarding Home Parents of Eskimo and Athabascan Indian Students," *Human Organization*, 32 (Apr. 1973), 191–99.

¹²Wülker, "Strukturprobleme," pp. 49–50; Jane Howard, "Indian Society, Indian Social Work," *International Social Work*, 14, No. 4 (1971), 16–31.

¹³A thoughtful discussion of the problem of intercountry adoptions is presented in John E. Adams and Hyung Bok Kim, "A Fresh Look at Intercountry Adoptions," *Children*, 18, No. 6 (Nov.-Dec. 1971), 214–21; Marianne Welter, "Comparison of Adopted Older Foreign Children and American Children" (New

York: International Social Service, 1966); Annabelle H. Cook, "Milan Conference on Adoption," *Social Work*, 17, No. 6 (Nov. 1972), 101–2.

[14]Georges Sicault, ed., *The Needs of Children* (New York: Free Press, 1963), pp. 21–23, 135–40; Eileen Davidson, "Maternal and Child Health Centers in Thailand," in *Social Services and the Standard of Living*, pp. 109–14. In Russia family life is adversely affected by the lack of equality of women (in contrast to their legal condition) and by the housing conditions, which are worse than those in western Europe during the industrial revolution in the nineteenth century. See Madison, *Social Welfare in the Soviet Union*, pp. 70.

[15]Friedlander, *Individualism and Social Welfare*, pp. 94–95, 385–86; Friedlander, *Child Welfare in Germany*, pp. 68–90; Henryka Veillard-Cybulska, "Aspects of Child Welfare in the People's Democracies," *International Child Welfare Review*, 19, No. 3 (1965) (USSR); 20, No. 1 (1966) (Poland); 21, Nos. 3 and 4 (Czechoslovakia and Hungary).

[16]Jacques Bernheim, "General Report to the Eighth Congress of the International Association of Youth Magistrates," Geneva, Switzerland, July 13–18, 1970 (unpublished report), pp. 16–17

[17]Leon D. Fisher, "The Experience of European Social Agencies in the Adjustment of Foreign born Children," *International Child Welfare Review*, No. 9 (Feb. 1971), pp. 35–37.

[18]Fisher, "The Experience of European Social Agencies," p. 36.

[19]Jonathan Power, "Key to European Boom," *The Nation*, 216, No. 16 (Apr. 16, 1973), 486–88.

[20]For foreign workers in Germany and their children see Eberhard de Hann, "Ausländische Kinder in unserer Gesellschaft" (Foreign Children in Our Society), *Neues Beginnen*, 22, No. 5 (Oct. 1971), 170–76.

[21]Sicault, ed., *The Needs of Children*, pp. 13–15; Alva Myrdal, *Nation and Family* (London: Kegan Paul, 1945), pp. 90–97; Walter Rau, "Der Friede ist unteilbar" (Peace Is Indivisible), in Ziock, ed., pp. 35–42.

[22]John E. Turner, "Relation of Health and Welfare Planning to Social Change and Development," in Charles I. Schottland, ed., *Social Work and Social Planning* (New York: National Association of Social Workers, 1964), pp. 17–19; Arnold Gurin, "Social Planning and Community," 21–27. For the special problems of child welfare in the Republic of Korea after the war of 1951 between North and South Korea see Charles G. Chakerian, *From Rescue to Child Welfare.*

[23]*Proceedings of the International Congress of Paris on Home-Help Services* (Washington, D.C.: U.S. Department of Health, Education, and Welfare, 1959). Pierre Laroque, "The Home-Helper and the Changes in the Family," ibid., pp. 3–23; Margareta Nordstrom, "The Importance of Training for Home-Helpers," ibid., pp. 24–29; Rudolf Pense, "The Place of the Home-Helper in Social Services," ibid., pp. 39–52. For the social problems of retirement, see R. J. Havighurst et al., *Adjustment to Retirement: A Cross-National Study* (New York: Humanities Press, 1969); see also *Proceedings of the International Congress on Home-Help Services*, Koenigstein, September 1965 (Washington, D.C.: U.S. Department of Health, Education, and Welfare, 1966).

[24]Nordstrom, "The Importance of Training," pp. 24–26; Laroque, "The Home-Helper and the Changes in the Family," pp. 12–14; George Nelson, ed., *Freedom and Welfare* (Copenhagen: Danish Ministry of Welfare, 1953), pp. 266–67, 468.

[25]Robert Prigent, "Report of Work Groups," in *Proceedings of the International Congress of Paris on Self-Help Services*, pp. 33–37.

[26]Roberta Hunt, "Homemaker Services," *Encyclopedia of Social Work, 1971* (New York: NASW, 1971), p. 586.

[27]Margaret Mead, "What is Happening to the American Family?" *Journal of Social Casework*, 28 (Nov. 1947), 322ff., Goode, *The Family*.

[28]Martin Wolins, "Some Theory and Practice in Child Care: A Cross-Cultural View," *Child Welfare*, 42 (Oct. 1963), 369–78; Hanokh Reinhold, "Dynamics of Youth Aliyah Groups," in Carl Frankenstein, ed., *Between Past and Future* (Jerusalem: Henrietta Szold Foundation, 1953), pp. 215–47; Effie Ambler, "The Soviet Boarding School," *American Slavic and East European Review*, 20 (1961), 237–52; Martin Wolins et al., "Adolescents in Kibbutz Care" (unpublished Master's thesis, University of California, Berkeley, 1966).

[29]Hermann Gmeiner, *Die SOS-Kinderdörfer-Moderne Erziehungsstätten für verlassene Kinder* (The SOS Children's Villages: Modern Educational Facilities for Abandoned Children), (Innsbruck: SOS Kinderdorf-Verlag, 1960), pp. 6–31; Martin Juckel, "Die SOS-Kinderdörfer," *Unsere Jugend*, 14, No. 12 (Dec. 1962), 535–40; F. Haider, "Die SOS-Kinderdörfer," *Neue Wege*, 9, No. 4 (1960), 6ff; J. Traub, "Zur Problematik der SOS-Kinderdörfer" (On the Problems of the SOS Children's Villages), *AFET Rundbrief*, 11, No. 5 (1962).

[30]Gmeiner, *Die SOS-Kinderdörfer—Moderne Erziehungsstätten*, pp. 32–39; J. Dodge, "S.O.S. Children's Villages in the World," *Child Welfare*, 51 (June 1972), 344–59.

[31]Gmeiner, *Die SOS-Kinderdörfer—Moderne Erziehungsstätten*, pp. 30–41; Juckel, "Die SOS-Kinderdörfer," pp. 539–40; *SOS-Messenger*, 6, No. 1 (1965).

[32]Martin Wolins, *Selecting Foster Parents* (New York: Columbia University Press, 1963), pp. 39ff; Child Welfare League of America, "Some Principles Basic in Home-Finding," *Child Welfare*, 30 (Jan. 1951), 14.

[33]Aaron L. Danzig, "Breaking the Age Barrier," *Vista*, 6, No. 5 (May–June 1971), 31–53. The International Gerontological Association comprises 55 gerontological societies of different nations—*Social Service Review*, 47 (Dec. 1973), 572.

[34]Magdelena Fürstenberg and Sigelinde Schulz, "Obdachlosigkeit: Problemfamilien im Ausland-Projekte, Modelle, Methoden" (Homelessness: Problem Families in Foreign Countries—Projects, Models, Methods), *Der Sozialarbeiter*, 3 (May–June 1972), 1–25.

[35]Fürstenberg and Schulz, "Obdachlosigkeit," pp. 8–9.

[36]Ibid., pp. 12–18.

## Selected References

*Books*

AINSWORTH, MARY D. SALTER, *Infancy in Uganda: Infant Care and the Growth of Love*. Baltimore, Md.: Johns Hopkins Press, 1967.

BECKER, THOMAS T., *Due Process in Child Protection Proceedings: Intervention on Behalf of Neglected Children*. Denver: American Humane Society, 1972.

BÉRAUD, JANINE, AND LOUIS MILLET. *Le Refus des jeunes* (The Rejection of Youth), Paris: Editions Universitaires, 1971.

BERELSON, BERNARD, ed., *Family Planning Programs: An International Survey*. New York: Basic Books, 1969.

BERRY, JULIET, *Social Work with Children*. London: Routledge & Kegan Paul, 1972.

BERTHET, ETIENNE, et al., *Assignment Children: Bilateral Aid to Children—Protection of Mother and Child—UNICEF in Action*. Neuilly, France: UNICEF, 1965.

BJÖRNSSON, BJÖRN, *The Lutheran Doctrine of Marriage in Modern Icelandic Society*. Oslo: University of Oslo Press, 1971.

BOLTON, F., AND J. LAISHLEY, *Education for a Multi-Racial Britain*. London: Fabian Research Series, 1972.

BOTT, E., *Family and Social Network*. London: Tavistock, 1957.

BOWLBY, JOHN, *Maternal Care and Mental Health*. Geneva: World Health Organization, 1952.

BRESNARD, SUZANNE, *Que feront nos enfants?* (What Will Our Children Do?) Paris: Le Centurion, 1972.

BRONFENBRENNER, URIE, *Two Worlds of Childhood: United States and U.S.S.R.* London: Allen & Unwin, 1970.

BRUEL, A., AND J. VERBRUGGHE, *Contribution du juge d'enfants à l'action educative* (The Contribution of the Juvenile Judge to the Educational Process), Lille (France): 1970.

BUDER, LEONARD, et al., *Where We Are: A Hard Look at Family and Society*. New York: Child Study Association of America, 1970.

CAILLY, PIERRE, *L'Éducation au futur: L'Orientation scolaire et professionelle de nos enfants* (Education for the Future: Academic and Professional Orientation of Our Children). Paris: Centurion, 1972.

CHAZAL, JEAN, *Séminaire sur la prévention de l'inadaption sociale des enfants dans les grandes villes*. (Seminar on the Prevention of Social Maladjustment of Children in the Cities). Paris: Centre International de l'Enfance, 1961.

DANIELS, ROGER, AND HARRY H. L. KITANO, *American Racism: Exploration of the Nature of Prejudice*. Englewood Cliffs, N.J.: Prentice-Hall, 1970.

DOLTRENS, ROBERT, *La Crise de l'éducation et ses remèdes* (The Crisis of Education and Its Remedies). Neuchâtel (Switzerland): Delachaux & Niestle, 1971.

DRIETZEL, HANS PETER, ed., *Family, Marriage, and the Struggle of the Sexes*. New York: Macmillan, 1972.

EISENSTADT, S. N., *The Absorption of Immigrants*. London: Routledge & Kegan Paul, 1954.

ESQUERRE-MONDIEGT, YVONNE, *L'École incostée: Techniques de la promotion humaine* (The Flexible School: Techniques for Human Development). Beauville-sur-Mer: L'amitié par le Livre, 1971.

FERGUSON, DAVID M., JOAN FLEMING, AND DAVID P. O'NEILL, *Child Abuse in New Zealand*. Wellington: Shearer, 1974.

FITZHERBERT, F., *The West-Indian Child in London*. London: Boll, 1967.

FRIEDLANDER, WALTER, AND EARL DEWEY MYERS, *Child Welfare in Germany: Before and After Naziism*. Chicago: University of Chicago Press, 1940.

GOODE, WILLIAM J., *The Family*. Englewood Cliffs, N.J.: Prentice-Hall, 1964.

GORECKI, JAN, *Divorce in Poland: An Analysis of Emotional and Social Problems of Divorce*. The Hague: Mouton, 1970.

GOTTLIEB, DAVID, AND ANNE LIENHARD HEINSON, *America's Other Youth: Growing Up Poor*. Englewood Cliffs, N.J.: Prentice-Hall, 1971.

HANDLER, JOEL F., ed., *Family Law and the Poor: Essays by Jacobus ten Broek*. Westpoint, Conn.: Greenwood, 1971.

HARMSEN, HANS, *Die Neue Ehe- und Famiengesetzgebung in der DDR, Polen und in der Tschechoslowakei* (New Family and Marriage Legislation in East Germany, Poland, and Czechoslovakia), Hamburg: Akademie für Staatsmedizin, 1967.

HAZARD, JOHN N., *Law and Social Changes in the U.S.S.R.* London: Stevens & Sons, 1953.

JANSEN, LUDWIG, AND GOTTFRIED KNOEPFEL, *Das Neue Unehelichengesetz* (The New Law on Illegitimacy). Frankfurt a/M.: Alfred Metzner, 1967.

JOUSSELIN, JEAN, *L'Organisation de la jeunesse en Europe* (The Organization of Youth in Europe). Strasbourg: Conseil de l'Europe, 1968.

KAIN, JOHN F., ed., *Race and Poverty: The Economics of Discrimination*. Englewood Cliffs, N.J.: Prentice-Hall, 1969.

KANDEL, DENISE B., AND GERALD S. COLEMAN, *Youth in Two Worlds*. New York: McGraw-Hill, 1972.

KAPUR, PROMILLA, *Marriage and the Working Woman in India*. New York: Humanities Press, 1971.

KNOWLES, LOUIS L., AND KENNETH PREWITT, *Institutional Racism in America*. Englewood Cliffs, N.J.: Prentice-Hall, 1969.

LANDER, ELIZABETH A., et al., *A Study of Black Adoption Families*. New York: Child Welfare League of America, 1971.

LEICESTER, JAMES H., AND W. A. JAMES FARNDALE, eds., *Trends in Services for Youth*. Oxford: Pergamon Press, 1967.

LUESCHEN, GUENTHER, AND RENÉ KÖNIG, *Jugend in der Familie* (Youth in the Family), Munich: Juventa, 1969.

MAAS, HENRY S., AND RICHARD F. ENGLER, *Children in Need of Parents*. New York: Columbia University Press, 1959.

MADISON, BERNICE Q., *Social Welfare in the Soviet Union*. Stanford, Ca.: Stanford University Press, 1968.

MAERKER, RUDOLF, *Jugend im anderen Teil Deutschlands* (Youth in the Other Part of Germany). Munich: Juventa Publ., 1969.

MILLER, HELLEN, *Korea's International Children*. New York: Lutheran Social Welfare Assn., 1971.

MITCHELL, J. PAUL, *Race Riots in Black and White*. Englewood Cliffs, N.J.: Prentice-Hall, 1970.

PEARLIN, LEONARD I., *Class Contest and Family Relations: A Cross-National Study*. Boston: Little, Brown, 1971.

PERRUCCI, ROBERT, AND MARC PILISUK, *The Triple Revolution Emerging: Social Problems in Depth*. Boston: Little, Brown, 1971.

PILISUK, MARC, AND PHYLLIS PILISUK, *Poor Americans: How the White Poor Live*. Chicago: Aldine, 1971.

PUGATCH-ZALEMAN, LENA, *Les Enfants de Vilna: Une expérience pédagogique* (The Children of Vilna: A Pedagogical Experiment). Tournai: Cartermau, 1970.

RAYNOR, LOIS, *Adoption of Non-White Children.* London: Allen & Unwin, 1970.

REUBENS, EDWIN P., *Planning for Children and Youth Within National Development Planning.* Geneva: UNICEF, 1967.

RHEINSTROM, MAX, *Marriage Stability, Divorce and the Law.* Chicago: University of Chicago Press, 1972.

ROEHL BLAVI-SPENLE, ANNE-MARIE, *L'Adolescent et son monde* (The Adolescent and His World). Paris: Editions Universitaires, 1969.

ROSENFELD, JONA M., *Strategies en vue d'interventions à long terme contre le désavantage social des familles.* Geneva: United Nations, 1970.

SCHELSKY, HELMUT, *Wandlungen in der deutschen Familie in der Gegenwart* (Changes in the German Family at the Present Time). Stuttgart: F. Emke (5th ed), 1967.

SCHLEMMER, FRANÇOIS, *L'Enfant placé* (The Child in Foster Care). Nyon (Switzerland): Editions de Lynx, 1972.

SCHULZ, DAVID A., *Coming Up Black: Patterns of Ghetto Socialization.* Englewood Cliffs, N.J.: Prentice-Hall, 1969.

SHERMAN, RICHARD B., *The Negro in the City.* Englewood Cliffs, N.J.: Prentice-Hall, 1970.

SIDEL, RUTH, *Women and Child Care in China.* New York: Hill & Wang, 1972.

STEIN, HERMAN D., *Planning for the Needs of Children in the Developing Countries.* Geneva: UNICEF, 1965.

TALMON, YOMINA, *Family and Community in the Kibbutz.* Cambridge: Harvard University Press, 1972.

TOWNSEND, PETER, ETHEL SHANAS, HENNING FRIES, AND DOROTHY WEDDESBURN, *Old People in Three Industrial Societies.* New York: Atherton, 1968.

TRISELIOTIS, J. P., *Evaluation of Adoption Policy and Practice.* Edinburgh: Department of Social Administration, 1970.

UNICEF, *Strategy for Children: A Study of UNICEF Assistance Policies.* New York: UNICEF, 1967.

UNITED NATIONS, *Youth in the Second Development Decade.* New York: United Nations, 1972.

VESSIGAULT, GABRIEL, *La Statut et la formation des cadres de jeunesse* (The Legal Status and the Organization of Youth Movements [in Europe]). Strasbourg: Conseil de l'Europe, 1969.

VOLLERT, MANFRED, *Erziehungsprobleme im Kinderdorf: Eine Untersuchung in den deutschen SOS-Kinderdörfern* (Educational Problems in the Children's Village: An Examination in the German SOS-Children's Villages). Stuttgart: E. Klett, 1970.

WOLFF, SULA, *Children Under Stress.* London: Penguin Press, 1969.

WOLINS, MARTIN, AND IRVING PILIAVIN, *Institution or Foster Family?: A Century of Debate.* New York: Child Welfare League of America, 1964.

WOLINS, MARTIN, AND MEIR GOTTESMAN, *Group Care: Israeli Approach: The Educational Path of the Youth Aliyah.* London: Gordon & Breach, 1971.

*Articles*

ADAMS, JOHN E., AND HYING BOK KIM, "A Fresh Look at Intercountry Adoptions," *Children* (Dec. 1971), pp. 214–21.

APTE, M. J., "Non-Statutory Child Welfare Services in Bombay-City," *Indian Journal of Social Work*, 32 No. 3 (1971), 233–46.

BÉKOMBO, MANGO, "L'Enfant, la famille et l'école en Afrique noire" (The Child, the Family, and the School in Black Africa), *Les Carnets de l'enfance*, 17 (March 1972), 62–74.

BÉLANGER, PIERRE W., "L'Enfant exceptionelle: phénomène social" (The Exceptional Child: Social Phenomenon), *Service social*, 20, No. 1 (1971), 85–97.

BERTHET, ETIENNE, "La Protection de l'enfance dans les pays en voie de développement" (The Protection of Children in the Developing Countries), *International Social Work*, 13, No. 2 (1970), 29–39.

CHATTERJEE, B., "Social Aspects of Family Planning in India," *Indian Journal of Social Work*, 32, No. 2, 137–50.

DASBACH, FERNANDO LOUIS, "Child Welfare: An East and West German Perspective on the Adoption of Children and Illegitimacy Statutes from 1949 to 1970" (doctor's dissertation, unpublished, Catholic University, 1972).

FANSHEL, DAVID, "Child Welfare," pp. 85–143 in Henry S. Maas, ed., *Five Fields of Social Service: Reviews of Research*. New York: National Association of Social Workers, 1966.

FRANKENSTEIN, CARL, "Youth Aliyah and the Education of Immigrants," pp. 248–66 in Carl Frankenstein, ed., *Between Past and Future*. Jerusalem: Henrietta Szold Foundation, 1953.

FRIEDMAN, RONALD, "Norms for Family Size in Underdeveloped Areas," pp. 157–80 in David M. Heer, ed., *Readings in Population*. Englewood Cliffs, N.J.: Prentice-Hall, 1968.

GILLETTE, ARTHUR, "Aims and Organization of Voluntary Services for Youth," *Community Development Journal*, 7 (1972), 99–129.

GREBLER, ANNE-MARIE, "Adoption in European Countries," *Child Welfare*, 43 (Dec. 1963), 495–99.

KOUNDA, KENNETH, "Children and Youth in Africa Today," *Les Carnets de l'enfance*, 17 (March 1972), 3–18.

LOX, F., "Le Problème des placements," *Le Service social*, 48, No. 5 (Sep. 1970), 193–214.

MAITREJAN, JEAN, "Les Maisons Familiales," *Theorie und Praxis der sozialen Arbeit*, 24, No. 5 (May 1974), 191–95.

PHADKE, SINDU, "Travelling Child Care for New Delhi's Nomad Workers," *Children Today*, 3, No. 1 (Feb. 1974), 16–19.

SALZBERGER, LOTTE, AND JONA M. ROSENFELD, "The Anatomy of 267 Social Welfare Agencies in Jerusalem," *Social Service Review*, 48 (June 1974), 255–67.

SCHOTTLAND, CHARLES I., "The Changing Roles of Government and Family," *Journal of Marriage and the Family*, 29 (Feb. 1967), 71–79.

SPIEGELMAN, J., "Challenge for the Third World: Preparing Girls for Parenthood," *Children Today*, 2 (Apr. 1973), 15–18.

STEVENS, EVELYN P., "Machismo and Marianismo," *Society*, 10 (Oct. 1973), 57–63.

THIRET, MICHELLE, "Les Adolescents en rupture de famille" (Adolescents in Broken Homes), *L'École des parents*, No. 5 (1972), pp. 4–14.

WOLINS, MARTIN, "Some Theory and Practice in Child Care: A Cross-Cultural View," *Child Welfare* (Oct. 1963), pp. 369–78.

ZIMMERMAN, C. Z., "The Future of the Family in America." *Journal of Marriage and the Family*, 34 (Feb. 1972), 323–33.

ZUCKERMAN, J. T., "Support and Custody of Children: International and Comparative Aspects," *International Social Work*, 12 (Feb. 1969), 18–26.

ZUMBACH, PIERRE, AND JEAN-PIERRE GAUME, eds., "Children of China," *International Child Welfare Review*, 19–20 (Dec. 1973), 3–52.

# International health conditions

## 5

The founding assembly of the United Nations in San Francisco in 1945 called for creation of a specialized agency for health. This agency, the World Health Organization (WHO) was discussed at a separate conference in France in 1946 and ratified in 1948, as explained in Chapter 2.[1]

## Infectious Diseases

Although there are no reliable statistics on health conditions in most countries of the world, there are sufficient indications that mortality rates and infectious and parasitic diseases are decreasing owing to improvements in medical science. One of the most relevant factors in the improvement of health conditions, especially in the developing countries, is the progress in the containment of malaria, yaws, leprosy, smallpox, poliomyelitis, and tuberculosis. The reduction and partial eradication of malaria has been achieved mainly by the conscientious work of the World Health Organization in cooperation with UNICEF, through establishment of malaria control projects and of basic health service centers offering preventive treatment, health education, and curative services. There remain regions of Africa with about 185 million people that are still plagued by malaria epidemics.

In the field of leprosy, there are over 2,800,000 patients registered, of whom only about 1,900,000 are under treatment. Estimates of the number of persons suffering from leprosy exceeds 10 million. If the estimates are accurate, only 18 percent of these sick persons are under treatment.[2] Leprosy control requires early detection and therapy with sulfones. Early treatment permits medical treatment on a large scale without requiring isolation of the patients in leprosy colonies and segregation from their families and the general population. Under modern treatment, only definite infectious cases of leprosy make a temporary isolation necessary. However, sulfone therapy is a slow process and patients need to be kept in treatment for a long period. Over 66 countries have received leprosy assistance from the World Health Organization and UNICEF. Recent research promises to find new and effective treatment methods by the use of BCG-vaccines and chemoprophylaxis.

Yaws has been a dreaded disease in Asia and the South Pacific for a long time. Recently intensive mass occulations with penicillin have caused a substantial decline of the disease, supported by the establishment of rural health centers in many parts of Asia and the South Pacific with the assistance of WHO and UNICEF.

Smallpox has nearly been eradicated in North America, Europe, and the Western Pacific under a program of WHO, but remains endemic in major parts of Africa, Asia, and, to a lesser degree, Latin America. There is hope for eradication by the extension of preventive treatment.

Poliomyelitis could be brought almost wholly under control by the use of polio vaccines, but in some tropical countries such systematic immunization still is lacking so that the disease is not completely eradicated yet.

One continuing serious health problem is tuberculosis. There are an estimated 10 to 20 million patients suffering from tuberculosis and from 2 to 3 million new cases each year. Tuberculosis still causes from 1 to 2 million deaths annually, three-quarters of them in the developing countries which obviously require better methods of diagnosis, prophylactic measures, treatment, and aftercare. BCG remains the most potent means of preventing the disease and can be given routinely even without a tuberculosis test in combination with a smallpox vaccination.

A number of severe diseases, the plague, yellow fever, trypanosomiasis, and venereal diseases, seemed to be fully under control but have recently reappeared. Venereal diseases particularly are a cause of worldwide concern. The large numbers of venereal infections—an estimated 50 million of syphilis and 150 million of gonorrhea—are caused by the break-up of rural family life as a result of urbanization and industrialization in the developing countries and by the changing sexual behavior of youth in most countries.[3] Public health authorities in most countries relaxed their controls on venereal diseases at a time when it was necessary to reinforce these measures and to develop even an international cooperative approach based on the assistance of private physicians, legislation requiring that all contacts be reported, and compulsory investigation and treatment.[4]

The plague is still endemic in Africa, Asia, and South America, particularly in Vietnam, Ecuador, Peru, Bolivia, and Brazil. Several studies of the World Health Organization reveal that it is necessary to locate the places where infections occur, to introduce surveillance, and to eliminate the rodents and flies that are carriers of the diseases.

Yellow fever is reappearing in the Caribbean islands, in Central and South America, and recently also in Africa (particularly Senegal) and Latin America (Bolivia, Brazil, and northern Argentina).

Trypanosomiasis (sleeping sickness) remains widespread in Africa south of the Sahara. Its resurgence has been facilitated by the interruption of surveillance of the disease and by the outbreak of new wars. Rapid population movement in this region has led to a large increase in the number of tsetse flies, and serious danger can only be removed by permanent land occupation and regular cultivation. In Latin America about 7 million persons are yearly infected with this disease, which frequently causes cardiac diseases, particularly among middle-aged persons.

Another dangerous development is the resurgence and spread of communicable diseases such as cholera, hepatitis, and bilharziosis to new areas. Cholera, which has been endemic in large regions of Asia (Korea, Hong Kong, Indonesia, and several islands of the Philippines), has now spread to some cities of Europe and Africa. New infections reached over 50,000 in recent years. Cholera control requires careful personal and communal hygiene, safe water, waste disposal, and sanitation not always available in the inflicted areas. Infectious hepatitis has so far resisted prevention and treatment. It is caused by a virus that infects the liver by drinks and food. There is hope that the development of a special serum may permit medical therapy. Bilharziosis, caused by snails in rivers, is second only to malaria as the cause of illness and death in several developing countries. More than 180 to 200 million cases are found in Africa, the Near East, Latin America, and the Western Pacific, but some progress in its treatment has been reported in the Arab Republic through systematic elimination of snails.[5]

Trachoma, respiratory virus infection, and filariasis show little change in their prevalence. Trachoma still remains the most dangerous cause of progressive sight loss. The disease impairs the sight of nearly 500 million persons in many nations, especially in the developing countries. No fully effective vaccine has been found, but antibiotic prophylaxis and therapy tend to reduce this disease. The therapy takes a long time and is difficult to carry on in field conditions, because it requires hospitalization or clinical treatment. Certain improvements in developing countries are reported as a result of better general living standards, more public health centers, and an increase in health education and awareness. Filariasis, an infection caused by mosquito bites, involves about 250 million persons in Africa, Asia, Latin America, and the Pacific. Its spread has been increased through urbanization, population movements, and a lack of adequate sanitation and sewage systems in many developing countries. There is no full consensus on the most effective medical therapy and on preventive measures except the eradication of the mosquitoes.

Deplorable health conditions exist for the nonwhite population of the Republic of South Africa, owing to its policy of Apartheid. In 1970 the infant death rate of its African tribes was 136.2 for 1,000 live births, compared with 2.1 for white infants. There is one doctor for every 450 whites, but only one for every 18,000 blacks, and only one black physician for 44,400 Africans. Conditions in the townships are extremely harsh and lead to much disease and social pathology for Africans. Since black laborers are not permitted to bring their families from the so-called reserves, the results of the long separations are prostitution and family disruption. Since their wages are very low, many blacks suffer from severe malnutrition, gastroenteritis, pneumonia, measles, diptheria, or dysentery. Estimates have been made that 20 percent of the black population suffers from tuberculosis. In the townships, medical responsibilities are divided among hospitals, clinics, and social services, each under different authorities. The clinics have no adequate finances or manpower; birth control programs are encouraged by the authorities. In the rural districts, mission hospitals are the best medical facilities, but they are so overcrowded they cannot accept many patients who need care.[6]

### Chronic and Degenerative Diseases

Chronic and degenerative diseases include mental deficiencies and nutritional diseases caused by malnutrition and sociocultural influences of the environment. These are common in the developing countries, but even in the industrialized countries cardiovascular diseases, malignant neoplasms, and accidents are among the most common causes of death, especially among the aged. Cardiovascular diseases, in the form of arteriosclerosis and degenerative heart diseases, are the cause of about half of all deaths in the developed nations.

Arterial hypertension is the most frequent disorder of the circulatory system, and the death rate from cardiovascular diseases increases steadily with advancing age. These diseases are caused by vascular lesions and rheumatic fever, especially in subtropical countries. In these regions the World Health Organization assists in establishing health clinics and centers with preventive programs and early therapy to diminish the high rate of vascular diseases causing disabilities and early death.[7]

The incidence of cancer varies in Europe, North America, Japan, Africa, and central Asia, but cancer is still considered the most dangerous of all diseases in the industrial countries. There are not yet any effective preventive or controlling techniques, though almost every country is trying to find such methods. Accidents have for some time been the major cause of death for persons in the industrial countries below 35, but even in the developing countries accidents, (falls, burns, poisoning, gassing, and suffocation) are an important danger.

Nutritional and other deficiency diseases are serious health problems in the developing countries, particularly in Asia and South America. They are frequently aggravated by measles and diarrhea in children, and by nutritional anemia in young children and pregnant and lactating women. Preventive measures like the use of iodized salt and nutritional education offer promise but have so far been used only in a few Asian and Latin American countries stimulated by the World Health Organization, the Food and Agriculture Organization and the United Nations International Children's Fund.

Mental disorders have decreased little during recent decades. They are frequently caused by drugs, alcohol, and inherited mental retardation. Prevention and cure require a program integrated with general public health care and the use of psychiatric outpatient clinics and general hospitals, and such programs do not exist in many countries of the world. It will be necessary to develop active community care facilities in order to supplement hospitals and clinics with the support of public health authorities and voluntary agencies.[8]

### Drugs

Narcotic drugs are now a worldwide problem and were considered such during the time of the League of Nations. In 1971 the Economic and Social Council of the United Nations decided to tighten international control over the production and traffic of hallucinogenic drugs and took measures to prevent their illicit import to countries in Europe and North America.[9]

During a session of the UN Commission on Narcotic Drugs in Geneva, in 1970, John Ingersoll, director of the United States Anti-Narcotics Law Enforcement Agency, suggested that socioeconomic measures such as the substitution of other crops, provision of other gainful employment, development of new market facilities, are needed to limit illicit opium cultivation, mainly in Turkey. These measures require the cooperation of the United Nations Food and Agriculture Organization and of the United Nations Development Program (discussed in Chapter 2). Turkey agreed to the proposed curtailment of the opium poppy, to alternative crops, and to the establishment of agroindustries, with compensations from the United States. The danger remains that illegal drug traffickers, shrewd persons devoted to their highly profitable business, will find other sources for opium in southeast Asia, the Middle East, Latin America and Africa.[10]

In 1971 the international assembly of INTERPOL (the international organization of police agencies) called attention to the decentralization of narcotic drug-processing centers from Marseilles to Iran, Turkey, Thailand, and Hong Kong. It emphasized the need for intensified international cooperation and for more effective support by the nation members of the United Nations. INTERPOL should be strengthened by increasing its staff of narcotic investigators and by regional assistance of the UN program of crop substitution and of preventing the illicit drug traffic.[11]

The widespread use of narcotic drugs in the United States is known all over the world.[12] There are no reliable statistics about the number of drug users, mainly among children and adolescents, but all estimates are very high. Numerous state laws make it a crime to sell, possess, or purchase "dangerous drugs" in the sense of the World Health Organization's formulation without medical prescription. The first approach to this danger employed punishment: imprisonment was expected to achieve rehabilitation, but it didn't. A second means, medical treatment in hospitals and clinics with minimal aftercare was not successful either. A third, more effective approach, has been to place addicts in institutions for an indeterminate time. The best-known such therapy centers are those of Synanon, but there is also Phoenix House in New York and Odyssey House.[13] The centers are directed by former addicts, which impresses the patients. Critics maintain that these therapies tend to be of very long duration and are more effective for young addicts than for older confirmed addicts. Organizations such as the Salvation Army, the Damascus Christian Church in New York and the Bronx, the Pentecostal Fundamentalist churches, the Black Muslims, and the Teen Challenge in Brooklyn use a religious approach for the treatment of drug or alcohol addiction. Their services have been effective among the addicts able to develop deep religious convictions, especially among Puerto Ricans in New York.

A very significant therapy was Leon Brill's "rational-authority approach," based upon the theories of Erich Fromm and Max Weber. Brill works at the Washington Heights Rehabilitation Center in New York in close cooperation with the New York City Office of Probation. His method uses strict controls and behavior limits to prevent antisocial acting out and relapse. Similar methods are applied by the Pennsylvania Division of Parole, the California Youth and Adult Corrections Agency in Sacramento, and the Federal Narcotic Addiction Rehabilitation

Agency. In medical therapy of drug addiction cyclazocine and methadone have so far been found most successful.[14]

The use of narcotic drugs in east Asia and countries in almost all continents is an old story and it cannot be discussed in this study. Their widespread use in Europe is a more recent event. In the Scandinavian countries, Germany, Switzerland, the Netherlands, and Belgium drug abuse is recognized as a most serious health problem and the main cause of juvenile delinquency and crimes.

As an example of measures to deal with these problems, the practice of the Netherlands may be cited. In Dutch prisons and correctional institutions there are a substantial number of juvenile drug addicts who have committed crimes. After passage of the law on opiates in 1968, the number of sentences for drug addicts, including offenders under 17 years of age, increased rapidly. The law prohibits the sale of cannabis and narcotic drugs and provides sentences up to four years of prison. The district attorney is entitled to help the drug addict to get rid of his addiction by permitting him to apply to a clinic and be treated there. If the offender is a danger to himself or others, he is placed in detention with psychiatric and social counseling and with the possibility of a commitment to a mental institution for six weeks. The use of opiates is severely punished with prison sentences, and foreigners are always expelled. Offenders 12 to 15 years of age and most of those 15 to 18 are placed in correctional institutions. For those 18 to 21 the judge of the juvenile court may order fines, correctional treatment, or probation until the age of 21. Several community centers in Amsterdam were for a long time extremely permissive about drug smoking and demonstrations, but in 1970 those hostels were closed. There is a community reception center for juveniles called *Jongeren Advies Centrum* for first aid and counselling, and another youth hostel, *de Laurier*, serves as a center for juveniles endangered by narcotic drugs. Therapy for drug addicts is offered by the famous Jellinek Clinic and by Cosmos, a meditation center with Yoga lectures and psychedelic music performances.[15]

## The Environment

Environmental Health receives increasingly more attention in industrial and in developing countries, but safe water supplies via pipes are still only available to about one-third of the populations of 75 countries in Asia, Africa, and Latin America. In Africa and Asia only 11 percent have good or fair water supplies. In many developing countries the lack of good water in rural regions is one of the main causes of a low level of living.

Urbanization, the flow of rural populations to the cities and metropolises, is a widespread phenomenon characteristic of our time. This immigration causes the rapid growth of the urban areas, overcrowding, insufficient housing, the spread of poverty, unemployment, crime, and serious health problems, including communicable diseases, as we saw in Chapter 3. The new pressure for health and social services cannot be adequately met because of the financial deficiencies of most of the developing countries without a much more generous international assistance which the superpowers are unwilling to grant without economic compensation.[16]

Pollution of water, air, and soil is another acute health problem. It is worst in the developed countries, but it is now appearing in the new countries. Pollution is the product of industrialization. It is expensive to protect the environment from the smoke of factories, and diesel and motor emissions and heated water from power plants. The increasing concentration of the urban population creates such a serious health hazard and a social problem that the World Health Organization is requiring worldwide legislation and research to prevent further use of pollutants and to introduce efficient control systems.[17]

### Medical Care in China

In the Republic of China there are clinics in the communes that provide health services for an annual contribution equivalent to about 50 American cents. These clinics are mostly staffed by so-called barefoot doctors, young women and men assigned to care for the health of families and children in rural regions of China who are trained in first aid, midwifery, treatment of simple ailments, and care of patients after hospitalization or operations. These barefoot doctors encourage family planning and the use of contraceptives. During the summer they do agricultural work, and during the winter they attend further training courses in hospitals. Accupuncture, inserting a fine needle into specific nerve points of the body, is widely used in China. It has been practiced as an anesthetic and cure of numerous diseases for about 5,000 years[18] and is now applied also in Western countries.

Medical care in China has been decentralized. Teams of physicians, nurses, and medical assistants are sent to the communes where they offer free medical services, collect herbs (which are used in the old tradition as effective medicines), and teach special aspects of hygiene, sanitation, and preventive medical treatment.[19]

### Changes in Public Health Organization and Planning

In the newly independent nations public health services have existed only on the national level, but now they are especially needed in the rural regions. These public health services, which include maternal and infant health centers, are often supported by allocations, personnel, and equipment from the World Health Organization and UNICEF. Many new nations initiated some health planning about 1960, but now need to expand health services to control diseases and train health personnel.[20]

In Asia and Africa only about 1.2 percent of the Gross National Products of nations is devoted to expansion of health services, compared with 3.5 percent in Europe and North America. Although during the past decade the increase of expenditures for health services was 12 percent of the GNP, compared with only 8 percent in the industrial countries, there remains a wide gap between the health levels of the two groups which the international agencies are attempting to reduce.

Health care is rendered in the different nations mainly under three systems: (1) private medical practice, (2) public health services, and (3) compulsory health insurance, which provides various forms of health services. The first system is characteristic for the United States. The second system is used in Great Britain, the Soviet Union, communist China, and in most communist nations in Eastern Europe. The third system, sometimes overlapping with public health services, is used in northern, central, and western Europe. It will be discussed in Chapter 8 in more detail.[21]

### Food and Nutrition

During and after the Second World War near famine conditions prevailed in numerous countries, particularly those occupied by enemy forces. After the war mass starvation was prevented by large food shipments by the United Nations Relief and Rehabilitation Administration and by the United States and Canada, as shown in Chapter 1. Later, during the 1960s, per capita food production decreased in wide areas of Africa and Asia owing to the emphasis on industrialization and urbanization, but again mass starvation was prevented by international aid and technical assistance from agencies of the United Nations. Still the population explosion and the food production crisis threatens the future of the developing regions. Some nations prefer to produce exportable goods and cash crops that bring them foreign valuta than to produce food for domestic consumption. Since in most developing countries most inhabitants still depend on agricultural production, the increase in their income from labor is seriously eroded by the continuous rise of population and by inflation in the prices of tools and materials from the industrial nations that the peasants have to purchase. Thus the demand for staple grains, potatoes, fats, oils, and sugar is not satisfied. Some countries can no longer meet the demand for meat, fishes, fruit, and vegetables, which were plentiful in former times. The consumption of nutritious foods varies greatly among different classes and income strata within such countries such as India, Pakistan, and Indonesia: the richer sections consume more than they need, while the poorer people who usually have to perform heavier work, suffer from malnutrition.[22]

The United Nations and its affiliated organizations are attempting a community development policy to change subsistence farming practices in developing countries to more market-oriented types of agricultural production, which would provide better nutrition for the growing population. This requires a systematic expansion of agricultural production, improvements in marketing methods by cooperatives and mutual support, modernization of rural institutions, better crop diversification, price stabilization, village cooperatives, and fair loan associations for credit giving. It will also be necessary to change the landlord and tenant system, with its inherent insecurity, high rents, exploitation of the tenants, and inequitable distribution of income, through the introduction of effective land reform measures in Asia and Latin American countries. Seasonal unemployment or underemployment and the exodus of youth to the cities need to be changed. To accomplish such changes, to integrate agricultural development with the increasing nutritional needs of the urban population, and to encourage the set-up of small and medium-sized food-processing industries in order to avoid spoilage of food and create new employment opportunities in rural regions and small cities will require regional development programs, as discussed in Chapter 3. In Japan the shortage of farm labor has led to the consolidation of small farms into larger units, and to the use of capital-intensive and labor-saving devices. Such methods have not yet made a major impact on the economies of most developing countries.[23] The establishment of low-cost transportation also is a prerequisite for better agricultural production and marketing, as is assignment of more development funds to improve agricultural production in the developing countries instead of to develop new industries. The objective is to increase the amount of the quality of agricultural products for exports and the domestic market, to install new industries based on use of native agricultural raw materials, and to modernize agricultural production methods.

The Food and Agriculture Organization (FAO) has done much to implement this policy in developing countries. In 1963 the FAO organized the World Food Congress, which established an Indicative World

Plan for the purpose of dealing for the next 20 years with food shortages in the developing countries by setting realistic targets for production and international trade in foods and fertilizers, framing sound land-use policies, providing wider employment opportunities for rural labor, balancing the agricultural and industrial development, strengthening economic cooperation among the new countries, improving long-distance transportation and freezing and freeze-drying facilities, and preserving food by ionizing radiation. There are also considerations for packing in lighter cans and using aluminum and plastic containers and safe food additives. People in tropical regions need educational programs on food spoilage and waste and on the use of protein-rich foods such as oil-seed cakes and soya proteins.[24]

The major educational efforts of the FAO have been directed toward pregnant and nursing mothers on how to nourish infants and preschool children. In order to raise the nutritional standards and to increase sane food consumption, FAO has tried to enlist the support of physicians, teachers, nurses, midwives, home economists, and community development organizers. Their strongest efforts have been in villages to encourage the active participation of the population. In most of these projects FAO has been helped by the World Health Organization, UNICEF, and the International Labor Organization (which provided equipment and materials, technical advice, and personnel).

Most developing countries need to transfer large unused areas to food production in order to prevent severe malnutrition and hunger. They also need to reduce the fertility rate by systematic family planning, which already is supported in India, Ceylon, Taiwan, Korea, Pakistan, and the Arab Republic.

### Rehabilitation of the Disabled

Rehabilitation programs for handicapped persons have played an important role, especially in the new countries. The large number of disabled at the end of the Second World War made such programs necessary, and the increasing number of accident victims occasioned by industrialization, urbanization, and rural migration to the cities has extended the need. Advances in medicine, the social sciences, and technology have led to the development of new rehabilitation techniques.[25]

The total number of handicapped persons who could take advantage of rehabilitative measures is not known, but in Great Britain there are over 650,000 in the Disabled Persons Register; in France 2 million people are known as handicapped; and in Russia 55,000 deaf persons are employed in sheltered workshops, and over 8,000 are in training for the disabled, and there are 300 workshops for the blind.[26] In Norway 5,000 disabled persons register annually with the labor exchanges; 3,000 of them are employed and 1,000 are placed in vocational training centers. In Finland the number of handicapped persons is estimated at 80,000, in Japan at 950,000.[27]

Rehabilitation services for disabled persons operate in most countries. International agencies assist in the establishment and operation of these rehabilitation centers. A few international rehabilitation services, for instance the All India Institute for Physical Medicine and Rehabilitation in Bombay and the *Hospital das Clinicas* in Sao Paulo, Brazil, have been set up with teams from many countries to serve as pilot projects and models for neighboring countries.[28]

Rehabilitation services in numerous countries are supported by the technical assistance from the United Nations, the World Health Organization, the International Labor Organization, and the United Nations International Children's Fund. In 1950 the United Nations Economic and Social Council adopted a resolution requesting the secretary-general to set up a well-coordinated program for the rehabilitation of physically handicapped persons. Experts are now sent to nations on request to develop rehabilitation programs, and fellowships are provided to train persons for these services. Following a recommendation of the International Labor Organization, vocational rehabilitation of the disabled with guidance, counseling, and placement is carried out, but there are differences of opinion whether the protection of the handicapped should be secured by legislation (in England, for example, a certain percentage of disabled persons must be employed by firms with more than a certain number of employees), or whether the cooperation of employers should be voluntary. The ILO included in its recommendation the suggestion that employment should be appropriate to national circumstances and consistent with national policy, and should not displace able-bodied workers. In Poland and other countries cooperatives of disabled persons have been founded, one of them producing soap and dental powder, and in 1949 a union of cooperatives for invalids was established that by 1959 included 363 cooperatives and employed over 50,000 handicapped persons. Sheltered employment is the regular form of helping the handicapped in most countries, often including medical treatment, vocational training, and placement in regular industries. Seminars are held from time to time under the auspices of the International Society for the Welfare of Cripples.

The medical treatment of the handicapped attempts to restore as much as possible their health and productivity, and tries to integrate them into the general society and to help their socioeconomic growth. The concept of rehabilitation is to use medical, psychological, economic, educational, vocational, and social resources to restore the entire life of the handicapped.

Until the beginning of this century rehabilitation of the handicapped was almost exclusively the function of private charities, foundations, and individuals. Recently the governments of numerous countries, including the new nations, are assuming responsibility for such rehabilitation, often in relation to their developing social security systems. Disability pensions (unless related to industrial accidents) seem not to be the most constructive solution; rather, an effective rehabilitation that enables the patient to resume work seems preferable because it usually pays the expense of the rehabilitation process within a few years in taxes and because of the social value of a satisfied, self-respecting human being and his family.[29]

In many countries special legislation, decrees, and regulations provide rehabilitation services instead of welfare to the handicapped, but sometimes the latter supplements rehabilitation services. In a few countries certain occupations are reserved for the disabled, in others quota systems secure their employment. Most such provisions were first enacted for disabled war veterans and later extended to other handicapped persons. The quota system has been criticized because it discriminates against the disabled by employing them because of their handicap rather than for their professional skills. In many countries civil service employment requires full physical health, but a few nations have abandoned this policy after experience proved that handicapped persons could do as well as able-bodied people.[30]

Medical treatment in rehabilitation includes examination, counseling, and therapy, including prosthetics such as artificial arms and legs, glass eyes, crutches, wheelchairs, hearing aids, safety canes, and the necessary training for the use of such instruments, and braille training for the blind—all free of charge for patients unable to pay for these services. Services for the training and employment of severely handicapped persons in several industrial countries (England, Sweden, Denmark, Norway, the Netherlands, West Germany, France, Belgium, and Italy) is organized with the purpose that these persons—the blind, the crippled, the deaf and mute, but also the mentally retarded, the very old, and those suffering from emotional disturbances—should feel more adequate and able to take care of themselves, even if their labor is not really needed on the labor market.[31] Japan and other countries still need a stronger integration of public and private rehabilitation services for the disabled, trained homekeepers for the home-bound disabled, and special services for the severely handicapped (those suffering from cerebral palsy and double and triple handicaps). There is also a widespread need for comprehensive rehabilitation programs and for trained personnel (doctors, nurses, vocational counselors, special teachers, social workers, and physical and occupational therapists), especially in the developing countries.

In the field of such rehabilitation the United Nations and its specialized agencies have provided much valuable assistance in Asia (India, Laos, Thailand), Latin America (Brazil, the Dominican Republic, El Salvador), Yugoslavia, the Arab Republic, and Indonesia. Special conferences and seminars on rehabilitation technique under international auspices contribute to better knowledge and skills in this field. The main trends in rehabilitation are the use of preventive measures, surgery, curative medical treatment, social and economic assistance, educational measures, regional rehabilitation centers based upon cultural and socioeconomic language and similarities, and the attempts to change public attitudes toward the handicapped, the chronically ill, and the mentally retarded. (In Queensland, Australia, the early placement of old patients suffering from severe organic brain diseases has proved to be successful.)[32]

### Health Services

A comprehensive comparison of health services in the countries of the world surpasses the bounds of this study. In most Western countries health-consciousness has been widespread.[33] Most of the developing countries base their health provisions on public health activities (permitting private medical practice only for the minority that has the means to pay physicians).

In Europe the medieval guilds in the Netherlands, Belgium, Germany, Switzerland, the Scandinavian countries, and England organized sickness insurance societies that served members and their families in case of serious illness via financial contributions. The first compulsory health insurance legislation for workers was enacted in Germany in 1883, followed by similar legislation in Austria, the Scandinavian countries, and in England in 1911 (see Chapter 8).

The public health service in England, Scotland, and Wales aims at prevention, diagnosis, and treatment of illness free of charge (with certain exceptions: reduction of social security benefits, special fees for private beds in hospitals, drugs and medicines, dental services, and some ophthalmic appliances). One has free choice of doctor, hospital, and therapies, and a change of the doctor is possible. Most physicians can combine work for the health service or for health insurance with private practice,[34] an option not available to doctors in public health programs under communist auspices. The aim of preventive health services, to avoid ill-health and incapacities in order to preserve the nation's manpower strength, is also prevalent in public health services under government authorities. Russia, for instance, has the Medico-Labor Expert Commissions, composed of three physicians, one trade-union representative, and a delegate of the local welfare department.[35] In many developing countries health services were first organized by the central ministry of health but have since been transferred to regional and local authorities (frequently subsidized by the national government),[36] where they are better equipped to provide adequate medical treatment, hospitalization, clinical after-care and the improvement of health conditions discussed previously.

Medical social work has long been an important part of public and private health services in the United States and Europe. The same is true here for school social work. In France and the Latin American countries social work, especially medical social work in welfare agencies, hospitals, clinics, health centers, and schools, has been closely connected with health services.[37] The United States and countries in Europe use medical social workers and school social workers as teams together with physicians, psychiatrists, and psychologists in clinics, hospitals, health centers, and schools, but the Soviet Union, the eastern European communist countries, and mainland China do not recognize social work as a professional discipline. Instead they use either state employees with administrative, legal, or psychological training or fellow workers or union members as functionaries for health and individual services. Japan, India, Pakistan, Burma, Thailand, the Philippines, Australia, and New Zeland all employ social workers trained in universities for medical social work.[38] Whatever the future of social work, whether in the direction of generic social work or work in methods such as casework, group work, or community organization (Chapter 11), social work in the framework of health services will remain very relevant.

In view of the rapid change of public opinion in various countries about the sexual behavior of the young, Kohlberg's research in Great Britain, Canada, the United States, Mexico, Turkey, Taiwan, and Israel showed that there are very different concepts in each of these countries on the moral aspects of sexual behavior, particularly among adolescents.[39]

## Notes

[1]Ralph Townley, *The United Nations* (New York: Scribner, 1968), pp. 253–54; Walter Friedlander, "International Social Welfare," in *Introduction to Social Welfare*, 3rd ed. (Englewood Cliffs, N.J.: Prentice-Hall, 1968), 543–45; Howard A. Rusk and Donald V. Wilson, "New Resources for Rehabilitation and Health," *The Annals*, 329 (May 1960), 97–106; United Nations, *1967 Report on World Social Conditions*, pp. 23–32; John Bryant, *Health and the Developing World* (Ithaca, N.Y.: Cornell University Press, 1969); Wilfred Malenbaum, "Progress in Health," *The Annals*, 393 (Jan. 1971), 109–21.

128     *International health conditions*

[2] *1967 World Social Report*, pp. 24–25. A survey of the methods of prevention and cure of various infectious diseases is discussed in Otto Jäger, *Probleme des Gesundheits-dienstes in Entwicklungsländern* (Problems of Public Health Services in Developing Countries) (Stuttgart: F. Enke, 1963), pp. 12–20, 69–83.

[3] *1967 World Social Report*, pp. 25–26.

[4] Ibid., p. 26.

[5] *1957 World Social Report*, pp. 26–27. River blindness, caused by a small black fly, infects millions of people in Africa. The World Health Organization is planning to eradicate this disease. See Thomas A. Blinkhorn, "Rivers That Eat the Eyes," *Saturday Review—World*, 1 (Dec. 18, 1973), 63–66.

[6] Raymond Hoffenberg, "Inequality in Health Care in South Africa," (New York: U.N. Unit on Apartheid, Dec. 1970); Ellen Hellman, *Sweto: Johannesburg's African City*, (Johannesburg: South African Institute of Race Relations, 1972); David Mechanic, "Apartheid Medicine," *Society*, 10, No. 3 (March–Apr. 1973), 36–44.

[7] *1967 World Social Report*, pp. 26–27; Wilfred Malenbaum, "Index of Progress in Health," *The Annals*, 393 (Jan. 1971), 109–21; *La Recherche médicale: Prorités et responsabilités* (Medical Research: Priorities and Responsibilities) (Geneva: World Health Organization, 1970). In northeast Brazil one out of every four babies dies from malnutrition before his first birthday.

[8] *1967 World Social Report*, pp. 28–30; Edwin M. Lemert, *Human Deviance, Social Problems, and Social Control* (Englewood Cliffs, N.J.: Prentice-Hall, 1967), pp. 3–30, 72–87.

[9] Kay Rainy Gray, "U.N. Notebook," *Vista*, 7, No. 1 (July–Aug. 1971), 8.

[10] Robert H. Steele, "The Business and Politics of Narcotics," *Vista*, 7, No. 5 (March–Apr. 1972), 36–39, 52.

[11] Steele, "The Business and Politics of Narcotics," p. 52.

[12] Leon Brill and Louis Lieberman, *Authority and Addiction* (Boston: Little, Brown, 1969); Leon Brill, "Three Approaches to the Casework Treatment of Narcotic Addicts," *Social Work*, 13, No. 2 (April 1968), 25–35; John A. Donell and John C. Ball, eds., *Narcotic Addiction* (New York: Harper & Row, 1966); Richard Cloward, "Illegitimate Means, Anomie, and Deviant Behavior," *American Sociological Review*, 24, No. 2 (Apr. 1959), 164–76; G. G. Barnes and P. Noble, "Deprivation and Drug Addiction: A Study of a Vulnerable Subgroup," *British Journal of Social Work*, 2 (March 1972), 299–311.

[13] Leon Brill, "Addiction: Drug," *Encyclopedia of Social Work, 1972*, pp. 24–38; Lewis Yablonsky, *Synanon: The Tunnel Back* (Baltimore: Penguin, 1969).

[14] Vincent Dole and Marie Nyswander, "A Medical Treatment for Diacetyl-Morphine, Heroin Addiction," *Journal of the American Medical Association*, 193, No. 8 (Aug. 1965), 646–50; Jerome H. Jaffe and Leon Brill, "Cyclazocine: a Long-Acting Narcotics Antagonist," *International Journal of the Addictions*, 1, No. 1 (Jan. 1966), 99–123.

[15] Walter Becker, "Bekämpfung des Drogenmissbrauchs in den Niederlanden" (The Fight Against Drug Abuse in the Netherlands), *Nachrichtendienst des Deutschen Vereins für öffentliche und private Fürsorge*, 52, No. 4 (Apr. 1972), 103–4; Paul W. Perch, "Drugs and Young People, Introductory Report," *International Child Welfare Review*, 11–12 (Dec. 1971), 32–39.

[16]Richard F. Behrendt, *Strategie für Entwicklungsländer* (Strategies for Developing Countries) (Frankfurt a/M.: S. Fischer, 1968), pp. 80–92, 623–26; *Zwischen Anarchie und neuen Ordnungen* (Between Anarchy and New Orders) (Freiburg i. B.: Rombach, 1969), p. 64; René Sand, "Health and the Standard of Living," in Gulestan Billimoria and Shirlin Dastur, eds., *Social Services and the Standard of Living* (Bombay, International Conference of Social Work, 1952), pp. 67–77; Rudie W. Tretton, *Cities in Crisis* (Englewood Cliffs, N.J.: Prentice-Hall, 1970); pp. 86–88; Philip M. Hauser, ed., *The Population Dilemma* (Englewood Cliffs, N.J.: Prentice-Hall, 1969) pp. 34–84.

[17]*1967 World Social Report,* pp. 30–31.

[18]Simone Atwood, "Women Inside China," *McCalls,* 77 (Nov. 1971), 141–44.

[19]Russell Johnson, "China Today," *Quaker Service* (Winter 1972), pp. 1–4.

[20]Ibid., pp. 31–32; Ben C. Berg, John B. Scrimshaw, and Andrew Call, *Nutrition, National Development, and Planning* (Cambridge: MIT Press, 1973).

[21]Otto Jäger, *Probleme des Gesundheits-dienstes,* pp. 25–46; John B. Turner, "Relation of Health and Welfare Planning to Social Change and Social Development," in Alfred H. Katz, ed., *Social Work and Social Planning* (New York: National Association of Social Workers, 1964).

[22]*1967 World Social Report,* pp. 38–40; Shirley Foster Hartley, *Population: Quantity vs. Quality* (Englewood Cliffs, N.J.: Prentice-Hall, 1972). See also Chapter 9; Ronald Freedman, "The High Fertility of the Less Developed Nations," in David M. Heer, ed., *Readings on Population* (Englewood Cliffs, N.J.: Prentice-Hall, 1968), pp. 157–80.

[23]*1969 World Social Report,* pp. 40–41. In 1972 the Massachusetts Institute of Technology, with the aid of a grant from the Rockefeller Foundation, established an international nutrition planning program to develop attacks against malnutrition in developing countries.

[24]*1967 World Social Report,* pp. 42–44; George M. Foster, "Some Social Factors Related to the Success of a Public Health Program," in Lyle Shannon, ed., *Underdeveloped Areas,* pp. 371–85; S. Chandrasakhar, "The Prospect of Planned Parenthood in India," ibid., pp. 386–93. Many countries do not fully recognize the need for adequate dental services. See also Lief Haanes-Olsen, "Dental Insurance in Sweden," *Social Security Bulletin,* 36 (Dec. 1973), 20–22.

[25]Howard A. Rusk and Donald V. Wilson, "New Resources for Rehabilitation and Health," *The Annals,* 329 (May 1960), 97–106; *1967 World Social Report,* pp. 101–4.

[26]Madison, *Social Welfare in the Soviet Union,* pp. 38, 143, 186, 183; Shiela Hewett, *The Family and the Handicapped Child: A Study of Heretical Palsied Children in Their Homes* (Chicago: Aldine, 1970).

[27]Seiji Matsumoto, "Work with the Physically Handicapped," in Dorothy Dessau, ed., *Social Work in Japan* (Kyoto: Social Workers' International Club of Japan, 1968) pp. 233–41.

[28]Rusk and Wilson, "New Resources for Rehabilitation and Health," p. 98.

[29]Leunart Levi, *Rehabilitation of Severely Handicapped Patients: Methods and Medical, Social, and Economic Results* (Stockholm: Ministry of Public Health, 1963); Klaus Dörrie, "Beschützende Werkstätten" (Sheltered Workshops), *Nachrichten-dienst,* 51, No. 3 (March 1971), 58–61 (experiences in Sweden, Norway, and Germany);

Charles G. Oakes, *The Walking Patient and the Health Care Crisis* (Columbia: University of South Carolina Press, 1973).
[30] *1967 World Social Report,* pp. 102–4.
[31] Beatrice G. Reubens, *The Hard-to-Employ: European Programs* (New York: Columbia University Press, 1970).
[32] R. A. Daniel, "A Five-Year Study of 693 Psychogeriatric Admissions in Queensland Wolston Park Hospital, Brisbane," *Geriatrics,* 27, No. 4 (Apr. 1972), 132–58.
[33] Richard M. Titmuss, *Essays on the Welfare State* (New Haven, Conn.: Yale University Press, 1959), pp. 133–51; A Sternback, "Research in Geriatric Psychiatry and the Care of the Aged," *Comprehensive Psychiatry,* 14 (Jan. 1973), 9–15.
[34] Richard M. Titmuss, "The National Health Service in England: Some Facts about General Practice," Titmuss, *Essays on the Welfare State,* pp. 152–77.
[35] Madison, *Social Welfare in the Soviet Union,* pp. 86–89.
[36] *1967 World Social Report,* p. 31.
[37] Parin Vakaria, "Social Work and Social Welfare Organizations in Other Parts of the World," *Encyclopedia of Social Work, 1965,* pp. 745–48; Friedlander, *Individualism and Social Welfare,* pp. 47–62; Elizabeth P. Rice, "Social Work Practice in Medical and Health Services," *Encyclopedia of Social Work, 1965,* pp. 470–76; Matilda Goldberg and June E. Mill, *Social Work in General Practice* (London: Allen & Unwin, 1972).
[38] Vakaria, "Social Work and Social Welfare Organizations," pp. 746–47; Fusa M. Asaka, "Medical Social Work in Japan," in Dorothy Dessau, ed., *Social Work in Japan,* pp. 149–59.
[39] Mary Calderone, "It's Society That Is Changing Sexuality," *The Center Magazine,* 5 (July–Aug. 1972), 58–68.

## Selected References

*Books*

ANDERSON, OLIN W., *Health Services in a Land of Plenty.* Chicago: University of Chicago Press, 1968.
ANDERSON, RONALD, BJÖRN SMEDLEY, AND OLIN W. ANDERSON, *Medical Use in Sweden and the U.S.A.* Chicago: University of Chicago Press, 1970.
BIRD, HERBERT G., AND JEAN DYE GUSSOW, *Disadvantaged Children: Health, Nutrition, and School Failure.* New York: Harcourt Brace Jovanovich, 1970.
BLUM, HENDRIK I., AND ALVIN R. LEONARD, *Public Administration: A Public Health Viewpoint.* New York: Macmillan, 1963.
BUDER, HUGUELLE, *Troubles psycho-moteurs chez l'enfant: Pratique de la rééducation psycho-motrice* (Psychomotor Troubles in Children: The Practice of Psychomotor Reeducation). Paris: Masson, 1970.
BURNS, EVELINE M., *New Directions in Public Policy for Health Care.* New York: Academy of Medicine, 1966.
CAMERON, DALE, AND A. R. MAY, *La Jeunesse et l'usage des drogues* (Youth and Drug Abuse). Geneva: Union Internationale de Protection de l'Enfance, 1972.

CANADA DEPARTMENT OF NATIONAL HEALTH AND WELFARE, *Health Services for Public Assistance Recipients in Canada.* Ottawa, 1957.

CANADIAN PUBLIC HEALTH ASSOCIATION, *The Development of Public Health in Canada,* Toronto, 1940.

CASELMAN, JO, et al., *Drugs: Middelen-mensen-samenleving.* Antwerpen: The Nederlandsche Boekhardel, 1971.

CENTRAL UNION FOR CHILD WELFARE IN FINLAND, *Care and Education of Exceptional Children in Finland.* Helsinki, 1971.

DAVIS, MICHAEL D., *Clinics, Hospitals, and Health Centers.* New York: Harper & Row, 1927.

DINNAGE, ROSEMARY, *The Handicapped Child.* London: Longman, 1972.

DUFF, RAYMOND S., AND AUGUST B. HOLLINGSHEAD, *Sickness and Society.* New York: Harper & Row, 1968.

DUNNELL, KAREN, AND ANN CARTRIGHT, *Medicine Takers, Prescribers, and Hoarders.* Boston: Routledge and Kegan Paul, 1972.

FEIN, RASHI, *The Doctor Shortage: An Economic Diagnosis.* Washington, D.C.: The Brookings Institution, 1967.

GINZBERG, ELI, AND MIRIAM OSTOW, *Men, Money, and Medicine.* New York: Columbia University Press, 1969.

GLASER, WILLIAM A., *Paying the Doctor: Systems of Remuneration and Their Effect.* Baltimore: Johns Hopkins Press, 1970.

GOLDBERG, MATILDA, AND JUNE E. MILL, *Social Work in General Practice.* London: Allen & Unwin, 1972.

HANLON, JOHN J., *Principles of Public Health Administration.* St. Louis: C. V. Mosby, 1969.

HILLEBOECET, HERMAN, et al., *Approaches to National Health Planning.* Geneva: World Health Organization, 1972.

JAEGER, OTTO A., *Probleme des Gesundheitsdienstes in Entwicklungsländern* (Problems of Health Services in the Developing Countries). Stuttgart: F. Enke, 1963.

JUNGER-TAX, J., *Jeunesse scolaire et drogues: une enquête dans quelques écoles belgiques* (School Children and Drugs: An Investigation in Several Belgian Schools). Brussels: Centre d'Etude de la délinquance juvenile, 1972.

KATZ, ALFRED H., AND J. S. FELTON, *Health and the Community.* New York: Free Press, 1965.

KLARMAN, HERBERT E., ed., *Empirical Studies in Health Economics.* Baltimore: Johns Hopkins Press, 1970.

KOSA, JOHN, AARON ANTONOWSKY, AND IRVING ZELA, *Poverty and Health: A Sociological Analysis.* Cambridge, Mass.: Harvard University Press, 1969.

LIEBERMAN, FLORENCE, PHYLLIS CAROFF, AND MARY GOTTESFIELD, *Before Addiction: How to Help Youth.* New York: Behavioral Publications, 1973.

MCLACHLAN, GORDON, *Challenges for Change: Essays on the Next Decade in the National Health Service,* London: Oxford University Press, 1971.

MAY, M. JOEL, *Health Planning: Its Past and Potential.* Chicago: University of Chicago Press, 1967.

MUNTENDAM, P., *Public Health in the Netherlands.* The Hague: Ministry of Public Health, 1968.

PENEHANSKY, ROY, ed., *Health Services Administration*. Cambridge, Mass.: Harvard University Press, 1968.

POPOV, G. A., *Principles of Health Planning in the U.S.S.R.* Geneva: World Health Organization, 1971.

QUERIDO, A., *The Development of Socio-Medical Care in the Netherlands*. London: Routledge and Kegan Paul, 1968.

READ, MARGARET, *Social and Cultural Backgrounds for Planning Public Health Programmes in Africa*. Brazzaville, Congo: World Health Organization, 1957.

ROSKIES, ETHEL, *Abnormality and Normality: The Mothering of Thalidomide Children*. Ithaca, N.Y.: Cornell University Press, 1972.

SEELIGER, JEANNINE, *Poverty and Health*. New York: Association for the Aid of Crippled Children, 1970.

SOMERS, HERMAN M., AND ANNE P. SOMERS, *Doctors, Patients, and Health Insurance*. Washington, D.C.: The Brookings Institution, 1961.

———, *Medicare and the Hospitals*. Washington, D.C.: The Brookings Institution, 1967.

SUSSMAN, MARVIN, et al., *The Walking Patient: A Study in Outpatient Care*. Cleveland, Ohio: Case Western Reserve University Press, 1967.

WEINERMAN, E. RICHARD, AND SHIRELY B. WEINERMAN, *Social Medicine in Eastern Europe: The Organization of Health Services and Education of Medical Personnel in Czechoslovakia, Hungary and Poland*. Cambridge, Mass.: Harvard University Press, 1969.

WOODS, D. E., *International Volunteers Contribute to Health in Developing Countries*. New York: Commission on Youth Service Projects, 1965.

WORLD HEALTH ORGANIZATION, *International Drug Monitoring: the Role of National Centres*. Geneva: World Health Organization, 1972.

*Articles*

MALETNLEMA, T. N., "The Nutritional Status and Health of Preschool Children in Karagswe District, Tanzania," *Children in the Tropics*, 70 (1971), 24–36.

MATHESON, SIMONE, "Nutrition Education for Children in Rural Africa," *Les Carnets de l'enfance*, 21 (March 1973), 34–50.

MELLANDER, C. M. S., "Nutrition of the Weaning Child," *Mother and Child*, 11, No. 2 (1972), 4–16.

PITTEL, STEPHEN M., et al., "Developmental Factors in Adolescent Drug Use," *Journal of the American Academy of Child Psychiatry*, 10, No. 4 (1971), 640–60.

RAJAN, V. N., "Medical Care Under Social Insurance in India," *International Labour Review*, 98 (Aug. 1968), 141–55.

SETHI, D. D., "Medical Benefits for Families in India," *International Social Security Review*, 23, No. 3 (1970), 435–44.

TITMUSS, RICHARD M., "The Hospital and Its Patients" and "The National Health Service in England," pp. 119–203 in Richard M. Titmuss, *Essays on the Welfare State*. New Haven, Conn.: Yale University Press, 1959.

———, "The Health and Welfare Complex," pp. 59–112, and "Dilemmas in

Medical Care," pp. 207–62, in Richard M. Titmuss, *Commitment to Welfare.* London: Allen & Unwin, 1968.

VERMA, PARSHETAN L., "Rehabilitation Opportunities for the Blind in India," *Indian Journal of Social Work,* 31 (1971), 439–47.

WATTS, E. RONALD, "Education for Better Nutrition of Children in Tropical Africa," *Les Carnets de l'enfance,* 17 (March 1972), 93–106.

# Mental health services

6

The mental health concepts of the advanced industrial nations cannot be transplanted to the developing nations, because a nation's conception of mental health is a function of the cultural, economic, and political conditions of that nation, and it is necessary to find out which mental health methods may be effective and which organizational and practical structure is needed to build a sound program of mental health.[1] The World Health Organization under the auspices of the United Nations has a section on mental health. Another nongovernmental organization, the World Federation for Mental Health (founded in 1948 in London), incorporates over 150 national mental health associations and representatives of psychiatry, medicine, psychology, social work, anthropology, and related disciplines. It not only promotes sound practices for the treatment of individual mental patients, it also develops sane human relations among all peoples and nations, and so functions as a major support of the United Nations and for the survival of all people on this earth. Its main activities are international yearly conferences, seminars, and study groups to help the developing countries set up effective institutions for the protection of mental health and community facilities for the prevention and treatment of mental disorders. But the fundamental purpose of the federation is to work toward a world community in which people can live together in peace and cooperation.[2] Intergroup relations play an important role in achieving these aims on the local level and in the treatment of the mental disorders of single patients.

In most Western countries the main form of psychiatric treatment is still therapy, supplemented by mental hospitals and clinics, but in the communist countries and the developing countries treatment is carried on exclusively in hospitals and outpatient mental health clinics as part of public health. This for instance is the case in Czechoslovakia (since 1958),[3] Russia,[4] and China.

In Japan, since enactment of the Mental Health Act of 1950, responsibility for treatment of the mentally ill and the retarded rests mainly on public health authorities even though the majority of hospitals and clinics are still privately owned and the mental health centers are public health facilities.[5] In England and Sweden the expenses of treating mental patients in hospitals and clinics are paid by the state authorities; no patient has to suffer because he can't afford treatment. Both countries also provide private psychiatric treatment under provisions of medical care.[6] The advantages of this method seem evident, but they are still disputed in those countries that continue to be afraid of "socialized medicine."

Very different methods of mental health services are applied in several African countries, such as Nigeria and Zaire. Because of the lack of trained physicians, psychiatrists, and health personnel, many villages in these countries still rely largely on native healers who have the confidence of the population and use traditional methods of magic based on superstition. These methods often work like hypnosis and are sometimes successful. In some places, particularly in regions which are far from the cities where psychiatrists and public health workers are employed, native healers cooperate with psychiatrists in the public health services in the villages or as group therapy guides in the cities.[7]

Few mental health services are available in the Sudan, where a large migration of people was necessary because of the flooding of the area after the building of the Aswan Dam. There are substantial numbers of patients suffering from psychoneurosis, schizophrenia, depression, psychosomatic disorders, and mental retardation in the Sudan, and the establishment of professionally staffed mental health centers is desirable.

In Ceylon the population is hesitant to reveal mental disorders because they are considered to be caused by "charmes," by malevolent spirits, or by supernatural, hostile forces invoked by enemies. This resistance is based upon Sinhalese folklore, and the Sinhalese make up two-thirds of the population of Ceylon.[8]

In Denmark and Sweden, and to a lesser degree in Finland and Iceland, the mentally ill and retarded are almost all cared for by the government, in general or mental hospitals or in state-subsidized social insurance facilities. Mental hospitals are setting up smaller homes for milder cases (foster home care); they are also setting up halfway houses in order to allow earlier dismissals and to make room in the main hospitals for the increasing demands for hospitalization.[9]

In India mental health problems are caused by hunger and malnutrition among the low-income masses in the villages and in urban areas, by wide-scale unemployment, and by apathy toward the wastage of food by animals (cows and apes that are considered holy, wild horses, rats, and other rodents). Gradual starvation is endemic, and mental disorders the natural accompaniment.[10] Voluntary organizations play a major role in preventive mental (as well as in educational, welfare, and general) health services in India (and most other southeast Asian countries). In India these organizations are often connected with religious associations and frequently belong to the upper classes. The Hindu religion has no organized priesthood and therefore is less inclined to resist social change, so progress in mental health is possible despite the superstitions discussed above. In contrast, Islam and its *Ulemas* (priests) oppose reform and consider mental health services a danger to their influence.[11]

In China mental health services, like all other social services, are performed by trained personnel, most of whom are paraprofessionals—"barefoot doctors" (peasants with training who work half-time in agriculture and half-time as medical workers), "red guard doctors" (urban laborers who work after a ten-day training course as medical aides in urban neighborhood health centers), and "worker-doctors" (factory workers who take a three-month training course and then work half-time as production workers and half-time as medical workers in the factory). These mental health workers are under the supervision of barefoot doctors or red guard doctors and so are not always supervised by physicians or even trained nurses, but they perform immunizations, treat minor illnesses, serve as health educators and marriage counselors, and encourage self-reliance and self-help.[12]

In Thailand numerous young men and women have migrated from the villages to the cities to find jobs as factory workers, laborers, or household help. Of those who have no success, some return to their villages, others remain in the cities and face unemployment and frustrations, which can lead to a break-up of families and serious mental health problems. Even their families in the home villages suffer the loneliness and isolation of losing their children.[13] Technical change, rapid industrialization, and urbanization in societies based upon the family as the main social factor and the symbol of stability and status represent a very difficult and dangerous problem, as discussed in Chapter 3. It will be necessary to develop efficient mental health services if we are to prevent such rapid social and economic change from working severe psychological damage. The dissolution of the extended family through emigration from the villages to the urban centers deprives the population of the villages of moral and economic security and exposes them to unemployment, delinquency, and crime. There also exists the danger of rising expectations; if these are frustrated it alienates the young from the wealthier natives and from foreign experts, advisors, and technicians who have come to help the country in its economic development. The progress in public health and elimination of epidemics and contagious diseases in the developing countries of Asia, Africa, and South America have not been accompanied by a comparable reduction in the birth rate. The result has been a dangerous growth of population, which we shall discuss in Chapter 9.[14]

In some developing countries and among native groups still involved in different cultural customs, particularly in Africa, Latin America, Asia, and the South Pacific, experience has shown that a team of psychiatrist, psychiatric nurse, and social worker working with the traditional healers, neighborhood priests, or medicine men in a mental hygiene center or clinic is fruitful because these persons have the confidence of the population, and the people are able to participate in old rituals more easily than they can trust modern methods of psychiatric therapy. On the other hand, the healers and medicine men may discover that in serious situations such as severe depressions and acute schizophrenia, the mental health center or hospital may be more effective.[15]

## *Drugs*

One mental health problem which in former times was limited to a few countries began in the late 1960s to assume international proportions. Drug abuse, especially among young persons, is now one of the serious dangers for mental health. Even when the exact medical consequences of some of the various types of drugs are not fully agreed upon, individual and group therapy of patients under the influence of drugs is generally needed, as are preventive methods to protect young persons against the serious dangers of drug abuse. Clinical services for drug addicts have been established in numerous countries, often in connection with public health services and hospitals. It is not the purpose of this chapter to deal with the drug question and its numerous problems, whether criminal punishment or medical treatment is indicated, which drugs should be limited to medical prescriptions, or how the traffic in narcotic drugs should be controlled (the literature on drugs has vastly expanded during recent years). In Western countries children and young people are often drawn to drugs out of curiosity, for thrills and excitement, through a desire to be accepted by their peer group, and in the hope of overcoming depressive feelings, psychic tensions, anxieties, sexual drives, inner conflicts, and environmental difficulties. The dangers were known for a long time in relation to the use of opium, heroin, cocaine, desomorphine, and ketobemodine, but the use of cannabis or marijuana was restricted in the international area only by the United Nations "single convention on narcotic drugs" (1961) at the request of the World Health Organization.[16]

The serious mental health problems in Africa were dramatically described at the International Conference of Social Work in Washington, D.C., in 1966 by Professor T. Adeloye Lambo of the Iban University in Nigeria. They have been caused by rapid urbanization, the vast migration of village people to the new cities, the instability of the population, the change of life rhythm involved in going after money and gains, large-scale unemployment, delinquency, and crime, as illustrated in Chapter 3.[17] Drug addiction has reached high proportions, mainly among unemployed adolescents who are isolated from their families because of the breakdown of the tribal discipline that prevented such deviance in the villages. Alcoholism, prostitution, venereal diseases, and crime also contribute to the mental health problem, as have the destruction of tribal coherence and the mixing of ethnic groups (in Ghana and the Ivory Coast) of people from both patriarchal and matriarchal societies, which sometimes leads to divorce or child stealing. Mental difficulties are aggravated by endemic diseases and infections, and by malaria and tuberculosis. Special programs are needed to combat these threats to mental health, not only in Africa, but also in the developing countries in Asia and Latin America. International assistance is necessary to develop such mental health facilities.[18]

## Notes

[1]Richard H. Williams and Lucy D. Ozarin, eds., *Community Mental Health: An International Perspective* (San Francisco: Jossey-Bass, 1968); Mervyn S. Susser, *Community Psychiatry: Epidemiology and Social Themes* (New York: Random House, 1968); David Mechanic, *Mental Health and Social Policy* (Englewood Cliffs, N.J.: Prentice-Hall, 1969), pp. 96–120.

[2]Otto Klineberg, "Growing Up for Cooperation or Conflict?" *World Mental Health*, 10, No. 2 (May 1958), 61–75.

[3]J. Prokupek, "Programs and Research in Czechoslovakia," in Williams and Ozarin, eds., *Community Mental Health*, pp. 113–17.

[4]Madison, *Social Welfare in the Soviet Union*, pp. 26–28. Asmus Jensen has criticized the very inadequate care in mental hospitals in Germany. See his "Antipsychiatrie, Sozialpsychiatrie, Soziale Psychiatrie," *Archiv für Wissenschaft und Praxis der sozialen Arbeit*, 4 (Dec. 1973), 269–78.

[5]Kazuo Itoga and Kiyoko Koike, "Treatment of Mental Patients in Japan," in Dorothy Dessau, ed., *Glimpses of Social Work in Japan*, rev. ed. (Kyoto: Social Workers International Club of Japan, 1968), pp. 258–60.

[6]Richard M. Titmuss, "Dilemmas in Medical Care," in Titmuss, *Commitment to Welfare* (New York: Pantheon, 1968), pp. 207–65; Royal Social Board, *Social Work and Legislation in Sweden* (Stockholm: Tiden, 1938), pp. 180–87, 201–10; Olaf Martensen-Larsen, "Neue Wege der Alkoholiker-Behandlung" (New Methods of Treating Alcoholics), *Gesundheit und Wohlfahrt*, 30, No. 2 (Feb. 1950), 77–85.

[7]T. Adeoye Lambo, "A Form of Social Psychiatry in Africa," *World Mental Health*, 13, No. 4 (Nov. 1961), 190–203; Williams and Ozarin, eds., *Community Mental Health*, 98–109; Claude Veil, "Mental Health in the Congo," *World Mental Health*, 14, No. 3 (Aug. 1962), 128–30; T. A. Baasher, "Mental Illness in Wadi Halfa," *World Mental Health*, 13, No. 4 (Nov. 1961), 181–85.

[8]M. G. Jayasundera, "Mental Health in a Ceylon Village," *World Mental Health*, 15 (Aug. 1962), 186–90.

[9]George R. Nelson, ed., *Freedom and Welfare: Social Patterns in the Northern Countries of Europe* (Copenhagen: Danish Ministry of Welfare, 1953), pp. 371–78.

[10]Arnold M. Rose, "Sociological Factors Affecting Economic Development in India," *Studies in Comparative International Development*, 3, No. 9 (1967–68), 169, 179–81.

[11]Ibid., p. 180.

[12]Joshua Horn, *Away with All Pests* (New York: Monthly Review Press, 1969), pp. 147–52; Jan Myrdal, *Report from a Chinese Village*, pp. 255–64; Ruth and Victor Sidel, "The Human Services in China," *Social Policy*, 2, No. 6 (March-Apr. 1972), 29–35; Ruth Sidel, "Social Services in China," *Social Work*, 17, No. 6 (Nov. 1972), 7–13; Paul T. K. Lin, "Medicine in China," *The Center Magazine*, 7 (June 1973), 13–21.

[13]Phon Sangsingreo, "Mental Health in Developing Countries," *World Mental Health*, 15, No. 14 (Fall 1963), 125–34.

[14]Sangsingreo, "Mental Health in Developing Countries," 127–32. Suggestions for improvement of mental health services in India were prepared by an international workshop on priorities in mental health care, held in 1971 under the leadership of A. Vankoba Rao in Madurai with delegates from India, Ceylon, Australia, Singapore, England, and the United Arab Republic.

[15]G. M. Carstairs, "Arab Workshop on Mental Health," *Bulletin World Federation for Mental Health* (Winter 1970–71), pp. 4–5.

[16] *The La Guardia Report: The Marijuana Problem in the City of New York* (Lancaster: Cattell, 1944); United Nations, *Single Convention on Narcotic Drugs* (New York, 1961); K. Biener, "Jugend und Rauschgift" (Youth and Drug Poisoning), *Fortschritte der Medizin*, No. 35/36 (1969), 1449–52; D. Heil, "Der Gebrauch von Cannabis unter Jugendlichen Zürichs" (The Use of Cannabis Among the Youth of Zurich), *Präventivmedizin*, 15, No. 5 (Sept.–Oct. 1970), 331–58; C. Andre St. Pierre, "Motivating the Drug Addict in Treatment," *Social Work*, 16, No. 1 (Jan. 1971), 80–88.

[17]T. Adeloye Lambo, "Mental Health Aspects of Urban Life," in International Council on Social Welfare, *Urban Development* (New York: Columbia University Press, 1967), pp. 100–116; M. Banton, *West African City* (London: Oxford University Press, 1957).

[18]Elizabeth Wickenden, "Social Priorities for the Modern City," in International Council on Social Welfare, *Urban Development*, pp. 117–29.

## Selected References

*Books*

ANDERSON, ODIN W., *Health Care: Can There Be Equity? The United States, Sweden and England.* New York: Wiley-Interscience, 1972.

APTE, ROBERT Z., *Halfway Houses.* London: G. Bell, 1968.

BESSON, JACQUES, *School and Training for the Mentally Insufficient.* La Tour de Feilz (Switzerland): Delta, 1969.

BLACK, BERTRAM J., *Principles of Industrial Therapy for the Mentally Ill.* New York: Grune & Stratton, 1970.

BLANKENBURG, PETER VON, AND HANS-DIETRICH CREMER, eds., *Handbuch der Landwirtschaft und Ernährung in den Entwicklungsländern* (Manual of Agriculture and Nutrition in the Developing Countries). Stuttgart: E. Ulmer, 1971.

BOGDAN, ROBERT, ed., *Being Different: The Autobiography of Jane Fry.* New York: Wiley-Interscience, 1974.

CANADIAN DEPARTMENT OF NATIONAL HEALTH AND WELFARE, *Mental Health Services in Canada.* Ottawa, 1954.

*Community Mental Health—an International Perspective.* Research Seminar on the Evaluation of Community Mental Health Programs. San Francisco: Chandler, 1967.

CUMMING, JOHN, AND ELAINE CUMMING, *Ego and Milieu.* New York: Atherton, 1963.

DAVID, HENRY P., *Child Mental Health in International Perspective.* New York: Harper & Row, 1972.

————, *International Trends in Mental Health.* New York: McGraw-Hill, 1966.

DICKS, HENRY V., *Fifty Years of the Tavistock Clinic.* London: Routledge & Kegan Paul, 1970.

GUNZBURG, H. C. *Centres éducatifs pour enfants déficients mentaux* (Educational Centers for Mentally Retarded Children), Brussels: Association nationale d'aide handicaps mentaux, 1969.

HOLLANDER, GAYLE D., *Soviet Political Indoctrination: Developments in Mass Media and Propaganda Since Stalin.* New York: Praeger, 1972.

HOLLINGSHEAD, AUGUST B., AND FREDERICK C. REDLICH, *Social Class and Mental Illness,* New York: Wiley, 1958.

JONES, KATHLEEN, *A History of the Mental Health Services.* London: Routledge & Kegan Paul, 1972.

JURJEVICH, RATIBOR RAY, *No Water in My Cup: Experiences and a Controlled Study of Psychotherapy of Delinquent Girls.* New York: Libra Publications, 1968.

KAHAN, V. L., *Mental Illness in Childhood.* London: Tavistock, 1971.

KLEIN, DONALD C., *Community Dynamics and Mental Health.* New York: Wiley, 1968.

LEISSNER, ARYCH, et al., *Advice, Guidance, and Assistance: A Study of Seven Advice Centres.* London: Longman, 1971.

LÉVY, CLAUDE, AND LOUIS HENRY, *Les Jeunes Handicaps mentaux.* Paris: Presses Universitaires, 1970.

MASLAND, R. L., S. B. SARASON, AND T. GLADWIN, *Mental Subnormality.* New York: Basic Books, 1958.

MECHANIC, DAVID, *Mental Health and Social Policy.* Englewood Cliffs, N.J.: Prentice-Hall, 1969.

MEYERS, JEROME K., AND BERTRAM H. ROBERTS, *Social Class, Family Dynamics, and Mental Illness.* New York: Wiley, 1965.

MILLET, LOUIS, *L'Agressivité* (Aggression). Paris: Editions Universitaires, 1970.

MYRDAL, JAN, *Report from a Chinese Village.* New York: New American Library, 1966.

NELSON, GEORGE R. *Freedom and Welfare: Social Patterns in the Northern Countries of Europe.* Copenhagen: Danish Ministry of Welfare, 1953.

PERLS, FREDERICK, RALPH F. HEFFERLINE AND PAUL GOODMAN, *Gestalt Therapy.* New York: Julian, 1962.

RAPAPORT, CHANAN, AND WIBOLD JETLICKI, *Social Planning and Research: Some Implications for Mental Health.* Jerusalem: Henrietta Szold Institute, 1970.

ROSENBLUM, J., ed., *Issues in Community Psychology and Preventive Mental Health.* New York: Behavioral Publications, 1971.

SALZBERGER-WITTENBERG, ISCA, *Psychoanalytic Insight and Relationships: A Kleinian Approach.* London: Routledge & Kegan Paul, 1970.

SCHEFF, THOMAS J., ed., *Mental Illness and Social Processes.* New York: Harper & Row, 1967.

SCHEUCH, ERWIN K., *Haschisch und LSD als Modedrogen* (Hashish and LSD as Drugs of Fashion), 3rd ed. Osnabrück: A. Fromm, 1971.

SCHULBERG, HERBERT C., AND FRANK BAKER, *The Mental Hospital and Human Services.* New York: Behavioral Publications, 1974.

STOLE, LEO, T. S. LANGNER, S. T. MICHAEL, AND K. K. OPLER, *Mental Health in the Metropolis.* New York: McGraw-Hill, 1967.

WEINER, HYMAN J., SHEILA A. AKABAS, AND JOHN J. SOMMER, *Mental Health Care in the World of Work.* New York: Association Press, 1973.

## Articles

BAVELIER, ALAIN, "L'Adolescence pathologique" (Pathological Adolescence), *La Tribune de l'enfance,* 74 (1970), 14–22.

BHOJAK, B. L., AND PACAS MEHTA, "An Investigation into the Causes Responsible for Social Rejection," *Indian Journal of Social Work* 30 (Apr. 1970), 315–25.

DYBWAD, GUNNAR, "Community Organization for the Mentally Retarded," pp. 108–21 in Alfred H. Kahn, ed., *Community Organization.* New York: Columbia University Press, 1959.

FRIEDMAN, ROBERT, "Structural Family-Oriented Therapy for School Behavior and Learning Disorders," *Social Welfare,* 49 (Apr. 1970), 187–95.

GARRETT, BEATRICE L., "Foster Family Services for Mentally Retarded Children," *Children,* 77 (Dec. 1970), 228–33.

HALL, JULIAN C., KATHLEEN SMITH, AND ANNA K. BRADLEY, "Delivering Mental Health Services to the Urban Poor," *Social Work,* 15 (Apr. 1970), 35–40.

KELLY, VERNE R., AND HANNA B. WESTON, "Civil Liberties in Mental Health Facilities," *Social Work,* 19 (Jan. 1974), 48–54.

KIZNER, NORA S., "Sexist Sociology," *The Center Magazine,* 7 (June 1973), 48–59.

LANDRY, MARC, "L'Adolescence en crises" (Adolescence in Crises), *L'École des parents,* No. 1 (1972), pp. 17–31.

LEVINE, RACHAEL A., "Consumer Participation in Planning and Evaluation of Mental Health Services," *Social Work,* 15 (Apr. 1970), 41–46.

LICOVANO, JAIME, "Group Psychotherapy with Adolescents in an Industrial School for Delinquent Boys," *Adolescence,* 5, No. 18 (1970), 231–52.

LUBIN, BERNARD, AND EUGENE E. LEWITT, "International Aspects of Clinical Psychiatry," pp. 280–89 in Lubin and Lewitt, eds., *The Clinical Psychologist: Background, Roles, and Functions.* Chicago: Aldine, 1967.

MENDLEVICZ, J., AND J. WILMOTTE, "La Prévention de suicide" (Prevention of Suicide), *Le Service social,* (Jan. 1970), pp. 31–37.

MORLEY, DAVID, "Comprehensive Care Through the Under-Five Clinic," *Les Carnets de l'enfance,* (March 1972), pp. 75–92.

O'REGAN, GERARD W., "Foster Family Care for Children with Mental Retardation," *Children Today,* 3 (Feb. 1974), 20–37.

PEEL, EVELYN, "Amendments to Australia's National Health Act," *Social Security Bulletin* 34 (Dec. 1971), 28–33.

PERCH, PAUL W., "Juvenile Drug Dependence," *International Child Welfare Review,* (Dec. 1971), pp. 34–60.

RENDU, DENISE, "Sexualité et société: Sexualité et existence incarné" (Sexuality and Society: Sexualism and Living Existence), *Rééducation,* 239–241 (1972), 45–89.

SKARNALIS, EDWARD, "Non-Citizen: Plight of the Mentally Retarded," *Social Work,* 19 (Jan. 1974), pp. 56–62.

TORREY, E. F., "What Western Psychotherapists Can Learn from Witchdoctors," *American Journal of Orthopsychiatry,* 42 (Jan. 1972), 69–76.

WATTS, E. RONALD, "Education for Better Nutrition of Children in Tropical Africa," *Les Carnets de l'enfance* (March 1972), pp. 93–106.

# International refugee services

7

As we saw in the history of international social welfare, services for refugees and displaced persons have become some of the most relevant social services. Internationally there have been governmental services like the League of Nations, the United Nations Relief and Rehabilitation Administration (UNRRA), the International Refugee Organization, the High Commissioner for Refugees, and the United Nations Relief and Work Agency for Palestine Refugees (UNRWA). There have also been numerous voluntary agencies, above all, the International Red Cross and its national societies in many lands, and other voluntary agencies in the U.S.A., Europe, and Taiwan. Refugees from mainland China to Hong Kong number nearly 3 million, and there are still refugees from the Russian Revolution (1917) and from Nazi persecution in central and eastern Europe. Assistance for some of these refugees is given through the Intergovernmental Committee for European Migration (though it disposes of limited funds).[1]

## The Scope of the Problem

After the First World War, 30,000 Greeks and Armenians fled from Turkey and have lived under miserable conditions in camps and hovels in Greece; thousands of Assyrians had fled to Iraq, Syria, and Lebanon, and after the Second World War the mass flight from the occupied territories of east Prussia, Silesia, northern Germany, Czechoslovakia, Poland, and Hungary brought millions to West Germany and Austria and even more from India and Pakistan to England and the United States. Millions of Tibetans fled to India from their homeland after the Chinese invaded Tibet, and in Africa untold masses have fled from the Portuguese colonies and from the Sudan, Nigeria, and South Africa to neighboring states. There are also refugees from East Pakistan in India. No wonder the World Federation for Mental Health has coined the phrase "Century

143

of the Homeless Man" to characterize the twentieth century.[2] Albert Schweitzer criticized the expulsion of the population of eastern and northern Germany by the Allied powers after the Second World War as the worst violation of historic truths and the right of man.[3] There are 3 million refugees from mainland China in Taiwan and Hong Kong, and numerous Chinese refugees from other parts of China have been absorbed in the southern provinces. Estimates indicate that there are now more than 2.3 million refugees.

## Refugee Agencies

The United Nations does not have the funds to solve this tremendous refugee problem, but the need for action scarcely can be doubted. An impressive statement about the moral and social obligation for such aid was made in 1957 by Odd Nansen, son of the famous Arctic explorer and first high commissioner for refugees under the League of Nations, at the Conference of the World Federation for Mental Health in Vienna. Nansen emphasized the humanitarian necessity for a fundamental change in the policies of aid to refugees and displaced persons to include blind, old, and disabled persons as well as young, able-bodied workers.[4]

Owing to the narrow policies of most governments, voluntary social organizations have had to assume major responsibilities for refugee services. Among these agencies are the International Red Cross and its national societies, and the major sectarian and humanitarian national and international organizations of many countries, among them the British and American Friends Service Committees (Quakers), the World Council of Churches, the International Conference of Catholic Charities, the International Conference of Catholic Organizations, the World Jewish Congress, and the Hebrew Immigrant Aid Society (HIAS). These agencies and their national sections have carried out a substantial part of individual and group services for refugees and displaced persons, helping, within the limits of their capacities, in their rescue, transportation, and resettlement.[5] In the United States 70 voluntary refugee aid societies are in operation, and there are many others in Great Britain, France, Germany, Austria, Italy, and Switzerland. But there are still vast masses of refugees and expellees in India, Pakistan, the African countries, and China.[6] The wars in Vietnam, Cambodia, and Laos and the civil war in East Pakistan added hundreds of thousands of refugees and expellees to the millions from earlier conflicts. The United Nations and its high commissioner for refugees do not have sufficient resources and funds available to deal with these formidable problems even with the support of the voluntary organizations engaged in this field. It seems necessary that a systematic coordination of all agencies for refugee aid of the United Nations and its affiliated governmental organizations, all agencies concerned with international community development (discussed in Chapter 3), and all voluntary organizations in this field undertake an integrated approach for the solution of the social, economic, and health problems of this disadvantaged section of mankind which is so deeply in need of human assistance. A global approach is absolutely necessary.

Specific psychosocial problems of political refugees in the Scandinavian countries and Switzerland have led to studies on the conditions of such refugees, particularly Hungarian and Czechoslovakian refugees, in countries which have offered them asylum. The results of these studies seem to indicate that serious conflicts of a social nature have been more frequent among male refugees than among female refugees, and that the latter group has been more easily assimilated in several countries.[7]

An example of a long-enduring refugee problem are the Spanish refugees who fled to France during the civil war of 1936–38 and who still live in severe poverty and under miserable conditions. Minimal pensions from the French government barely permit them to survive, and force them to choose between being cold and being hungry. Spanish Refugee Aid, an international voluntary organization with headquarters in New York, is supported by a group in England called Help the Aged, by a Swiss committee called *Aide aux Refugiés Espagnoles,* by a Swedish group, *Individuell Manniskohjalp,* a German group, *Deutsches Komitee zur Hilfe für Spanische demokratische Flüchtlinge,* and by several trade union committees. All these organizations are inadequate.

### Bangladesh

The same characteristics are evident in the problems of the Palestinian refugees and of the East Pakistani refugees who fled to India. While most of them returned to Bangladesh, international activities and the investment of substantial economic sacrifices are necessary and should be arranged under the auspices of the United Nations. These would have to include scholarships, schools, adult training facilities, economic rehabilitation, and health services, especially for sick and disabled refugees suffering from tuberculosis, diabetes, and the need for dental care. These people, particularly some tribes that have not been permitted to return to Bangladesh, need clothing, work tools, and any type of employment as long as they are able to work. All attempts to cope with this tragic refugee problem through the United Nations and its affiliated agencies and through the contributions of numerous countries and religious and other private social agencies and foundations have not been able to meet the human and health needs of these 10 million refugees, among them over 3 million children, before and after they returned to Bangladesh.

Many Muslims among the refugees found some of their crops preserved by the present cultivators, but most Hindus (the bulk of the refugees) found their land fallow and no stocks to share. They faced a serious food shortage and were forced to rebuild their burned villages without money, materials, or tools. The fishing communities had lost their equipment and all livelihood. Hundreds of thousands had been killed, including professionals. Millions within Bangladesh had been displaced, moved into squatter settlements near the larger cities, especially Dacca, without food and employment. This condition still contains great potential for social and political unrest and for disease. International aid will remain an urgent necessity for years to come.[8]

### Africa

In Africa serious refugee problems have been caused by political tensions (tribal warfare and unrest), particularly in the Sudan, the Portuguese colonies, and East Africa. In former times, church organizations have tried in Africa to help refugees, but the size of their numbers in recent years has made the problem too large for religious charities. The civil war in the Sudan forced about 178,000 to flee to Zaire, Ethiopia, Central Africa, Kenya, Tanzania, and Uganda. These refugees present a most difficult problem.[9]

In 1972 the United Nations high commissioner for refugees estimated that there were more than 1 million refugees in Africa—40,000 from Guinea in Nigeria, 12,000 from Burundi in Rwanda, 70,000 from Rwanda in Uganda, 34,000 from Zaire and 71,000 from the Sudan in Uganda, 475,000 from Angola in Zaire, 33,000 from Mozambique in Tanzania, and 63,000 from Portuguese Guinea in Senegal. Although most of these refugees are integrated into the economies of their host countries, they remain a severe social and economic burden for the countries of emigration.[10]

Another difficult refugee problem is the people who have fled from the Republic of China to Hong Kong or Taiwan. Official Hong Kong statistics indicate that during 1972, 5,816 Chinese fled to Hong Kong and were temporarily detained by the Hong Kong police. The Taiwan Free China Relief Association estimates that in 1972 the total number of refugees from China was 25,000. They either remain in Hong Kong or settle in Taiwan, where they receive scholarships for schools and universities and training for other work.[11]

Tibetan refugees were forced to flee in 1961 when the Chinese invaded and threatened the lives of natives and of the Dalai Lama. About 14 thousand refugees were settled in India in agriculture, and about 3,400 in small industries; 2,400 went to Nepal, 1,800 to Bhutan, and smaller numbers to Sikkim or Switzerland. Nearly 8,000 refugees remain unsettled. They work on road construction and odd jobs in India, Nepal, and Bhutan, often separated from their families and children.[12]

Even in Europe the refugee problem has not been fully solved. The Intergovernmental Committee for European Migration in Geneva was created in 1951 to help displaced persons from the Second World War and refugees of the Cold War from Hungary, Czechoslovakia, Russia, and Poland to settle overseas.[13]

### *Uganda*

In 1972, 40,000 to 45,000 Asian residents in Uganda were expelled by the decree of Uganda President Idi Amin, forced to leave the country without being able to take any belongings with them. During the meeting of the General Assembly of the United Nations in New York in the fall of 1972, British Foreign Secretary Sir Alec Douglas Home urged the United Nations to demand that Uganda extend the deadline for the expulsion and permit the Asians to take their property with them. The secretary-general of the United Nations succeeded, with the support of the presidents of the African states of Somalia, Tanzania, and Zaire and of the Economic Commission for Africa of the United Nations, in persuading President Amin to accede to these requests. Great Britain accepted expellees with British passports, and the United Nations high commissioner for refugees has started to collect a special relief fund for those expellees who are stateless, with the cooperation of the International Red Cross and of all other United Nations Agencies (IRO, WHO, UNICEF, UNESCO).[14]

According to recent reports from various refugee service organizations, the number of refugees is more than 23 million: more than 17 million in Asia; more than 1,800,000 in the Middle East; more than 1 million in Africa; about 700,000 in Europe; and more than 1,600,000 in North and South America.[15]

Among the American voluntary agencies that help refugees with medical supplies, food, clothing, and resettlement are the International Rescue Committee, the U.S. Committee on Refugees, the Save the Children Federation, CARE, the Thomas A. Dooley Foundation, and numerous missionary and sectarian agencies supported by the relief organizations of several European countries. Refugees in the United States from Cuba are under the auspices of the Department of Health, Education, and Welfare and the Social and Rehabilitation Service.[16] All these agencies try to find solutions for these many refugees, the "homeless and nearly forgotten people" in this century who have not been satisfactorily settled in other countries.

## Notes

[1]Elfan Rees, "The Refugee Problem: Joint Responsibility," *The Annals*, 329 (May 1960), 15–22; Julia J. Henderson, "The Challenge of Worldwide Social Conditions," ibid., 1–14; see also p. 63, footnote 13. Valuable pioneer work also has been achieved by the International Social Service (formerly the International Migration Service) with headquarters in Geneva and New York.

[2]*World Mental Health*, 10, No. 1 (Feb. 1958), 2.

[3]Albert Schweitzer, *After Ten Years—A European Problem—Still No Solution* (Frankfurt a/M.: Wirtschaftsdienst, 1957), p. 5; Fred K. Hoehler, *Europe's Homeless Millions* (New York: Foreign Policy Association, 1946), pp. 11–21, 78–92; Arnold M. Rose, *Migrants in Europe: Problems of Acceptance and Adjustment* (Minneapolis: University of Minnesota Press, 1969). Refugees are in India from Tibet and Pakistan; in 35 nations in Africa; in the United States from Cuba, the Middle East, and Vietnam; and in Austria from Hungary and Czechoslovakia.

[4]Odd Nansen, "Responsibility for Refugees," *World Mental Health*, 10, No. 1 (Feb. 1958), 3–8.

[5]Gwen Gardner, "Employment and Integration Project for Foreign Refugees," ibid., pp. 21–34.

[6]The fate of the refugees from Nazi Germany is ably described in Norman Bentwich, *The Refugees from Germany* (London: Allen & Unwin, 1936); Alfred A. Häsler, *Das Boot ist voll—Die Schweiz und die Flüchtlinge, 1933–45 (The Boat Is Full—Switzerland and the Refugees, 1933–45)* (Zurich: Fretz & Wasmuth, 1967); Regina Kägi-Fuchsmann, *Das gute Herz genügt nicht* (A Good Heart Is Not Enough) (Zurich: Ex-Libris Verlag, 1968), which also discusses refugees from Austria, France, and Spain. Another valuable source book about the refugees from Nazi persecution is Kurt R. Grossmann, *Emigration: Die Geschichte der Hitler-Flüchtlinge, 1933–1945* (Emigration: The Story of the Refugees from Hitler, 1933–1945) (Frankfurt a/M.: Europäische Verlagsanstalt, 1969). The problem of the refugees from Bangladesh is described in "Despair in Calcutta," *The Social Service Review*, 45, No. 3 (Sep. 1971), 318–19.

[7]L. Faris, "Cultural Isolation and the Schizophrenic Mentality," *American Sociological Journal*, 40 (1934), 155ff; O. Oedegaard, "Immigration and Insanity," *Acta Neurologica* (Stockholm: University of Stockholm Press, 1932); S. A. Prins, "L'Individu en fuite," pp. 27–36 in H.B.M. Murphy, ed., *Personnes Déplaces* (Paris: UNESCO, 1955); Emil Pintér-Eber, F. Cavalli, and R. Pfeiffer, "Die psychosozialen Probleme der Flüchtlinge im Wohlstandsstaat" *Präventivmedizin*, 15, No. 6 (Nov.–Dec. 1970) 463–74.

[8]Erna Sailer, "Report on the Mission of High-Level United Nations Consultants to Bangladesh," *World Refugee Report 1972* (Apr. 1972), pp. 6–8.

[9]Lawrence Fellows, "A Far More Costly War than Vietnam: The Unknown War in the Sudan" *World Refugee Report, 1970,* pp. 25–28.

[10]Abdulrahim Abby Farah, "Problems of African Social Development." *Social Welfare Forum 1972* (New York: Columbia University Press, 1972), pp. 138–52.

[11]Newsletter of Free China Relief Association, 2, No. 1 (Apr. 1973), 1–4.

[12]Ernest Gross (Tibetan Foundation), ibid., pp. 22–23. A general survey of the refugee situation was given by R. Norris Wilson, "The National Conference on World Refugee Problems," *World Refugee Report 1970* (1971), pp. 11–16.

[13]John F. Thomas, "European Migration," ibid., pp. 9–10.

[14]Gray, Kay Rainy, "UN Notebook," *Vista,* 8, No. 3 (Nov.–Dec. 1972), 7–12, 46–48.

[15]Dorothy Lally, "International Social Welfare Services," *Encyclopedia of Social Work* (1972), pp. 683–84; U.S. Committee for Refugees, "The Facts About Today's Refugees" (New York, 1973); United Nations, *Addendum to the Report of the United Nations High Commissioner of Refugees,* (New York, 1969).

[16]Lally, "International Social Welfare Services," pp. 683–84.

# References

*Books*

ABRAMS, CHARLES, *Man's Struggle for Shelter in an Urbanizing World.* Cambridge, Mass.: Massachusetts Institute of Technology, 1964.

BERNARD, WILLIAM S., "Services for the Foreign Born," *Encyclopedia of Social Work 1971,* (New York: National Association of Social Workers, 1971), pp. 458–464.

BRANDT, ULRICH, *Flüchtlingskinder* (Refugee Children). Munich: J. Barth, 1964.

COLSON, ELIZABETH, *The Social Consequences of Resettlement.* Manchester: University Press, 1971.

DAVIE, MAURICE R., *World Immigration* (with Special Reference to the USA), New York: Macmillan, 1936.

_____, *Refugees in America.* New York: Harper, 1947.

FLEMING, DONALD, AND BERNARD BAYLIN eds., *The Intellectual Migration: Europe and America, 1930–1960.* Cambridge, Mass: Harvard University Press, 1969.

GROSSMANN, KURT, *Emigration: Geschichte der Hitler-Flüchtlinge 1933–1945* (Emigration: History of the Hitler Refugees 1933–45), Frankfurt a/M.: Europäische Verlagsanstalt, 1969.

GUKIINA, PETER M., *Uganda: A Case Study in African Political Development* Notre Dame: University of Notre Dame, 1972.

HIRSHMAN, IRA A., *The Embers Still Burn.* New York: Simon & Schuster, 1949.

HOEHLER, FRED, *Europe's Homeless Millions.* New York: Foreign Policy Association, no. 54, 1945.

HUGO, GRANT, *Appearances and Reality in International Relations.* New York: Columbia University Press, 1970.

KATZ, JACOB, *Out of the Ghetto: The Social Background of Jewish Emancipation, 1770–1870.* Cambridge: Harvard University Press, 1973.

KUNKEL, JOHN H., *Society and Economic Change.* London: Oxford University Press, 1970.

LABOUISSE, HENRY R., *Nigerian Emergency: a UNICEF Report: Aid to Children and Mothers on Both Sides of the Conflict.* Geneva (Switzerland): UNICEF, 1969.

MARTIN, JEAN I., *Refugee Settlers.* Canberra: Australian National University Press, 1965.

———, *Refugee Groups in Adelaide.* Canberra: Australian National University Press, 1972.

MOONE, SEUNG GYN, *Outmigration from Families of Orientation in Two Rural Communities.* Seoul, Korea: National University Press, 1972.

PILISUK, MARC, *International Conflict and Social Policy.* Englewood Cliffs, N.J.: Prentice-Hall, 1972.

PUSIC, EUGEN, *Social Welfare and Social Development.* The Hague-Paris: Mouton, 1972.

REES, ELFAN, *We Strangers and Afraid.* New York: Carnegie Endowment for International Peace, 1959.

SCHECHTMAN, JOSEPH B., *The Refugees in the World: Displacement and Integration.* New York: A. Barnes, 1963.

SIMPSON, JOHN HOPE, *The Refugee Problem.* London: Oxford University Press, 1939.

TABORI, PAUL, *The Anatomy of Exile.* London: Harrap, 1973.

VERNAUT, JACQUES, *The Refugee in the Postwar World.* London: Allen & Unwin, 1954.

*Articles*

CLAIBORNE, LOUIS E., "Law and Race in Britain," *The Annals of the American Academy of Political and Social Science,* 407 (May 1973), pp. 167–78.

FARAH, ABDULRAHIM ABBY, "Problems of African Social Development," *Social Welfare Forum 1972.* New York: Columbia University Press, 1972, pp. 135–40.

HENDERSON, JULIA J., "The Challenge of World-Wide Social Conditions," *The Annals of the American Academy of Political and Social Science,* 329 (May 1960), pp. 1–14.

MILLER, JOAN, "Community Development in a Disaster Community," *Community Development Journal,* 8 (Oct. 1973), 161–66.

REES, ELFAN, "The Refugee and the United Nations," *International Conciliation* (June 1953), pp. 269–314.

———, "The Refugee Problem: Joint Responsibility," *The Annals of the American Academy of Political and Social Science,* 329 (May 1960), pp. 15–22.

SCHOTTLAND, CHARLES I., "Translating Social Needs into Action," *International Social Work* (Bombay), 14 (April 1971), pp. 3–17.

# Social security

8

Legislation and social welfare services to prevent or mitigate economic deprivation, health defects, and human suffering vary widely in the different countries of the world, but social changes, especially industrialization and urbanization, are inducing most countries to introduce and plan comprehensive programs of social assistance and social insurance. We shall not attempt here to compare the many laws and operations of social assistance and insurance systems in the nations of today; instead we shall outline some of the major trends to indicate the direction of this development.[1]

In contrast to earlier programs of relief and charity, the industrial nations and recently many developing countries have introduced public assistance and social insurance systems[2] which aim to prevent misery and protect the respect and dignity of the poor, the handicapped, and sick persons who do not deserve to be treated as beggars, and to provide a system of social services which meets the general and individual needs of human beings. This change in treatment of the poor began in Europe at the end of the last century when municipal or regional governments assumed responsibility for the care and rehabilitation of the destitute instead of leaving it to overseers who considered every poor person a criminal and vagabond unwilling to work and who distributed relief on a starvation level.

## The Bases of Social Security

In the United States and most other industrial nations social security is based upon one or more of three fundamental programs: (1) public assistance in case of need (sometimes called *social assistance*); (2) social insurance benefits, based upon contributions of the beneficiary and his employers (and often upon tax contributions as well), combined with medical and related services, and paid as a matter of right; and (3) pensions, whether restricted to certain groups, such as former public officials, war veterans and the like, or unrestricted, or as universal pensions paid on the basis of categories such as the aged or the disabled. In Asia, Africa, and South America most of what poor relief they had was distributed by religious charities located in larger cities. Rarely did it reach the rural population, where the sole source of relief in case of need and sickness was the family or kinship group.[3] Before the twentieth century poor relief in Europe and America was generally accepted as a necessary burden of local government, disliked by its recipients as a disgrace and hated by the taxpayers. In England relief caused the Chartist movement with its riots and futile petitions to Parliament, and in France it contributed to the Revolution of 1789. In other European countries it also created severe dissatisfaction and resentment among the poor, especially among trade unions in the nineteenth century. In the United States the economic depression of 1929 led to abandonment of the outmoded principles of poor relief, because for the first time large segments of the population suffered from loss of farms and jobs and so shared the fate of the disabled and poverty striken, a group that had been very small before this period.[4] The Social Security Act of 1935 established the modern public assistance system. This includes categorical assistance programs for the aged, the blind, the severely disabled, and families with dependent children. The first three are now financed and administered by the federal government, while a fifth category, general assistance, is mainly financed by the state or local communities. When social insurance programs do not sufficiently protect part of the population, most countries have a system of public assistance based on a means test, which serves as a "safety net" or "residual service" or a "last resort" for destitute people who need economic and social help.[5]

### The French System

In France the overwhelming influence of individualistic thinking and the dominance of the agrarian sector during most of the nineteenth century combined to prevent recognition of the need for a system of protection through a program of social insurance and public assistance until the end of the century. The majority insisted that charitable poor relief was sufficient to meet the needs of the destitute. Eventually the influence of the British social legislation and the example of the German social insurance legislation of the 1880s persuaded the French political parties that some public social protection was unavoidable.[6] A useless old-age pension law was enacted in 1910, and social insurance legislation was enacted in 1928, but the Second World War kept it from going into effect until the end of the war and the retreat of the German occupation armies. The decision to enact this social insurance legislation was influenced by the decline of the birth rate during the war and the need to consolidate and strengthen numerous legal provisions for assistance and medical services which included elements of social insurance concepts in France.[7] Before this legislation, all applicants for public assistance in France except orphans and the mentally insane were denied any legal right for public relief. If a community did not have sufficient funds for public relief and no charitable church or private aid was available, the *département* (provincial or regional authority) was expected to supply the necessary funds. The legal basis of this municipal poor relief was the statute of 27 *vendemaire* II of October 15, 1793. Later amendments required that each community establish a relief board of five citizens, and that each *département* set up an almshouse for destitute persons and a "foundling's home" for orphans and abandoned children.[8]

### The German System

In Germany social insurance programs were originated under Bismarck as a political weapon against the trade unions and the socialist movement, but they developed later as an independent system. At present about 95 percent of the population is insured against illness, industrial accidents, and disease, old age, invalidity, and unemployment. Persons in economic need who are not covered by social insurance are maintained by public or private assistance. Most benefits are increased with a rise in the cost of living. Most social insurance benefits are financed by contributions from employers and workers and from taxes related to the income of the employees, but industrial accident insurance (workmen's compensation) is financed by the employers only. The insurance programs are administered by independent, self-governing boards composed of equal numbers of representatives from management and labor. Emphasis is on preventing unemployment. Unemployed workers are not forced into retraining, but labor offices offer higher benefits for accepting retraining than for unemployment compensation. Unemployment benefits are paid for 52 weeks, after which an unemployment assistance of about 60 percent of the insurance allowance is paid to workers unable to find work.

Health insurance protects about 90 percent of the population, providing free medical service, hospitalization, and specialist treatment. For the first six weeks of illness workers receive full wages from their employer, and thereafter the health insurance agency pays 75 percent of the employee's former earnings for up to 18 months for the same illness.

Industrial accident insurance covers accidents at work, accidents on the way to and from work, and industrial diseases. It includes medical treatment, operations, occupational aids, and cash benefits. When a person loses 20 percent of his or her earning capacity, he or she is entitled to a disability insurance pension.

Old-age insurance benefits were increased in 1957 by legislation that provided annual increments based upon years of work and the rise of cost of living. Widows receive six-tenths of the husband's security allowance, orphans and disabled persons a similar benefit.[9]

In the last decades of the nineteenth century social insurance programs were developed in Europe, first, as we saw, in Germany, then in most other European countries.[10] Social insurance benefits were not introduced in the United States until 1935, following the Great Depression, because governments and the trade unions had resisted such legislation in the mistaken belief that private enterprise was able to provide individual security. Modern social insurance legislation was not enacted in France until 1945.[11] England had established social insurance on a limited basis in 1909 and 1911, but the Beveridge Plan of 1941 expanded the program. In all Western countries social insurance is now acknowledged as the best method of preventing destitution and securing at least a minimum of security for people unable to gain their own livelihood. In the developing countries in Asia, Africa, and Latin America, however, public assistance and social insurance programs take a secondary position behind community development, increased economic production, social planning, women's education, child care, and the training of young leadership.

### The Spanish and Communist Systems

In Spain a social security program was established by legislation in 1966 and amended in 1972. The benefits are financed by contributions from employers, workers, and government subsidies. Legislation covers most groups of the population, and financing is scheduled to be at a uniform rate in 1975.[12]

In some communist countries social insurance programs are administered either by the state or through trade unions under the direction of the Communist party. Individual social work in public assistance or personal service is not considered necessary under the assumption that personal needs could be met by representatives of the labor unions and do not require professionally trained social workers.[13]

Social insurance programs are financially based on contributions from employers and workers, and, in many countries, from general taxation. The costs of industrial accident insurance (workmen's compensation) are paid by the employers alone. The British National Health Service is financed via general taxation and not with individual contributions, as was the old health insurance program.[14] The question of income ceilings for computing the financial base for old-age insurance programs in Austria, France, West Germany, Sweden, and the United States is discussed in a study by Horlick and Lucas entitled "Role of the Contribution Ceiling in Social Security Programs: Comparison of Five Countries," published in the *Social Security Bulletin*, 34, No. 2 (Feb. 1971), 14–31.

### Different Philosophies

In the industrial countries the emphasis is on effective social insurance programs, whereas in the developing countries there is greater interest in programs of community development, child and youth welfare services, recreation, and education. This is understandable, given the differences in age composition: in many of the developing countries 95 percent of the population is under 60 years of age. Therefore we find that recreation facilities, camps, and educational and vocational training programs receive priorities rather than programs for the aged, handicapped, and mentally deficient. The interest in the training and employment of social workers and health personnel is increasing, but most of it is still in the cities and metropolitan centers. Rural villages show less inclination to employ social workers and usually do not have the funds for such positions, so in many countries (especially in Asia) the state agencies are the ones that employ village workers for child and family welfare services.

In most developing countries the large majority of the population still lives in villages and gains its livelihood as peasants on small holdings or as tenants and sharecroppers; therefore the governments try to secure a minimum income for the rural masses instead of social insurance programs for the aged, the disabled, or the sick. Despite a decrease in the operation of the joint family system, individual help in cases of natural disasters or failures of crops is still mostly left to family members or the clan. Only slowly is the value of social insurance protection under statewide systems being recognized.[15] However, the rural population is becoming aware of the need of social insurance protection in their old age, in disabilities, and in cases of loss of the breadwinner, such that in the future we can look for an increase in social insurance legislation that will include a general all-risk insurance to provide crop and livestock insurance that would reduce the insecurity of the peasant and sharecropper who is exposed to the uncertainties of weather, floods, droughts, pests, price changes on which he has no influence, lack of credit under reasonable conditions, and usury by excessive interests on loans, in addition to the usual dangers of sickness, accidents, old age, and invalidity. Some improvement in these conditions should be produced by the measures introduced in the community development programs (see Chapter 3)— the establishment of rural cooperatives and self-help programs which would assist in stabilizing the income of the rural population in the developing countries. One example of such an improvement in the economic security of the farm population is Japan, where in 1947, an old livestock insurance program was merged with crop insurance, then strengthened by reinsurance through prefectural federations and the national government.[16] In the United States insurance protection for farmers is offered by the Crop Insurance Corporation (created by legislation in 1938 and amended in 1947), which covers earthquakes, drought, freeze, inundations, insect damage, plant diseases, and fires. Similar insurance schemes are growing in other countries, but they will not be sufficient in case of major natural disasters. For these there is the United Nations Program for Assistance in Cases of Natural Disasters and the World Food Program (discussed in Chapter 2), which the International Red Cross and the League of Red Cross Societies are trying to create for emergency relief. Unfortunately, at times political considerations prevent urgently needed emergency relief. This happened in 1970, during the Biafran civil war, when there were many starving children of that country, and again in 1971, to the millions of refugees from East Pakistan (now Bangladesh).

### Miscellaneous Programs

In order to achieve a greater economic security for export crops on the world market, several nations have asked the United Nations to promote a stabilization of prices for such crops as sugar cane in India and Pakistan and coffee and cocoa in South America and Africa through the United Nations Conference on Trade and Development (see Chapter 2 above). These international agreements, however, in general protect the large producers more than the vast numbers of small farmers, peasants, and sharecroppers who are in need of such protection.[17]

Another essential program of economic and social security (usually found in the advanced industrial countries) is minimum wage legislation. It was first enacted in New Zealand in 1894, Australia (1896), and Great Britain (1909). In the United States Massachusetts initiated a program in 1912, then most other states, and finally the federal government. Before 1920 this legislation in the United States applied only to women, who usually were not organized or protected by collective bargaining. But under the National Industrial Recovery Act federal minimum wage laws now cover all workers.[18]

In the industrialized countries social security legislation usually protects both the urban and the rural population, but in most developing countries it is limited to a small proportion of the latter group. This is caused by the financial problems of most governments and the low income of the farm workers, especially the tenants, sharecroppers, and migratory workers which prevents collection of their contributions. An exception exists in Mexico, where since 1954 seasonal workers as well as peasants and tenants are covered by social insurance legislation.[19] Special social insurance programs for farmers have been developed in the form of pension systems in France, Poland, Austria, Germany, Denmark, Sweden, Switzerland, Finland, the Netherlands, Norway, Greece, Italy, Luxembourg, Belgium, and recently in Japan. In some of these programs (for instance in Great Britain) this supplemental benefit is only granted to persons whose income does not exceed a certain amount, or (in France, Poland, and West Germany) to farmers who dispose of their agricultural property.[20]

In developing countries in which the large majority of the population is very poor, no system of public assistance and no social work or psychiatric treatment can be expected to solve some problems of poverty in the near future. In such countries probably only a revolutionary ideology would appeal to the destitute masses because it would give them hope for a rising standard of living.[21]

In addition to regular old-age insurance benefits for retired people, a "constant attendance allowance" has been added in several countries that enables older citizens to remain in their own homes instead of being placed in institutions such as old-age or nursing homes; in Great Britain, France, Germany, Sweden, Austria, Belgium, and Spain such allowances have been granted mainly to recipients of workmen's compensation for industrial accidents and for the disability pensions.[22] In several industrialized and a few developing nations a guaranteed income or demogrant system provides different levels of basic economic security to the entire population.

For industrial workers and their families in the developing countries, where the immigration to the cities is rapidly increasing, social security programs are also badly needed, since in rural areas protection through the family, relatives, the clan and the tribe is quickly disappearing. In many Asian and African nations there are "provident funds," financed by employers and workers, which offer a certain security in case of industrial accidents. Most of these provide medical care, hospitalization, maternity aid, and sometimes also unemployment insurance. In parts of Africa "family allowances" follow the example of the French legislation in colonial times. But few countries have a comprehensive social insurance program which offers an adequate protection: many groups are still excluded, the costs of contributions are too high, and medical benefits are often not covered. In order to improve progress in this area, the Technical Assistance Program of the International Labor Organization exists to assist countries in the planning and preparation of new legislation, in revising old laws to adapt them to present needs and economic conditions, and by expanding or modernizing older social security systems. In India, Italy, Japan, and in several African nations these activities have included establishment of medical care services, seminars, and training courses.[23]

### The Industrial Experience

In the industrial countries, social security legislation is attempting to improve present laws by closing gaps in coverage and by covering self-employed persons, farmers, and members of the professions. In the fields of old-age, invalidity, and survivors insurance there have been improvements of legislation recently in Austria, Canada, Czechoslovakia, Denmark, Finland, France, West Germany, Italy, the Netherlands, Norway, Switzerland, Turkey, the Soviet Union, the United Kingdom, and Yugoslavia. Family allowances have been extended in Canada, France, Germany, Ireland, Holland, and Spain. Workmen's compensation (industrial accident insurance) has been improved in Belgium, Czechoslovakia, Japan, the United Kingdom, and the United States. Unemployment insurance is improved in Japan, Spain, and the United Kingdom.[24]

In the industrialized nations social insurance legislation was aimed first at protecting workers, the aged, invalids, disabled and sick persons, and their survivors on the basis of their contributions to the insurance program. Recently, however, the needs of young adults in these countries have led to new legislation to protect younger members of society, such as apprentices and students, who do not have significant employment and thus cannot make adequate contributions to social insurance programs against the dangers of ill health, accidents, disabilities, and unemployment, and to provide security for them through such special measures as family allowances and extended insurance programs. Such legislation has been enacted in Austria, Canada, Denmark, Finland, Germany, Italy, the Netherlands, Norway, Switzerland, Spain, Israel, New Zealand, Australia, France, and Japan.[25]

The International Labor Conferences of 1962 and 1967 made relevant recommendations for legislation on industrial accidents, old age, invalidity, and survivors insurance laws. They also emphasized the need for social insurance for migratory workers and for better insurance for medical care.

Social insurance is now accepted internationally as the main method of protection against poverty in case of old age, disability, sickness, unemployment, or industrial accident. The future of public assistance is more doubtful. That there remains need for a system of public assistance for persons not covered under social insurance legislation in the developing countries seems certain. But even in the industrialized countries, particularly the United States, Great Britain and the European countries, after the experience of the last decades public assistance seems still necessary as a supplement to social insurance benefits and will probably continue to be used in this capacity even after some program of "negative income taxes" or of a "social derogrant" has been introduced.[26] The guaranteed annual income, a much-discussed plan for all individuals and families that is favored by labor organizations, would be valuable only if this guaranteed income were adequate for the living standards of the country enacting such legislation and providing the finances necessary for its implementation.

### The Soviet Union

In the Soviet Union no supplementation through public assistance has been introduced, despite the meagerness of social insurance benefits. Only emergency grants are given the aged and disabled in cases of utmost deprivation. The kind of social welfare system the Soviets will develop for people in great need is difficult to predict.[27]

In 1968 and 1971 amendments to the Russian social insurance legislation increased the minimum benefits in old-age retirement and invalidity insurance which had been started in 1965, and included the workers on collective farms in the program of social insurance. These changes were intended to relieve Russia's labor shortage by encouraging retired older workers to return to employment. About 30 percent of the people who receive old-age or disability insurance benefits are retired collective farmers, some of them also supported through arrangements with mutual aid societies. All workers with young children are protected by a guaranteed annual minimum income supplement to their disability and survivors benefits. Further improvements are scheduled under the Five-Year Plan of 1971–75.[28]

Public assistance is granted to persons qualified for social security benefits and, since 1964, to members of the farm collectives. In general it is restricted to persons under the jurisdiction of the Trade Union Council. Destitute people may apply for relief to the local Soviet or to the local Social Security Office in order to receive some emergency relief. Severely disabled persons without relatives to help them are also entitled to some public assistance, but disability grants are very minimal, sometimes only 8 percent of the minimum wage, and different in different republics.[29]

In India and other Asian countries, social insurance programs and public assistance systems do not yet operate as they do in the Western countries. The amount of poverty, the lack of housing for the destitute, and cultural factors such as superstition and the still powerful caste system prevent the use of those methods that have secured economic and social security in the industrialized nations. The main hope for social improvement, especially in the villages, lies in the kinds of community development programs discussed in Chapter 3.[30]

The Social Security system of the United States is frequently praised in the international literature, but it has a serious deficiency that needs to be considered when making international comparisons. The Scandinavian, German, and Austrian social insurance benefits secure a *moderate* income for the beneficiaries, but the United States and British programs still operate on a concept of austerity and a type of "subsistence minimum." This concept has led to a strange caste system. Beneficiaries who are totally dependent upon the social security benefits for the aged or the disabled receive such inadequate incomes that they have a steady need for additional public assistance or private charity. On the other hand, beneficiaries who are entitled to an additional pension from government, labor union funds, private savings, annuity allowances, industrial shares, or other interests enjoy a security that was the original goal of social insurance legislation for all beneficiaries. The first category cannot achieve a decent standard of living without social assistance (in Britain these are called "supplementary benefits"), which does not fulfill the purposes of social insurance concepts.[31] Such people have become a "pensioners proletariat," people who live in poverty and without economic security. In the Appalachian mountain region, for example, many aged miners are denied promised supplementary pensions from the United Mine Workers' Union, and so must ask for public assistance.[32]

In several countries a system of universal pensions for the aged guarantees a minimum income in old age without qualifying conditions beyond proof of age; but the costs of such a program are high, compared with social insurance benefits, public assistance allowances, or specific categorical pensions. Persons with substantial earnings are excluded in some systems. Such pension programs exist in Denmark, Canada, Finland, Iceland, Sweden, New Zealand, and Norway, and several countries have combined such a program with a social insurance system which provides income-related benefits.[33]

### Children's Allowances

As already mentioned, in recent times *family allowances* or *children's allowances* have become an essential part of social security, social insurance programs, and social assistance systems. The first countries to introduce such family support were France and Belgium, during the nineteenth century. They were established first in the navies and the fishing fleets of these countries, in order to secure the wives of the men overseas. Later, miners, whose accidents were particularly frequent, were added, to help families in urgent need of support before industrial accident insurance legislation had been enacted.[34] Some children's allowances were based upon the private initiative of employer groups that were interested in attracting reliable workers or in keeping them during periods of labor shortage without a general increase of wages. After the First World War France expanded such family allowances to all categories of workers and subsequently (1931 and 1932) to the entire population.

Statewide family allowance laws were enacted earlier, in New Zealand (1926), New South Wales (Australia), (1927), and Belgium (1930). The motivation in France for family allowances had originally been humanitarian, and later became one of population policy. In Sweden and Germany the opposite was true. They both started from demographic considerations, which led to a humanitarian and civil rights program. Children's allowances are now in operation in 62 nations—in all European countries except Malta, 20 African countries, five countries in Oceania and southeast Asia, three countries in the Middle East (Lebanon, Iran, and Israel), six countries in South America, and Canada. They are established in every major industrial nation but the United States and Japan. The conditions which led to the enactment of children's allowance legislation differed in different countries and cannot be fully examined in this study, but a partial aim of every program was to redistribute income in favor of the poor (who often have more than the average number of children) and thus assist in eliminating unemployment, stabilizing purchasing power, and improving the nutrition and upbringing of children. A basic objective of children's allowances is to share the burden of raising the young generation with the general population instead of imposing most of it on a small segment of the working population. In about 15 of the 60 countries using this system the financing is carried by government.

In Germany the financial burden was transferred from employers to general taxation, and in France it remains the obligation of employers.[35] In Russia "family allowances" are granted to unmarried and married mothers, but are considered rather inadequate.

The vast majority of the social security programs now in existence only provide minimum benefits, are not adequate to secure a decent standard of living, and so are in need of supplementary measures.[36]

A systematic planning of the international development of social security programs is a task for the future, as Kahn explains.[37] Kahn emphasizes that there will be no universal system of social security planning and social services for all countries on this globe owing to cultural, social, and economic diversity among various countries and because of differences in professional qualifications, social stratification, and value systems.[38] But he has the vision that under changing economic and social conditions effective social security programs finally will evolve in all countries of this earth.

## Notes

[1]David Braybrooke and Charles E. Lindblom, *A Strategy of Decision* (New York: Free Press, 1963); Shirley Jenkins, ed., *Social Security in International Perspective* (New York: Columbia University Press, 1969).

[2]An excellent survey of the organization and functions of such welfare and social insurance programs is presented in Dorothy Lally, *National Social Service Systems, A Comparative Study and Analysis of Selected Countries* (Washington, D.C.: U.S. Department of Health, Education, and Welfare, 1970).

[3]Parin Vakaria, "Social Work and Social Welfare Organizations in Other Parts of the World," *Encyclopedia of Social Work 1965*, pp. 741–49; George M. Foster, *Traditional Cultures and the Impact of Technical Change* (New York: Harper & Row, 1962).

[4]Walter A. Friedlander, *Introduction to Social Welfare* (Englewood Cliffs, N.J.: Prentice-Hall, 1969), pp. 113ff.

[5]Vera Shlakman, "The Safety-Net Function in Public Assistance: A Cross-National Exploration," *The Social Service Review*, 46, No. 2 (June 1972), 193–212.

[6]Gaston V. Rimlinger, *Welfare Policy and Industrialization in Europe, America, and Russia* (New York: Wiley, 1971), pp. 60–62; H. Derouin, A. Gory, and F. Worms, *Traité théorique et pratique d'assistance publique* (Theoretical and Practical Treatise on Public Aid), (Paris: Cotillon, 1900); René Sand, *Le Service social à travers le monde* (Social Service Throughout the World), (Paris: Armand Colin, 1931); Walter Friedlander, *Individualism and Social Welfare: An Analysis of the System of Social Security and Social Welfare in France* (New York: Free Press, 1962), pp. 27–37; E. Labrousse, *Le Mouvement ouvrière et les idées sociales en France* (The Labor Movement and Social Ideas in France), (Paris: Tournier et Constans, 1949).

[7]Pierre Laroque, "Social Security in France," in Jenkins, ed., *Social Security in International Perspective*, pp. 171–89.

[8]André Laporte, *L'Assistance publique et privée en France* (Public and Private Aid in France), (Paris: Libraries Techniques, 1952).

[9]Rimlinger, *Welfare Policy,* pp. 89–192

[10]Other European countries introduced social insurance with the humanitarian aim of assisting the poor, the sick and disabled, and the aged. In *Denmark* accident insurance began in 1898, in *Sweden* as voluntary sickness societies in the 1870s with support of the trade unions. George R. Nelson, *Freedom and Welfare* (Copenhagen: Danish Ministry of Social Welfare, 1953), pp. 388–445.

[11]Friedlander, *Individualism and Social Welfare in France,* pp. 170–98; Richard M. Titmuss, *Essays on the Welfare State* (New Haven, Conn.: Yale University Press, 1959), pp. 34–55, 56–74; Vakharia, "Social Work and Social Welfare Organizations," pp. 746–47.

[12]Max Horlick, "Social Security Revisions in Spain," *Social Security Bulletin,* 36, No. 4 (Apr. 1973), 36–39.

[13]International Labour Conference, *Social Security: Principles and Problems Arising out of the War* (Montreal, 1944), pp. 2–3; Madison, *Social Welfare in the Soviet Union,* pp. 53–60.

[14]Richard M. Titmuss, *Commitment to Welfare* (New York: Pantheon, 1968), pp. 91–103; Titmuss, *Essays on the Welfare State,* Chapter 3, "Pension Systems and Population Change," pp. 56–74.

[15]United Nations, *Report on World Social Condition 1967,* p. 80; Sayid Safar Hasan, "Social Security in India: Limited Resources, Unlimited Needs," Jenkins, *Social Security in International Perspective,* pp. 190–208; Kenneth Borelli, "Social Security in Central America," *International Social Work,* 14, No. 1 (1971), 4–15.

[16]*Report on World Social Condition 1967,* p. 82.

[17]Ibid., p. 83.

[18]Clair Wilcox, *Toward Social Welfare* (Homewood, Ill.: Irwin, 1969), pp. 212–13.

[19]Ibid., p. 86. In mainlaind China health insurance premiums are paid by the rural communes for their members and by factories for their workers; hospitals arrange insurance contracts with factories, trade unions, and workers' cooperatives for their members, and premiums are paid from "welfare funds"; hospitalization is free for those members, but other persons or their families have to pay one-half of hospitalization costs. Edgar Snow, "Population Care and Control in China," *The New Republic* (May 1, 1971), pp. 22–23.

[20]Dalmer D. Hoskins, "Special Retirement Programs for Farmers," *Social Security Bulletin,* 34, No. 10 (Oct. 1971), 24–30.

[21]Oscar Lewis, "The Culture of Poverty," in Marc and Phyllis Pilisuk, eds., *How the White Poor Live* (Chicago: Aldine, 1971), pp. 25–26.

[22]Elizabeth K. Kirkpatrick, "Constant Attendance Allowances," *Social Security Bulletin,* 36, No. 4 (Jan. 1973), 35–36.

[23]United Nations, *Report on World Social Situation 1967,* pp. 88–89; George A. DeVos, "Achievement Orientation, Social Self-Identity, and Japanese Economic Growth," *Asian Survey,* 5 (Dec. 1965), 575–89.

[24]Ibid., pp. 89–90; Max Horlick and Robert Lucens, "Social Security Programs: Comparison of Four Countries," *Social Security Bulletin* (Feb. 1971), 19–31; Franco Illuminati, *La Tutela della Salute e l'Assicurazione de Malatta* (Protection of the Health and Security of Women) (Florence: Institute Studi Previdenzali, 1970); Pierre

Laroque, "Social Security in France," in Jenkins, ed., *Social Security in International Perspective*, pp. 170–87; Robert J. Lampman, "Transfer and Redistribution as Social Process," ibid., pp. 29–54.

[25]Max Horlick, "Social Security Provisions for Young Adults in Industrialized Countries," *Social Security Bulletin*, 34, No. 11 (Nov. 1971), 29–36; UNESCO, *Statistical Yearbook* (Paris, 1968), pp. 79–91.

[26]Eveline Burns, "Social Security in Evolution," *The Social Service Review*, 39, No. 2 (June 1965), 129–40; Richard M. Titmuss, "New Guardians of the Poor in Britain," in Jenkins, ed., *Social Security in International Perspective*, pp. 151–70; Robert Theobald, *Free Men and Free Markets* (New York: Potter, 1963), pp. 168–84; John S. Morgan, "An Emerging System of Income Maintenance: Canada in Transition," in Jenkins, ed., *Social Security in International Perspective*, pp. 105–28; Henning Friis, "Issues in Social Security Policies in Denmark," ibid., pp. 129–50; Laroque, "Social Security in France," pp. 171–89; Friedlander, *Individualism and Social Welfare in France*, pp. 152–209; Stephanie Münke, "Soziale Sicherung und ihre Reform in Mitteldeutschland" (Social Security and Its Reform in East Germany), in F. Sitzler, ed., *Die Sozialpolitik in der sowjetistischen Besatzungszone Deutschlands* (Social Policy of the Russian Occupation Administration in Germany) (Berlin: Duncker & Humblot, 1957), pp. 39–56.

[27]Madison, *Social Welfare in the Soviet Union*, pp. 60–61; Charles Schottland, et al., *Social Security Programs in the Soviet Union* (Washington, D.C.: U.S. Department of Health, Education, and Welfare, 1960), pp. 34–77; 91–100; Rimlinger, *Welfare Policy*, pp. 257–301.

[28]Joseph G. Simania, "Recent Changes in Russian Social Security," *Social Security Bulletin*, 35, No. 10 (Oct. 1972), 33–35, 62.

[29]Robert I. Davis, "The Soviet Concept of Social Welfare," *Social Welfare Forum 1972*, pp. 117–19, 126–28; Rimlinger, *Welfare Policy*, pp. 252–301.

[30]Arnold Rose, "Sociological Factors Affecting Economic Development in India," *Studies in Comparative International Developments*, 3, No. 9 (1967–68) 169–81; for U.S.A. see Norman V. Lourie, *New Strategies for Social Development* (New York: International Council on Social Welfare, 1970), pp. 16–20.

[31]Richard Titmuss, "New Guardians of the Poor in Britain," in Jenkins, ed., *Social Security in International Perspective*, pp. 159–70; Friis, "Social Security Policies in Denmark," pp. 133–44; Laroque, "Social Security in France," pp. 175–82; Alfred J. Kahn, "Social Security as System," ibid., pp. 211–27.

[32]Bruce Jackson, "In the Valley of the Shadows," *Trans-action*, 8, No. 5 (June 1971), 29–38.

[33]George F. Rohrlich, *Social Security for the Aged: International Perspectives* (Washington, D.C.: U.S. Government Printing Office, 1969), pp. 12–14.

[34]Roger Picard, "Family Allowances in French Industry," *International Labour Review*, 9, No. 2 (Feb. 1924), 161–62; Günther Prévot, *Die Wohlfahrtseinrichtungen der Arbeitgeber in Frankreich und Deutschland* (Welfare Institutions of Employers in France and Germany) (Leipzig: Verein fur Sozialpolitik, 1905); Friedlander, *Individualism and Social Welfare*, pp. 158–70; Ida Merriam, "Income Maintenance and Social Services," *Bulletin of the International Social Security Association*, No. 10–12 (Oct.–Dec. 1964), p. 358–61; Dominique Ceccaldi, *Histoire des prestations familiales in France* (Paris: Caisses d'allocations familiales, 1957); Leif Haanes-Olsen, "Children's Allowances: Their Size and Structure in Five Countries," *Social Security Bulletin*, 35, No. 5 (May 1972), 17–28.

³⁵Haanes-Olsen, "Children's Allowances," pp. 25–28; Rimlinger, *Welfare Policy,* pp. 60–62.

³⁶Richard M. Titmuss, "New Guardians of the Poor in Britain," in Jenkins, ed., *Social Security in International Perspective* (New York: Columbia University Press, 1969), pp. 151–70; David Braybrooke and Charles E. Lindblom, *A Strategy of Decision* (New York: Free Press, 1963), p. 71

³⁷Kahn, "Social Security as System," pp. 211–27.

³⁸Ibid., p. 225.

## Selected References

*Books*

AARON, HARRY, *Social Security: International Comparisons in Studies in the Economics of Income Maintenance.* Washington, D.C.: Brookings Institution, 1967.

ACHINGER, HANS, J. HÖFFNER, HANS MUTHESIUS, AND L. NEUNDÖRFER, *Neuordnung der sozialen Leistungen* (Reorganization of Social Services—in Germany). Koeln: Groom Publications, 1955.

ATKINSON, A. B., *Poverty in Britain and the Reform of Social Security.* London: Cambridge University Press, 1969.

AUERBACH, WALTER, *Beiträge zur Sozialpolitik* (Contributions to Social Policy). Neuwied (Germany): H. Luchterhand, 1972.

BENDIX, REINHOLD, AND SEYMOUR M. LIPSET, *Class, Status and Power.* New York: Free Press, 1953.

BHATACHARYA, VIVEK R., *Some Aspects of Social Security Measures in India.* Delhi: Metropolitan Book Co., 1970.

BLUM. J., *Lord and Peasant in Russia from the Ninth to the Nineteenth Century.* Princeton, N.J.: Princeton University Press, 1961.

BOGS, WALTER, *Grundfragen des Rechts der sozialen Sicherheit und seiner Reform* (Basic Questions on the Right for Social Security and Its Reform). Berlin: Duncker & Humblot, 1955.

BUCKTON-JAMES, DOROTHY, *Poverty, Politics, and Change.* Englewood Cliffs, N.J.: Prentice-Hall, 1972.

CARLSON, V., *Economic Security in the United States.* New York: McGraw-Hill, 1962.

DEWAR, MARGARET, *Labor Policy in the U.S.S.R., 1927–1928.* London: Royal Institute of International Affairs (1956), pp. 160ff.

DOBB, MAURICE, *Soviet Economic Development Since 1917.* New York: International Publishers, 1948.

GEORGE, VICTOR, *Social Security and Society.* London: Routledge & Kegan Paul, 1973.

GIL, DAVID G., *Social Policy: Analysis and Synthesis.* Cambridge: Harvard University Press, 1971.

GLASSER, WILLIAM A., *Paying the Doctor: Systems of Remuneration and Their Effect.* Baltimore, Md.: Johns Hopkins Press, 1970.

GORDON, MARGARET S., *The Economics of Welfare Policy.* New York: Columbia University Press, 1963.

HANSEN, H., *Die Finanzen der socialen Sicherung im Kreislauf der Wirtschaft* (The Monetary Background of Social Security Within the Circuit of the Economy). Kiel: University Press, 1955.

HAYEK, F., *The Road to Serfdom.* Chicago: University of Chicago Press, 1944.

JECHT, H., *Oekonomische Probleme der Produktivitätsrente.* (Economic Problems of the Earnings of Productivity). Stuttgart: Kohlhammer, 1956.

JENKINS, SHIRLEY, ed., *Social Security in International Perspective.* New York: Columbia University Press, 1969.

JANTZ, K., *Sozialreform und Sozialrecht. (Social Reform and Social Law).* Berlin: Duncker & Humblot, 1959.

KAIM-CAUDLE, P. R., *Comparative Social Policy and Social Security.* Cambridge: Cambridge University Press, 1973.

LALLY, DOROTHY, *National Social Service Systems: A Comparative Study and Analysis of Selected Countries.* Washington, D.C.: U.S. Department of Health, Education, and Welfare, 1971.

LAMPMAN, ROBERT, *Ends and Means of Reducing Poverty.* New York: Markman, 1971.

LIEFMANN-KEIL, E., *Oekonomische Theorie der Sozialpolitik.* (Economic Theory of Social Politics). Berlin: Springer, 1961.

MAAS, HENRY S., ed., *Five Fields of Social Service: Review of Research.* New York: National Association of Social Workers, 1966.

MACKENROTH, GERHARD, *Die Reform der Sozialpolitik durch einen deutschen Sozialplan* (The Reform of Social Politics through a German Social Plan). Frankfurt a/M.: Verein für Sozialpolitik, 1961.

MADISON, BERNICE Z., *Social Welfare in the Soviet Union.* Stanford, Ca.: Stanford University Press, 1968; pp. 195–209.

MENDELSOHN, RONALD, *Social Security in the British Commonwealth.* London: Athlone Press, 1958.

MERIAM, IDA C., PAUL FISCHER, AND MAX HORLICK, eds., *Social Security Programs Throughout the World.* Washington, D.C.: U.S. Department of Health, Education, and Welfare, 1971.

MILLER, MARGARET, *The Economic Development of Russia, 1905–1914,* 2nd ed. London: Cass, 1967.

NEMITZ, CURT, *Sozialistische Marktwirtschaft* (Socialist Market Economy). Frankfurt a/M.: Europäische Verlagsabst, 1960.

PEN, FERN, *Income Distribution: Facts, Theories, Policies.* New York: Praeger, 1971.

PILCH, MICHAEL, AND VICTOR WOOD, *Company Pension Schemes,* 2nd ed. London: Gower Press, 1971.

PILISUK, MARC, *International Conflict and Social Policy.* Englewood Cliffs, N.J.: Prentice-Hall, 1972.

RICHTER, MAX, *Die Sozialreform: Dokumente und Stellungnahme* (The Social Reform: Documents and Recommendations). Bad Godesberg (Germany): Asgard, 1955–68.

RIMLINGER, GASTON, *Welfare Policy and Industrialization in Europe, America, and Russia.* New York: John Wiley, 1971.

ROBERTS, PAUL CRAIG, *Alienation and the Soviet Economy.* Albuquerque: University of New Mexico Press, 1971.

ROBSON, WILLIAM A., AND BERNARD CRICK, eds., *The Future of the Social Services.* Harmondsworth (England): Penguin Books, 1970.

RODGERS, BARBARA H., JOHN GREVE, AND JOHN S. MORGAN, *Comparative Social Administration.* New York: Atherton, 1968.

ROENER, MILTON I., *The Organization of Socio-Medical Care Under Social Security.* Geneva: International Labor Office, 1969.

ROHRLICH, GEORGE F., *Social Security for the Aged: International Perspectives.* Washington, D.C.: U.S. Government Printing Office, 1969.

ROSENTHAL, ALBERT H., *The Social Program of Sweden,* Minneapolis: University of Minnesota Press, 1967.

RUBINOW, J. M., *Workmen's Insurance and Compensation Systems in Europe.* Washington, D.C.: U.S. Department of Labor, 1912.

RUNCIMAN, W. G., *Relative Deprivation and Social Justice.* London: Routledge and Kegan Paul, 1966.

SCHOTTLAND, CHARLES I., *The Social Security Program of the United States.* New York: Appleton-Century-Crofts, 1963.

THEOBALD, ROBERT, ed., *The Guaranteed Income.* New York: Doubleday, 1965.

TIFFANY, DONALD W., JAMES R. COWEN, AND PHYLLIS M. TIFFANY, *The Unemployed: A Social-Psychological Portrait.* Englewood Cliffs, N.J.: Prentice-Hall, 1970.

TITMUSS, RICHARD M., *Commitment to Welfare.* London: Allen & Unwin, 1968.

TOWNSEND, PETER, ed., *The Concept of Poverty: Working Papers on Methods of Investigation and Life Style of the Poor in Different Countries.* New York: American Elsinor Co., 1970.

VALENTINE, CHARLES A., *Culture and Poverty: Critique and Counter Proposals.* Chicago: University of Chicago Press, 1968.

WINTERSTEIN, HELMUT, *Sozialpolitik mit anderen Vorzeichen: Zur Frage einer stärken Betonung von persönlicher Freiheit und Selbstverantwortung in der Westdeutschen Sozialpolitik* (Social Politics with Different Symptoms: The Question of Stronger Emphasis on Personal Freedom and Self-Responsibility). Berlin: Duncker & Humblot, 1964.

*Articles*

ABRAHAMSON, R., "The Reorganization of Social Insurance Institutions in the U.S.S.R.," *International Labor Review,* 31 (March 1935), 370–80.

BURNS, EVELINE M., "Welfare Reform and Income Security Policies," *Social Welfare Forum 1970.* New York: Columbia University Press, 1970, pp. 46–60.

CARTWRIGHT, P. W., "Unemployment Compensation and the Allocation of Resources," pp. 65–81 in M. Abramovits, ed., *The Allocation of Economic Resources.* Stanford, Ca.: Stanford University Press, 1959.

EASON, W. W., "Labor Force," pp. 86–106 in A. Bergson and S. Kuznets, eds., *Economic Trends in the Soviet Union.* Cambridge: Harvard University Press, 1963.

FISHER, PAUL, "Major Social Security Issues: Japan 1972," *Social Security Bulletin,* 36 (March 1973), 26–38.

FORM, WILLIAM H., "Technology and Social Behavior of Workers in Four Countries: A Sociotechnical Perspective," *American Sociological Review*, 37 (Dec. 1972), 727–38.

FRIEDLANDER, WALTER A., "Social Security in France," pp. 152–209 in Walter A. Friedlander, *Individualism and Social Welfare in France*. New York: Free Press, 1962.

HAANES-OLSEN, LEIF, "Children's Allowances: Their Size and Structure in Five Countries," *Social Security Bulletin*, 35 (May 1972), 17–22.

HERMANN, J., "Lösungen für das dritte Alter" (Solutions for the Third Age), *Theorie und Praxis der sozialen Arbeit*, 24 (Apr. 1973), 150–53.

JANTZ, KURT, "Pension Reform in the Federal Republic of Germany," *International Labor Review*, 93 (Feb. 1961), 154–60.

JOFFE, WILLIAM M., "New International Standard for Medical Care Under Social Security Programs," *Social Security Bulletin*, 31 (Oct. 1969), 21–32.

KANEW, J., "Planning of Health Insurance and Health Services in Developing Countries," *International Social Security Bulletin*, 20 (Apr. 1967), 456–93.

LAUTERBACH, HERBERT, "The German Child Allowances Law," *Bulletin of the International Social Security Association*, 8 (Apr. 1955) 184–95.

MINKOFF, JACK, "The Soviet Social Insurance System Since 1921." Ph.D. dissertation, Columbia University, 1959.

NASH, EDMUND, "Labor Aspects of the Economic Reform in the Soviet Union," *Monthly Labor Review* (June 1966), pp. 597–602.

PERRIN, G., "The Future of Social Security," *International Social Security Bulletin*, 22 (Jan. 1969), 3–27.

PRESTHUS, ROBERT, ed., "Interest Groups in International Perspective," *The Annals*, 413 (May 1974), 1–172.

RHEIN, MARTIN, "The Strange Case of Public Dependency," pp. 169–89 in Marc Pilisuk and Phyllis Pilisuk, eds., *How the White Poor Live*. New York: Transaction, 1971.

RIMLINGER, GASTON V., "The Trade Union in Soviet Social Insurance," *Industrial and Labor Relations Review*, 14 (Apr. 1961), 412–16.

RIS, VLADIMIR, "The Sociology of Social Security," *Bulletin of the International Social Security Association*, 17 (Feb. 1964), 3–34.

SCHORR, ALVIN, "Income Maintenance," *Social Welfare Forum 1970*, pp. 34–45.

SHLAKMAN, VERA, "The Safety-Net Function in Public Assistance: A Cross-National Exploration," *Social Service Review*, 46 (June 1972), 193–212.

STEVENSON, OLIVE, "The Problems of Individual Needs and Fair Shares for All," *Social Work Today*, 1 (Apr. 1970), 15–21.

TAIRA, K., AND P. KILBY, "Differences in Social Security Development in Selected Countries," *International Social Security Review*, 22 (Jan. 1969), 139–53.

YOUNG, L. C., "Mass Sociology: The Chinese Style," *American Sociologist*, 9, No. 3 (Aug. 1974), 117–25.

# *Environmental problems and the population explosion*

*9*

For the first time in our history the rapid increase of the world's population presents a serious threat to the survival of mankind. The population is now about 3.5 billion, but if the rate of increase remains stable, it is expected to grow to about 7 billion by 2000. There is danger of an enormous famine, but it may not be so serious if we can increase food production more rapidly than the population. One would, under such circumstances, no longer eat meat, as there would no longer be room for cows, sheep, and pigs, and the waters will be too polluted for fish, but artificial food and seaweed might still prevent wholesale starvation.[1]

## *The Effects of Modern Medicine*

Medical science and public health have reduced infant mortality and increased the healing of sick persons to such a degree that leaders of the developing nations are seriously concerned over the threat of excessive population growth without a comparable increase in economic progress and food production. About 56 percent of the world's population (in Asia) exists on only 13 percent of the world's food production because of a lack of social and economic development that impedes the struggle against hunger, malnutrition, and poverty. This prevents an improvement of the standards of living of the masses in most developing countries, while small elite power groups get rich, in spite of foreign and international assistance. Resources for economic and social development are absorbed to feed the rapidly increasing population and cannot be used for the urgently needed schools, health facilities, hospitals, and housing for the poor. Often both parents have to work, especially when the family has moved from the village to the city, so that children and adolescents are deprived of love and proper care, are without proper education and recreation, are insecure, resent their parents and societies, and become easy prey to delinquent gangs.

In a few decades even the older generation is going to suffer because of the rapid population growth. Housing conditions are deteriorating owing to the lack of sufficient new housing for the migration from the rural regions to the cities and to the increasing costs of housing. And despite all endeavors to improve schools and adult literacy courses, population growth increases the number of illiterate persons in most developing countries. The increase in population causes more unemployment because there are not enough jobs for unskilled laborers. The result is that malnutrition, poverty, and hunger threaten the stability of governments because they can't meet the growing demands for social, economic, and medical provisions.[2]

### Population and Family Planning

Alva Myrdal has explored the psychological and economic reasons for the decline in birth rates in the developed countries and comes to the conclusion that they are closely intertwined. They are not easily studied, however, since a multitude of traditions, religious beliefs, conventions, folkways, habits, ideals, and social patterns are involved.[3] Family planning is determined also by the number of children already in the family and the personal inclinations of the parents.

Since the Second World War, the progress of medicine, the health measures of the United Nations and its affiliated agencies (particularly those of the World Health Organization, as we discussed in Chapter 2), and industrialization have created the world's population explosion, by reducing the mortality rate through the elimination of epidemics, the improvement of water supplies, and sanitation. But a lowering of the birth rate requires a change in family patterns and an educational process that produces a sense of social responsibility that differs from tradition. Religious customs in India and China regard the birth of a son as a link between the ancestors and the living, and until recently the religious leaders of Islam prohibited the use of contraception.[4]

In most developing countries, the rural population is still accustomed to relying on children for labor on the farm and for social security in sickness and old age, and therefore is not inclined to accept family planning and birth restriction until there are three or four living children. An interesting example is family planning in Taiwan. After the end of the Second World War there was a declining mortality rate, and average life expectancy is now over 60 years. But despite wide acceptance of family planning, many families still desire one or two sons according to traditional Chinese values, so that there will be a male heir who will care for the parents in old age or disability.[5]

In low-income countries where the population is doubling every 20 to 25 years, the educational system faces intolerable burdens. However many schools and teachers are employed, the number of illiterates still increases, and health resources do not suffice. In rural regions the percentage of unemployment and underemployment is growing despite immigration to the cities and industrial centers. The dissatisfactions of increasing masses of the population, together with air and water pollution and congestion in the cities lead to unrest and attacks against the ruling government and increasing amounts of crime and delinquency. Population growth leads to further contamination of the streams and oceans, to further erosion of the soil, and to new housing problems.[6]

### Movement to the Cities

A special danger in population explosion is that in some of the developing countries, particularly in India, Africa, and Latin America, large numbers of the rural population are beginning to leave the rural villages and to move to the larger cities and thus create a serious problem in many metropolitan areas. The *bustees* in India, the *barrios* in Latin America, and the "shanty-towns" in Africa are a serious new problem for their inhabitants as well as for their governments and countries. If this movement should develop into an avalanche, there is the danger that these peoples living in misery, squalor, and unemployment will revolt against a society which denies them human dignity and basic human rights. While this danger is present in all countries, it is particularly serious in the agricultural developing countries where technological progress, machinery, and scientific methods of crop increase permit a larger output of wheat and millet, thus permitting the production of more stable foods. But this development favors the wealthier farmers and landowners without helping the small peasants, tenants, and poor sharecroppers. Thus, in India, numerous small holdings are deteriorating and their rural population is driven to migrate to the cities where unemployment and lack of housing are throwing them into utmost misery.

So far this increasing danger of an avalanche into the cities has not been countered by an international policy of combined urban and rural planning by the international agencies.[7] Among the recommendations to meet these social problems is "sites and services," a planning device which sets aside special areas for the settlement of rural migrants with facilities for transportation and communication and thus allows them to integrate into the urban community and to develop the necessary skills for work and employment. But it is doubtful whether the necessary time for such a peaceful development will be available in view of the urgent social problems in the poorer countries.

The United Nations attempts to secure a safer environment in all countries by coordinating a global crusade for cleaner air, unpoisoned soil, purer water, and quieter surroundings by asking all nations to agree upon international standards for achieving these goals. The United Nations Conference on the Human Environment in Stockholm in June 1973 issued these suggestions. Over 100 "earthwatch stations" are set up to implement these goals under supervision of the United Nations Agency on the Human Environment in Nairobi, Kenya, directed by Maurice F. Strong who had served as secretary-general of the United Nations Conference on the Human Environment. This agency will also attempt to organize the use of the various sources of energy, in cooperation with the International Institute for Environmental Affairs in New York at the United Nations Headquarters.[8]

### The Stockholm Conference

At the Stockholm Conference Margaret Mead emphasized for the nongovernmental organizations of the United Nations that the limited resources of the earth need to be distributed more fairly among all nations. The world economy must become balanced with the environment, and people, while conforming to their different cultures and traditions, must assume responsibility for a population policy which does not surpass the productivity of their natural resources. Nations no longer can use aggression and destructive competition. Social policies are needed everywhere to reduce human stress, physical deterioration, inadequate diets (particularly in infancy), lack of decent housing, and intolerable noise, and to provide adequate assistance to people in need. A significant redistribution of the world's resources in favor of the developing countries is necessary. The UN General Assembly approved the work of the Stockholm Conference in its December 1972 session and established a governing council of 58 nations to which the recommendations of the Stockholm Conference were referred.[9]

Even in the United States, the richest country of this earth, 25 million families who are poor suffer from unwanted children, who grow up without adequate nutrition, health services, good clothing, or education. Planned family education and birth control facilities are needed to improve these conditions.

Birth Control and Family Planning have been successfully achieved in Japan and mainland China. In both countries the birth rate, which was extremely high until the end of the Second World War, has been reduced to from 1.5 to 2 percent. Contraceptive measures are encouraged by public health centers and distributed free of charge to women who cannot afford to buy them in pharmacies. In China abortion is provided only as a last resort, when contraceptive devices have not been available or did not succeed in preventing pregnancy, and in these instances they are free of charge. Birth control pills are freely distributed by public health centers, doctors, nurses, the "barefoot doctors," and medical assistants (often medical students) who work among the peasants in the villages and rural collectives, doing medical auxiliary services on the level of a nurse. The population likes their help.[10]

Chile is an illustration of the serious consequences of the high birth rate in Latin American countries combined with declining food production. Until recently there was adequate domestic food production, but now it is necessary to import food stuffs. While the population increases annually at a rate of 3 percent, agricultural production goes down. According to official statistics, about one out of every two children under 15 years of age suffers from malnutrition.[11]

Until fairly recently private organizations such as the International Parenthood Federation, the Ford Foundation, the Rockefeller Foundation, and the Population Council assumed the major responsibility for developing an efficient system of planned parenthood. There were also a few bilateral programs, such as the agreement between the Swedish and United States governments to assist in spreading the idea of birth control. The International Planned Parenthood Federation consists of over 60 private family planning organizations and supports these agencies by financial assistance and technical advice, particularly in countries where the governments have not yet assumed responsibility for the family planning program. The International Family Planning Federation helps in the design and supervision óf such programs through the Population Council, established in 1952, which administers a fellowship program for the study of 600 fellows in demographic and biomedical sciences, maintains resident advisors in 11 countries, and conducts research projects into contraceptive technology. Bilateral programs in the area of family planning have been organized in Denmark, Sweden, Britain, Holland, Norway, Japan, the United States, India, Ceylon, Pakistan, Korea, and Malaysia.

Sweden has been a prominent pioneer in the field of population control, in its generous allocation of funds to the United Nations Population Trust Fund (established in 1967), the World Health Organization, the United Nations Educational, Social, and Cultural Organization, and the United Nations Children's Fund. The United States also supports these activities of the United Nations, and contributed $500,000 to the

Population Trust Fund. Smaller contributions were made by Britain and Denmark.[12]

In 1966 the United Nations General Assembly requested that the Economic and Social Council, the Population Commission, the Regional Economic Commissions, and the specialized agencies assist in developing and strengthening national and regional facilities for the establishment of training, research, information, and advisory services in the field of population, bearing in mind the different character of population problems in each country and region. However despite many conferences and discussions, no sufficient action has resulted so far. More important has been the work of the United Nations Population Division, which was able to explain the urgency of the problem and to clarify the necessity of coordinated action. In Latin America the regional demographic centers and the regional economic commissions have been able to convince leading personalities in several governments of the need for action. The United Nations has sent missions to India, Pakistan, Columbia, and several African countries for information about family planning and has recruited ten population program officers who are working in Asia, Africa, and Latin America. The World Health Organization assists by advice on the "health aspects of population dynamics," and the World Bank has started a population project in Jamaica.

Despite an increasing insight into the importance of population policy and good will among many national and international agencies, family planning programs are still inadequate. Attitudes toward family planning differ among the continents and even among regions of the same country. Bureaucratic difficulties and rivalries among the numerous organizations have caused inaction. Those difficulties need to be overcome. The United Nations system is qualified to work constructively in the solution of the urgent problem of population control.

Most demographers still consider the population explosion a serious danger for the developing nations, especially for India, Pakistan, Bangladesh, and several Latin American and African countries, but R. Buckminster Fuller is convinced by his sociological and historical studies that with the increasing industrialization of all nations the steep birth rate will decrease and a natural equilibrium will develop in all countries within a fairly short time.[13]

Family planning programs have been successful in countries where they were integrated with general community development activities and involved the use of interprofessional teams of demographers, economists, planners, social workers, and health personnel.[14] Within the framework of the United Nations the United Nations Development Program (UNDP) offers the best concentration point for the realization of family planning and population policy. The UNDP is working with specialized agencies and may contact all kinds of government divisions, whereas WHO approaches ministries of health and UNESCO ministries of education. But it seems necessary to develop more integrated policies in order to achieve more effective actions in the line of family planning. To this purpose other institutions besides government agencies and private organizations already active in family planning should be approached, such as research institutes and universities, which should be assisted with advice and funds from the Population Trust Fund and should be encouraged to implement effective family planning activities. Religious and political objections against birth control should be encountered and disputed as prejudice. The priority of the population question must be clearly emphasized. The present Population Trust Fund must be substantially enlarged, and the specialized agencies of the United Nations (WHO, UNICEF, ILO, FAO, UNESCO) must place more urgency on demographic training and the development of family planning. This applies especially to the World Health Organization, which so far has not taken the lead in family planning policies by including family planning in basic public health services.[15]

## The Case of India

The most tragic problem of the population explosion and its consequences of diseases, contamination, pollution, and destruction of human life is found in India. Indian cities, such as Bombay, Calcutta, and Delhi, are severely overcrowded. There is inadequate water, sanitation, housing, and transportation; corruption; despair; and a hopeless dichotomy between the old Indian and the modern Western civilizations. In many cities the population has increased fivefold since the beginning of this century and there is widespread unemployment because of the high birth rate and the stream of refugees from Pakistan and villages. During the nights the homeless sleep on the pavements; they suffer from hunger and cold and diseases. Squatters were taken out of Delhi, but the size of the housing deficiency cannot be solved by such measures. The International Development Association, an affiliate of the World Bank, has tried to assist Bombay by reconstructing its harbor to relieve the city of overpopulation, but the human needs of the poor are not ameliorated by industrial development.[16] Similar conditions prevail in Calcutta, where a cholera epidemic brought by masses of refugees from East Pakistan after the war in Bangladesh increased the danger of starvation and death. As early as 1959 the World Health Organization found that it would not be possible to eradicate cholera because it would be necessary to rebuild all city services, water supply, sewage, housing, transportation, and utilities.

The Ford Foundation organized the Calcutta Metropolitan Planning Organization, an all-Indian group, which has tried to develop a satellite port, but this endeavor has been hampered by political and personal difficulties. The population, housing, and health problems of most Indian cities are so extreme because of the millions of people involved and because of their abysmal poverty and the cultural obstacles to an improvement of health conditions.[17]

Assistance to increase food and agricultural production is of utmost importance in India. It is also needed in large parts of South America and Africa. One successful program for training farmers in modern farming methods, developing new crops, and teaching families better nutrition is the Rural Vocational Training Project at Guerina in Senegal, which has been conducted by the Senegalese government in cooperation with the United Nations Development Program, the International Labor Office, and the Food and Agriculture Organization. Its example and success have led to similar training and education experiments for the benefit of the rural population in other developing countries.[18]

### Pollution

In addition to overpopulation, the threat of atomic war and the poisoning of the environment are other dangers to human survival.[19] In order to call these dangers to the attention of all peoples, the United Nations held a "Conference on the Human Environment" in Stockholm in 1972. The conference agreed to establish a special environmental agency within the United Nations to administer environmental funds, review and approve programs, coordinate environment-related work, and provide assistance for the peaceful settlement of disputes in this area. The conference faced tremendous obstacles. Assistance to foreign countries is necessary, but it also increases the danger of overpopulation. Family planning is needed, but is seen by some developing countries as genocidal. Industrialization is demanded by most developing nations, but causes pollution and higher consumption (which the poor countries request as "social justice").[20] The survival of this earth depends upon the insight that peace among men is necessary before the environment can be saved.

In order to secure human survival, Elisabeth Mann-Borgese has suggested the establishment of an international earth resource management organization, which would include protection of the resources of the seabed beyond the limits of national jurisdiction according to principles already adopted by the General Assembly of the United Nations. Such an international agency would establish regulations that all earth resources remain the common heritage of all mankind; that no nation, commercial company, or individual could acquire earth resources in conflict with the international regime; and that the exploration and use of these resources could be carried out only for the benefit of mankind as a whole, with consideration of the needs of the developing nations. Such an organization would have to operate a seabed protection system, a satellite system, a scientific institute which would coordinate research on satellite findings, and training facilities for experts of all nations in this field. It would also have to set up a planning board under the auspices of the United Nations General Assembly, to develop a system for distribution of the earth resources that would eliminate the present unfair division between rich and poor nations.[21]

## Notes

[1]United Nations Association of the United States of America, *World Population: A Challenge to the United Nations and Its System of Agencies* (New York: United Nations, 1970), pp. 11–16, 27–29; George Wald, "A Better World for Fewer Children," *The Progressive* (Apr. 1970), 26–28; Paul R. Ehrlich, "Looking Backward from 2000 A.D.," ibid., pp. 23–25; Phon Sangsingkeo, "Implications of Rapid Population Growth," *World Mental Health*, 15, Nos. 3–4 (Fall 1963), 131–34; Paul R. Ehrlich and Anne H. Ehrlich, *Population—Resources—Environment* (San Francisco: Freeman, 1970); Irene B. Taeuber, "Population Growth in Less Developed Countries," in Philip M. Hauser, ed., *The Population Dilemma* (Englewood Cliffs, N.J.: Prentice-Hall, 1969), pp. 34–84.

[2]Sangsingkeo, "Implications of Rapid Population Growth"; Ronald Freedman, "The High Fertility of the Less Developed Nations," in David M. Heer, ed., *Readings on Population* (Englewood Cliffs, N.J.: Prentice-Hall, 1968), pp. 157–75; François Cloutier, "Population Problems and Mental Health," *World Mental Health*, 15, Nos 3–4 (Fall 1963), 143–49; Stanley Johnson, "Food, People, and Technology," *Vista*, 7, No. 1 (June 1972), 28–32, 57.

[3]Alva Myrdal, *Nation and Family* (London: Routledge and Kegan Paul, 1945), pp. 27, 48–54, 100, 132; Kingsley Davis, "The Demographic Consequences of Changes in Productive Technology," in Robert Aaron, ed., *Economic and Technical Change* (Paris: International Social Science Council, 1958), pp. 193–227; Wilbert E. Moore, *The Impact of Industry* (Englewood Cliffs, N.J.: Prentice-Hall, 1965), pp. 72–82.

[4]William J. Goode, *The Family* (Englewood Cliffs, N.J.: Prentice-Hall, 1964), pp. 110–12; Kingsley Davis and Judith Blake, "Social Structure and Fertility," *Economic Development and Cultural Change*, No. 4 (Apr. 1956), pp. 211–35.

[5]Freedman, "High Fertility," pp. 159–63; Wilbert E. Moore, *Social Change* (Englewood Cliffs, N.J.: Prentice-Hall, 1963), pp. 39–41, 70–72, 100–101.

[6]Johnson, "Food, People, and Technology," pp. 11–16; Rudie W. Tretten, *Cities in Crisis* (Englewood Cliffs, N.J.: Prentice-Hall, 1970), pp. 86–89; Ruth Mulvey Harmer, *Unfit for Human Consumption* (Englewood Cliffs, N.J.: Prentice-Hall, 1971), pp. 38–55; Thomas R. Ford and Gordon F. De Jong, *Social Demography* (Englewood Cliffs, N.J.: Prentice-Hall, 1970), pp. 3–16, 404–34, 670–77.

[7]Laurence Hewes, "When Rural Migration Becomes an Avalanche," *The Center Magazine,* 7, No. 2 (Apr. 1973), 8–9; Wilbert E. Moore, "The Migration of Native Laborers in South Africa," in Lyle W. Shannon, ed., *Underdeveloped Areas* (New York: Harper & Row, 1957), pp. 79–87.

[8]United Nations, *World Energy, the Environment, and Political Action* (New York, 1973); Barbara Ward and René Dubos, *Only One Earth: The Care and Maintenance of a Small Planet* (New York: Norton, 1972).

[9]The 109 special recommendations of the Stockholm Conference are contained in *Science and Public Affairs,* 28, No. 7, 1–46. See also James E. Atkins, "International Cooperative Efforts in Energy Supply," *The Annals of the American Academy of Political and Social Science,* 410 (Nov. 1973), 75–85; Elizabeth Mann-Borgese, "Energy Politics and the International System," *The Center Magazine,* 7 (Feb. 1974), 26.

[10]Milso Macura, "Demographic Factors in Urban Development," in Ellen Winston and Eugen Pusíc, eds., *Urban Development: Its Implications for Social Welfare* (New York: Columbia University Press, 1967), pp. 273–82; Edgar Snow, "Population Care and Control," *The New Republic* (May 1, 1971), pp. 20–23.

[11]Ernest Greenwood, "Chile: A Nation Westward Bound" (Mimeographed, Berkeley: University of California, 1971), p. 6; Kingsley Davis, "Population and Change in Backward Areas," in Shannon, ed., *Underdeveloped Areas,* pp. 68–78.

[12]Johnson, "Food, People, and Technology," pp. 18–21. For the problem of hunger and malnutrition see Ernesto Pollitt, "Poverty and Malnutrition: Cumulative Effect on Intellectual Development," *Les Carnets de l'enfance,* 14, (Apr.–June 1971), 40–52; Aldo Buffa, "Technologie de l'alimentation et développement," (Technology of the Nutrition of Development), ibid., pp. 56–68; Carl L. Biemiller, "Tomorrow's Seas," *Vista,* 3, No. 2 (Sep.–Oct. 1967), 43–53, No. 3 (Nov.–Dec. 1967), 50–59; Frank Barton, "Africa's Food Problem, *Vista* 1, No. 3 (Nov. 1965), 33–40.

[13]R. Buckminster Fuller, "Geoviews," *World* 14, No. 2 (July 3, 1973), 16–40; E. J. Kahn, Jr., "A Capitalist the Socialists Can Trust," ibid., pp. 33, 40.

[14]Johnson, "Food, People, and Technology," pp. 26–28; William L. Langer, "Population Growth and Increase in the Means of Subsistence," in Heer, ed., *Readings on Population,* pp. 2–15; A. M. Carr-Saunders, *The Population Problem* (Oxford: Clarendon Press, 1922); B. Singh, *Five Years of Family Planning in the Country-Side* (Lucknow: Institute of Sociology and Human Relations, 1958); Richard Gardner, "Seven Billion Soon," *Vista,* 3, No. 5 (March–Apr. 1968), 20–29; Hauser, *The Population Dilemma,* pp. 35ff.

[15]Johnson, "Food, People, and Technology," pp. 37–46; John R. Rees, "Mental Health and Population Problems," *World Mental Health,* 14, No. 3 (Aug. 1962), 102–3; Ronald Freedman, "Norms for Family Size in Underdeveloped Areas," in Heer, ed., *Readings on Population,* pp. 157–75; Julia J. Henderson, "Developing Population Policy in Relation to Social Change and Social Welfare" (paper read at the International Conference on Social Welfare, The Hague, The Netherlands, August 1972).

[16]Edward Rice, "The Cities of India," *Vista,* 5, No. 4 (Jan–Feb. 1970), 29–35; Kingsley Davis and Hilda H. Golden, "Urbanization and the Development of Preindustrial Areas," in Heer, ed., *Readings on Population,* pp. 40–56; Kingsley Davis, "Institutional Patterns Favoring High Fertility in the Underdeveloped Areas," in Shannon, ed., *Underdeveloped Areas,* pp. 88–95.

Environmental problems and the population explosion **179**

[17]Rice, "The Cities of India," p. 35; Myrdal, G., *Beyond the Welfare State,* pp. 200–221; Jagdish N. Bhagwati and Padma Desai, *Planning for Industrialization* (New York: Oxford University Press, 1971); P. J. Eldridge, *The Politics of Foreign Aid in India* (New York: Schocken, 1970), pp. 175, 181; Behrendt, *Soziale Strategie für Entwicklungsländer,* (Social Strategy for Developing Countries), pp. 493–500.

[18]Elizabeth Bosne, "A Journey to Senegal," *Vista,* No. 4 (Jan. 1970), 48–51.

[19]United Nations Association, *World Population;* Barry Commoner, "Motherhood in Stockholm: The U.N. Environmental Conference: Ecological Crusaders Are About to Clash with Seekers of Social Justice," *Harper's,* 244, No. 1465 (June 1972), 49–54.

[20]R. Stephen Berry et al., "What Happened in Stockholm," *Science and Public Affairs,* 28, No. 7 (Apr. 1973), 1–46.

[21]Elisabeth Mann-Borgese, "Interlocked: Disarmament and Development," *The Center Magazine,* 5, No. 2 (Apr. 1972), 3–5.

## Selected References

*Books*

ALBERTSON, PETER, ed., *Managing the Planet and Margery Barnett.* Englewood Cliffs, N.J.: Prentice-Hall, 1972.

ARMSTRONG, TERRY, ed., *Why Do We Still Have an Ecological Crisis?* Englewood Cliffs: N.J.: Prentice-Hall, 1972.

ATTINGER, E. O., ed., *Global Systems Dynamics.* New York: Wiley-Interscience, 1970.

BEHRENDT, RICHARD F., *Sociale Strategie für Entwicklungsländer* (Social Strategy for the Developing Countries). Frankfurt a/M.: Fischer, 1969.

————, *Zwischen Anarchie und neuen Ordnungen* (Between Anarchy and New Regulations). Freiburg i. B: Herder, 1967.

BERELSON, BERNARD, *Beyond Family Planning.* New York: Studies in Family Planning, 1969.

————, *National Family Planning Programs.* Ann Arbor; University of Michigan Press, 1967.

BERG, ALAN, *The Nutrition Factor.* Washington, D.C.: Brookings Institution, 1973.

BILLING, WILLARD A., AND GEORGE O. TOTTEN, eds., *Developing Nations: Quest for a Model.* New York: Van Nostrand, 1970.

BOSE, ASHISH P., P. B. DESAI, AND S. P. JAIN, *Studies in Demography.* Chapel Hill: University of North Carolina Press, 1971.

BOULDING, KENNETH, *Beyond Economics.* Ann Arbor: University of Michigan Press, 1968.

BROWN, LESTER, *World Without Borders,* New York: Random House, 1972.

CHAMBERLAIN, NEIL C., *Beyond Malthus: Population and Power.* Englewood Cliffs, N. J.: Prentice-Hall, 1972.

CHANDRASEKHAR, S., *Infant Mortality, Population Growth, and Family Planning in India.* Chapel Hill: University of North Carolina Press, 1972.

**180**     *Environmental problems and the population explosion*

CHASTEEN, EDGAR R., *The Case for Compulsory Birth Control.* Englewood Cliffs, N.J.: Prentice-Hall, 1972.

COLLVER, O. ANDREW, *Birth Rates in Latin America: New Estimates of Historical Trends and Fluctuations.* Berkeley: University of California Institute of International Studies, 1965.

DUBOS, RENÉ, *The Nation's Health.* Washington, D.C.: American Public Health Association, 1972.

DUNCAN, GORDON W., ELIZABETH J. HILTON, PHILIP KREAGER, AND ARTHUR A. LANSDALE, eds., *Fertility Control Methods: Strategies for Introduction.* New York: Academic Press, 1974.

EHRLICH, PAUL R., *The Population Bomb.* New York: Ballantine, 1968.

FREIJKO, THOMAS, *The Future of Population Growth.* New York: Wiley-Interscience, 1970.

FRIEDMAN, RONALD, AND JOHN Y. TAKESHITA, *Family Planning in Taiwan: An Experiment in Social Change.* Princeton, N.J.: Princeton University Press, 1969.

GALBRAITH, JOHN KENNETH, *The New Industrial State.* Boston: Houghton-Mifflin, 1967.

GALLAGHER, ART JR., ed., *Perspectives in Developmental Change.* Lexington: University of Kentucky Press, 1968.

HARTLEY, STANLEY FOSTER, *Population: Quantity Versus Quality.* Englewood Cliffs, N.J.: Prentice-Hall, 1972.

HEER, DAVID M., ed., *Readings in Population.* Englewood Cliffs, N.J.: Prentice-Hall, 1968.

HOROWITZ, DAVID, *The Abolition of Poverty.* New York: Praeger, 1969.

JACOBS, NORMAN, *The Sociology of Development: Iran as an Asian Case Study.* New York: Praeger, 1966.

JENKINS, SHIRLEY, ed., *Social Security in International Perspectives: Essays in Honor of Eveline M. Burns.* New York: Columbia University Press, 1969.

KEYFITZ, NATHAN, AND WILHELM FLIEGEN, *World Population: An Analysis of Vital Data.* Chicago: University of Chicago Press, 1968.

KÖNIG, RENÉ, *Probleme der Mittelschichten in Entwicklungsländern* (Problems of Middle-Income Strata in Developing Countries). Koeln: Westdeutscher Verlag, 1964.

LEISS, WILLIAM, *The Domination of Nature.* New York: Braziller, 1972.

LERNER, DANIEL, *The Passing of Traditional Society.* New York: Free Press, 1958.

LIVINGSTON, ARTHUR, *Social Policy in Developing Countries.* New York: Humanities Press, 1969.

McNAMARA, ROBERT S., *Address to the Board of Governors of the World Bank Group.* Washington D.C.: World Bank, 1972.

MANN-BORGESE, ELISABETH, *Pacem in Maribus: Ocean Enterprises.* Santa Barbara, Ca.: Center for the Study of Democratic Institutions, 1970.

MATRAS, JUDAH, *Population and Societies,* Englewood Cliffs, N.J.: Prentice-Hall, 1972.

MEADOWS, DUELLA, DENIS L. MEADOWS, JORGEN READERS, AND WILLIAM W. BEHRENS, *The Limits of Growth: A Report for the Club of Rome—Project on the Predicaments of Mankind.* New York: Universe Books, 1972.

MECHANIK, ERNEST, *The World Development Plan: A Swedish Perspective.* Washington, D.C.: Population Crisis Committee, 1971.

PASSELL, PETER, AND LEONARD ROSS, *The Retreat from Riches: The Gross National Product and Its Enemies.* New York: Viking, 1972.

PILISUK, MARC, *International Conflict and Social Policy.* Englewood Cliffs, N.J.: Prentice-Hall, 1972.

PINKUS, JOHN A., ed., *Preshaping the World Economy: Rich and Poor Countries.* Englewood Cliffs, N.J.: Prentice-Hall, 1968.

PIOTROW, PHYLLIS T., *World Population Crisis: The United States Response.* New York: Praeger, 1973.

ROTHSCHILD, DONALD, *Racial Bargaining in Independent Kenya: A Study of Minorities and Decolonization.* New York: Oxford University Press, 1973.

SCHAPPER, H. R. *Aboriginal Advancement to Integration: Conditions and Plans for Western Australia.* Canberra: Australia National University Press, 1970.

SIMON, PAUL, AND ARTHUR SIMON, *The Politics of World Hunger.* New York: Harper & Row, 1973.

SPENCER, DANIEL L., AND ALEXANDER WORONIAK, eds., *The Transfer of Technology to Developing Countries.* New York: Praeger, 1967.

SPOONER, BRIAN, ed., *Population Growth: Anthropological Implications.* Cambridge: MIT Press, 1972.

STYKOS, J. MAYONE, *Ideology, Faith, and Family Planning in Latin America.* New York: McGraw-Hill, 1971.

THOMLINSON, RALPH, *Thailand's Population: Facts, Trends, Problems, and Policies.* Bangkok: Thai Waitana Panish Press, 1971.

TIEN, H. YUAN, *China's Population Struggle: Demographic Decisions of the People's Republic, 1949–1969.* Columbus: Ohio State University Press, 1973.

TITMUSS, RICHARD M., *Income Distribution and Social Change.* London: Allen & Unwin, 1962.

TRACY, STANLEY J., ed., *Report on World Population.* St. Louis, Mo.: George Washington University Press, 1945.

WARD, BARBARA, AND RENÉ DUBOS, *Only One Earth: The Care and Maintenance of a Small Planet.* New York: Norton, 1972.

WENK, EDWARD JR., *The Politics of the Oceans.* Seattle: University of Washington Press, 1973.

WESTHOFF, CHARLES F., AND ROBERT PARKER, JR., eds., *Demography and Social Aspects of Population Growth.* Washington, D.C.: U.S. Government Printing Office, 1972.

WILMER, D., R. P. WALKEY, I. PINLERTON, AND M. TAYBACK, *The Housing Environment and Family Life.* Baltimore, Md.: Johns Hopkins Press, 1962.

WOGAMAN, PHILIP J., ed., *The Population Crisis and Moral Responsibility.* Washington, D.C.: Public Affairs Press, 1973.

YOUNG, LOUISE B., ed., *Population in Perspective.* New York: Oxford University Press, 1968.

YUAN-TIN, H., *China's Population Struggle: Demographic Decisions of the People's Republic, 1949–69.* Columbus: Ohio State University Press, 1973.

ZATUCHNI, GERALD I. ed., *Post Partem Family Planning: A Report on The International Program.* New York: McGraw-Hill, 1970.

*Articles*

BURCH, T. K., AND G. A. SHEA, "Catholic Parish Priests and Birth Control: A Comparative Study in Colombia, the United States, and the Netherlands," *Studies in Family Planning,* 2 ( (June 1971), 121–38.

CHATTERJEE, B., "Social Aspects of Family Planning in India," *Indian Journal of Social Work,* 32 (Feb. 1971), 139–50.

DAVIS, KINGSLEY, "Population Policy: Will the Current Program Succeed?" *Science* (Nov. 10, 1967), pp. 730–39.

DEANNE, DOUGLAS, ed., "Les Questions de la population," ICVA Document No. 19 (Geneva, Switzerland, 1974).

DEYAZIGI, VICTORIA GARCIA, "Family Planning in Latin America," *World Federalist,* 19 (Mar. 1974), 8–17.

FABIAN, ANNE-MARIE, "From Achtstundentag zum Weltbeschäftigungsprogramm" (From the Eight-Hour Day to a Worldwide Employment Program), *Gewerkschaftliche Monatshefte* (Dec. 20, 1969), pp. 729–36.

GOLDMAN, MARSHALL I., "Growth and Environmental Problems of Non-Capitalistic Nations," *Challenge,* 1 (July–Aug. 1973), 45–51.

HEIDERMANN, INGRID, "Entwicklungshilfe und afrikanische Standpunkte" (Development Aid and African Points of View), *Gewerkschaftliche Monatshefte,* 20 (Sept. 1969), 590–604.

HUTTMAN, E., "Stigma in Public Housing: International Comparisons." Ph.D. dissertation, University of California, Berkeley, 1970.

LARKIN, MARGARET, "Family Planning in Mexico," *The Nation,* 203 (Nov. 14, 1966), 508–11.

MORGAN, JOHN S. "Welfare and the Steady State: An Essay Review," *Social Service Review,* 47 (March 1973), 81–92.

PAUL, ARTHUR, "Emerging Repercussions of Economic Development," *The Asian Foundation Quarterly* (Fall 1971), pp. 2–10.

RUBINGER, MARCOS M., "Social Participation as an Instrument for the Development and Formation of Society in Latin America," *International Labour Review,* 97, No. 6 (June 1968), 551–70.

SCHNORR, LEO F., "Demography and Human Ecology: Some Apparent Trends," *Annals of the American Academy of Political and Social Science,* 39 (July 1970), 120–28.

TAYLOR, HOWARD C. JR., AND BERNARD BERELSON, "Maternity Care and Family Planning as a World Program," *American Journal of Obstetrics and Gynecology,* 100 (1968), 885–99.

# Violence, delinquency, and crime

## 10

The seriousness of the problem of violence, delinquency, and crime owing to their increasing dimensions is indicated by the appalling magnitude of these deviations in most parts of the world. Almost every country, industrialized as well as developing, has had this problem during the last decades. However, since ruling groups in all countries are afraid of violent actions as threats to their dominance, we may question whether their anxiety does not exaggerate the real danger of violent movements.[1] In some instances violent actions have been encouraged by the ruling government, such as the so-called cultural revolution of youth in mainland China as a defense of the Mao Tse-tung regime. And in the United States some contend that, contrary to the widespread public belief, violent crime has not significantly increased during recent years. In France the number of juvenile offenders in prisons increased from 500 to 4,500 between 1956 and 1966, and the number of juvenile delinquency court cases went from 15,000 to 45,000. In Japan during a similar period the figure climbed from 18.2 percent to 28.7 percent of all criminal offenses, and there are similar statistics for Ceylon.[2]

### Increases in Crime

In many developing countries there is a tendency to neglect the danger of delinquency and the potential for crime caused by the migration of large masses from the rural areas to the growing cities, large-scale unemployment in urban areas, and lack of education and training for youth. But delinquency and crime are also high in the industrialized nations. For instance, in the United States the report of the President's Commission on Law Enforcement and Administration of Justice describes the increase of crime in the United States for the past three decades as very substantial, but warns that it is necessary to distinguish crimes of violence from those against property, and cautions against

**183**

dealing with all offenses as a unitary problem.[3] It also emphasizes that improved reporting of crimes will lead to an increase in crime statistics. In West Germany an increase in crimes and delinquency has been observed, but not an appalling increase in violent crimes.[4] It is questionable whether the increase of offenses by children under 14 is really as substantial as some statistics indicate.

France was the first European country to develop national criminal statistics (in 1825); the other western European countries followed suit later in the same century. But criminal statistics are of social value only if it is possible to coordinate them with the data on population growth, immigrations, and other facts which determine the social significance of statistical data on crime and delinquency.[5] As illustrations statistical data from several countries may be quoted:

*Juvenile Delinquents Sentenced by Juvenile Courts in France*[6]

| | | | |
|---|---|---|---|
| 1944 | 23,484 | 1954 | 13,504 |
| 1945 | 17,578 | 1955 | 13,975 |
| 1949 | 22,761 | 1956 | 14,778 |
| 1950 | 19,239 | 1957 | 16,366 |
| 1951 | 14,624 | 1958 | 12,886 |
| 1952 | 14,624 | 1959 | 22,123 |
| 1953 | 13,140 | 1960 | 26,894 |

*Juvenile Delinquents Sentenced in Great Britain*[7]

| | | | | | |
|---|---|---|---|---|---|
| 1938 | 55,511 | 1948 | 71,998 | 1953 | 63,770 |
| 1944 | 68,069 | 1949 | 65,660 | 1954 | 59,991 |
| 1945 | 73,620 | 1950 | 69,591 | 1955 | 48,594 |
| 1946 | 62,355 | 1951 | 75,857 | 1957 | 64,128 |
| 1947 | 58,243 | 1952 | 72,834 | | |

*Juvenile Delinquents Sentenced in Austria*[8]

| | | | |
|---|---|---|---|
| 1937 | 6,384 | 1950 | 5,695 |
| 1946 | 4,834 | 1951 | 5,856 |
| 1947 | 5,688 | 1952 | 5,696 |
| 1948 | 7,645 | 1953 | 6,324 |
| 1949 | 6,161 | 1954 | 6,584 |

*Juvenile Delinquents Sentenced in Sweden*[9]

| | | | |
|---|---|---|---|
| 1946 | 1,955 | 1952 | 2,231 |
| 1947 | 2,310 | 1953 | 2,209 |
| 1948 | 1,672 | 1954 | 2,144 |
| 1949 | 1,858 | 1955 | 2,232 |
| 1950 | 1,942 | 1956 | 2,636 |
| 1951 | 2,267 | | |

*Juvenile Delinquents Sentenced in West Germany*[10]

| | | | | |
|---|---|---|---|---|
| 1951 | 30,495 | | 1955 | 33,882 |
| 1952 | 30,000 | | 1956 | 37,183 |
| 1953 | 28,317 | | 1957 | 42,434 |
| 1954 | 29,219 | | | |

*Convicted Juvenile Offenders in East Germany*[11]

| | | | |
|---|---|---|---|
| 1951 | 4,346 | 1961 | 8,532 |

*Convicted Juvenile Offenders in Yugoslavia*[12]

| | | | |
|---|---|---|---|
| 1950 | 1,819 | 1954 | 3,687 |
| 1952 | 2,335 | 1955 | 4,401 |
| 1953 | 3,710 | 1956 | 4,414 |

*Juvenile Offenders Prosecuted in Finland*[13]

| | | | |
|---|---|---|---|
| 1951 | 11,992 | 1954 | 16,033 |
| 1952 | 12,619 | 1955 | 16,445 |
| 1953 | 15,040 | 1956 | 18,926 |

*Juvenile Offenders Convicted in Belgium*[14]

| | | | | | |
|---|---|---|---|---|---|
| 1946 | 4,751 | 1950 | 2,572 | 1954 | 2,379 |
| 1947 | 3,537 | 1951 | 2,370 | 1955 | 2,060 |
| 1948 | 3,408 | 1952 | 2,499 | 1956 | 2,510 |
| 1949 | 2,605 | 1953 | 2,172 | 1957 | 2,119 |

*Switzerland*[15]

There is not yet a criminal statistic for juvenile offenders for the entire country, but some studies indicate that in the most populous cantons no increase in juvenile delinquency has occurred when one takes into consideration the respective growth of the total population and the increase in foreign migratory workers.

These examples indicate that more countries in Europe have an increase in the number of juvenile offenders convicted for punishable activites than have a decrease, but that in some countries, there has been a decrease.

*Juvenile Offenders Sentenced by Family Courts in Japan*[16]

| | | | | | |
|---|---|---|---|---|---|
| 1949 | 59,779 | 1952 | 105,534 | 1955 | 107,347 |
| 1950 | 70,146 | 1953 | 101,815 | 1956 | 110,916 |
| 1951 | 116,232 | 1954 | 105,534 | 1957 | 123,948 |

*Serious Offenses Sentenced by the Family Court of Osaka*

| | | | |
|---|---|---|---|
| 1960 | 8,017 | 1963 | 7,093 |
| 1961 | 7,838 | 1964 | 7,217 |
| 1962 | 7,206 | | |

In rural regions of Israel the stealing of fruit by juveniles, frequently the children of new immigrants, has been reported as a new type of offense.[17] In Greece the stealing of motorcycles and cars for temporary use has been done on such a large scale that a special law was enacted in 1957 ordering up to one year of prison for this offense.[18]

Juvenile delinquency and adult crime in industrialized and developing countries are so high and threatening that it seems necessary to plan strategies for the prevention and control of delinquency and crime on an international level and to arrange for mutual assistance based on international treaties in extraditing criminals who have sought refuge in other countries. In such treaties the particular conditions of each nation need to be considered.[19] Because of conditions of technological and economic change in most countries, flexible policies need to be set up so that provisions of mutual cooperation for prevention and control of delinquency and crime do not become obsolete before they are fully implemented.

### Correctional Institutions in Europe

In continental Europe correctional institutions are administered by the states or federal governments, not by counties and cities, and by civil servants with legal training who maintain only limited contact with juvenile delinquents. Seldom are custodial or probation officers promoted to administrative positions within the correctional system. In England personnel for prisons, borstals, and approved schools are recruited for this task and receive specialized training. There is much interaction between staff and inmates, and progressive methods are used in classification and counseling. Often the British probation service is used as a model. In France and Italy probation means leniency combined with surveillance. In Europe most probation officers also serve in parole and aftercare, and have been trained as social workers, but in France there are two different types of probation workers: the *agent de probation* exercises surveillance, whereas the *assistante sociale* serves as social worker and counselor. Both functions are supervised by a magistrate of the juvenile or penal court.

Advanced systems of corrections exist in the Netherlands and Denmark. There has been integration into social and economic planning, but little "intervention practice." In most European countries the correctional program is not change oriented. The administration of corrections is entrusted to bureaucracies with powerful juridical support. But the influence of psychology and psychiatry is growing slowly, and probation services accept research into their results. Schizophrenic and brain-injured offenders are excluded from correctional treatment. At the Van

Howen Clinic in Amsterdam and the Herstedvester Institution in Copenhagen modern methods of psychotherapy and probation services are
applied to offenders sentenced to long-term confinement. In Sweden
probation services are carried out by volunteers who are supervised by
professional consultants. In the Netherlands six private agencies with
public subsidies provide probation services.

In Germany probation services are complicated because they are
based on federal laws, but state and local agencies administer probation
performance. In Denmark the child welfare system administers social
services for families and children, youth clubs for adolescents, and obser-
vation centers for diagnosis and therapy plans. Residential treatment
facilities are under lay child welfare boards. Parents may appeal decisions
to the National Child-welfare Authority or to the courts.

In the USSR juvenile courts and special treatment of juvenile
offenders were abandoned in 1921 by the transfer of such cases to the
penal courts. Juvenile offenders are assigned to correctional institutions,
labor colonies, and military wards, mainly by "people's patrols" and
"comrades' courts."[20]

### Juvenile Delinquency

Juvenile gangs present a special problem. It is a group delinquency
committed by children and adolescents, sometimes under adult leadership, who join casual, informal street corner groups or closely knit delinquent bands. In England they are known as Teddy Boys, in Italy as
*vitelloni,* in Germany as *Halb-Starke,* in the Soviet Union and Poland as
hooligans, in Japan as Mambo boys and girls, in South Africa as *tsotsio,*
in Australia and New Zealand as bodgies and widgies, in France as *blousons
noires,* and in the United States as street gangs. Many violent disturbances
occur after rock-and-roll festivals and concerts, leading to serious riots
and sometimes homicides.[21] Riots after such concerts offer opportunities
to many youngsters to indulge their longings for kicks, violence, excitement, and brawls, rather than for really criminal action.

In contrast to these fairly harmless groups of juveniles are the youth
gangs, groups of youngsters who have joined with the understanding that
they are willing to commit serious criminal offenses. A well-known example of this is the hooligan gangs in Russia during the 1920s. These gangs
threatened not only peasants in villages but even police and army units.
They committed arson and murders and were finally subdued only
through large military actions.

In Russia the entire system of correctional services is based upon
the Pavlovian theory that environmental influences are the causes of

deviance and crimes. Individual treatment and rehabilitation were neglected, and the results have not been satisfactory.[22] The deterrent com-
ponents of hard labor in Siberian prison camps and extremely long
sentences have not induced prisoners to become decent, law-abiding
citizens. However, at a 1971 symposium on juvenile delinquency in
Prague, Russian delegate G. M. Minkowski mentioned that Russia has
introduced socioeducative and preventive methods for dealing with delinquent youngsters through social welfare organizations and municipal
agencies, and courses to prevent juvenile delinquency.[23] In Czechoslovakia the Institute of Criminology is employing research methods on
crime prevention and new methods of treating young delinquents.[24]

In Portugal the problem of limiting the competence of juvenile
courts to civil proceedings was recently discussed. The Portuguese Civil
Code of 1967 expanded the jurisdiction of the juvenile courts, but there
were problems which were solved through the introduction of special
family courts in 1971.[25]

Yugoslavia has only two correctional schools for juvenile delinquents, where young offenders may be kept until they reach the age of
23. One of them is an institution for girls in Croatia. It is administered
by the girls themselves, with open school attendance and apprenticeships
in town, and with leisure time and recreational activities in the school.[26]

In Germany the so-called *Rocker-Gruppen* developed from riot
groups after rock-and-roll festivals in several German cities; they are
juvenile gangs that terrorize the public, assault their victims, commit
armed robbery and extortion, rape young girls, and rob older persons.[27]
The number of criminal acts committed by youth gangs in mainland
China during the cultural revolution is not known, but serious crimes by
such gangs are reported from numerous countries, among them Sweden,
Norway, Finland, England, the United States, Ireland, Argentina, Uruguay, and Australia. Gang activities often lead to vandalism and sexual
crimes. Alcoholic excesses are responsible for juvenile crimes in numerous countries, including those in Africa and Latin America, and stimulate
the gang members to vandalism and to sexual attacks.[28]

In Israel juvenile gangs are either Arab guerillas or Jewish immigrants from Africa, Yemen, or Asia. Their total number is moderate.

### Prevention and Rehabilitation

In view of the increasing number of adult and juvenile crimes in
most parts of the world, there exists the need for concerted international
preventive and rehabilitative measures to stem this tide. The problem of

crime cannot be evaluated solely on the basis of its material damage, but needs to be seen in connection with the broader societal consequences for the entire world. Preventive strategies have to include measures for raising the general standards of living and education, for improving health and social services, and for creating work opportunities under governmental and private auspices.[29]

One important aspect of preventive measures is the need for broader application of probation and parole services than those that now operate in most countries. Most such services still suffer from insufficient funding and from a lack of well-trained personnel to rehabilitate offenders and prevent recidivism. An interesting suggestion for improving probation services came from Switzerland.[30] This plan consists of introducing the comprehensive, continuous social service of a probation officer immediately after arrest so that an offender and his family will have an understanding, sympathetic counselor who would visit the arrested offender in the investigating stage in detention and prison, would contact and advise the family, and generally create an atmosphere of trust still missing among the vast majority of persons apprehended in connection with delinquent or criminal procedures. Such service would create far better conditions for the rehabilitation of the offender and support for the family, wife, and children. The present system generates hostility toward society and so increases the danger of recidivism.

A more effective system of prevention of delinquency and crime requires better cooperation among all nations in the field of a "unified social defense policy." This would involve development of particular methods to meet the needs of special groups such as juvenile delinquents, drug abusers, and homosexuals in the light of the cultural, social, and religious conditions of the various countries. For the establishment and administration of such programs, university training centers operating in cooperation with departments of criminology seem desirable. Such centers might be able to develop research studies to investigate the most effective means of achieving such preventive measures as recruitment and training of personnel. The United Nations and its specialized agencies can help where sufficient personal and economic resources are unavailable.[31]

In Germany an interesting experiment in assistance to prisoners released after serving their sentence is conducted. "Contact advisors" are employed by the Federal Labor Office to work in the penal institutions in close cooperation with the courts, probation officers, and outside employers to find jobs for released prisoners, according to their capacities, before they leave the penal institution. This prepares prisoners for life after release. But beyond assistance such as loans for travel, clothing, and equipment, it remains necessary to change the attitude of the population toward exprisoners, in order to break the vicious circle of crime-prison-recidivism.[32]

### International Aspects

The rapid increase of crime and delinquency in both the industrial and the developing countries motivated the UN secretary-general in 1971 to request that United Nations work in the field of social defense be greatly expanded to include technical assistance programs and a conference of ministers of justice in 1973. Before the Commission for Social Development the secretary-general emphasized that there must be "comprehensive action conceived at the highest level," and a follow-up of the proposals made in 1970 at the International Congress on the Prevention of Crime and the Treatment of Offenders in Kyoto, Japan. This congress (10,000 delegates from 85 countries) unanimously declared that it was urgently necessary that all governments coordinate and intensify their crime prevention efforts in cooperation with other international organizations.[33]

Some crime is caused by rising expectations among the young generation in the developing countries, but there are also new transnational crimes, such as aerial hijacking, kidnapping of diplomats and political prisoners, and drug abuse. These crimes occur in the developed and in the developing nations. For instance, in the Development Plan of Kenya for 1964–70 there is the statement that the maintenance of law and order is the very first task of government for the promotion of economic and social development.[34]

Expenses for the social and economic control and prevention of crime are growing heavier. In France and the United States in recent years it has grown at a rate of more than 5 percent of the gross national product annually. To prevent social breakdown and crime under conditions of rapid social and economic change, it is not sufficient to enlarge the police force; instead, a new comprehensive policy needs to be developed in the community, and preventive measures must be given priority. In Africa it is noted that economic and social progress in all countries is accompanied by an increase in crime, while in Asia there is doubt whether health and education really lead to reduced crime. Delegates of the Arab states declared that economic development often causes disintegration of the extended family, work of women, the weakening of the family control, and considerable unemployment in the cities, because rural migrants cannot find jobs.

Asian countries attempt to prevent the disintegration of family and communities through industrialization and commercialization by better education and youth protective measures, with properly staffed schools promoting constructive behavior and wholesome social and economic development. Latin American countries have special problems: violent demonstrations of youth groups (frequently university students) with political objectives, "white-collar crimes," such as fraud and corruption, and "upper-class delinquency" by persons of economic power who desire higher gain. There is a need for new legislation to punish such crimes.

At the Kyoto Conference there was a unanimous recognition of the value of the United Nations Research Institute for Social Defense in Rome and of the UN Institute for Crime Prevention in Japan, and there was a proposal to put a similar institute in Latin America. The UN Commission for Social Development is establishing closer relationships with the Commission on Narcotic Drugs and the Commission on Human Rights to create a more effective worldwide program of crime and delinquency prevention.

In Europe the seventeen countries belonging to the Council of Europe, represented by the directors of their prison services, agreed in 1972 to establish common rules for the treatment of prisoners, based on the United Nations standards for the treatment of prisoners adopted by the United Nations General Assembly in 1955. The rules emphasize the principle that the deprivation of liberty shall be effected in material and moral conditions which shall ensure respect for human dignity. The objective is to prevent a complete break between the prisoner and his family or friends and so facilitate the transition from prison to community after the prisoner serves his sentence. These rules were approved in 1972 by the European Committee on Crime Problems.[35]

In an important area of international law, the United States has shown an amazing lack of consistency. The U.S. was the prime mover of the unanimous United Nations decision (in 1946) that genocide is a crime under international law. This proposition has been ratified by 75 nations, but to date the United States has not yet ratified it, probably out of fear that this accusation might be raised in connection with internal racial strife.[36]

## Notes

[1]Marvin E. Wolfgang, "A Preface to Violence," *The Annals*, 364 (March 1966), 1–7; Lewis A. Coser, "Some Social Functions of Violence," ibid., pp. 8–18; Walter B. Miller, "Violent Crimes in City Gangs," ibid., pp. 96–112; Richard M. Brown, *American Violence* (Englewood Cliffs, N.J.: Prentice-Hall, 1970), pp. 163–66.

[2]United Nations, *1967 Report on the World Social Situation*, 46; "Social Defense Planning," *International Social Development Review*, No. 2 (1970), 24–27; L. N. Smirnov, *Third United Nations Congress on the Prevention of Crime and the Treatment of Offenders* (Stockholm, 1965).

[3]*The Challenge of Crime in a Free Society* (Washington, D.C.: U.S. Government Printing Office 1967), pp. 18–30; Don C. Gibbons, *Changing the Lawbreaker* (Englewood Cliffs, N.J.: Prentice-Hall, 1965), pp. 253–82.

[4]Gerhard Potrykus, "Kriminalstatistik 1968," *Unsere Jugend*, 21, No. 10 (Oct. 1969), 442ff; and "Kriminalstatistik 1969," ibid., 22, No. 10 (Oct. 1970), 464–69; Gerd Neiss, "Kinderkriminalität?" ibid., 22. No. 2 (Feb. 1970), 49–56.

[5]Wolf Middendorff, *Jugendkriminologie: Studien und Erfahrungen (Youth Criminology: Studies and Experiences)*, (Ratingen: A. Henn, 1956), pp. 23–33.

[6]Henri, Joubrel, *L'Enfance dite coupable* (Childhood Pronounced Guilty), (Paris: Editions Universitaires, 1946), pp. 9–10; *Rééducation*, Nos. 140–141 (May 1962); Walter Friedlander, *Individualism and Social Welfare* (New York: Free Press, 1962), p. 113.

[7]United Kingdom Home Department, *Penal Practice in Changing Society* (London, 1959), p. 1; Wolf Middendorff, *New Forms of Juvenile Delinquency* (New York: United Nations, 1960), pp. 9–10; Middendorff, *Jugendkriminologie*, p. 29.

[8]Middendorff, *Jugendkriminologie*, p. 29; Jalkotsky, *Verdorbene Jugend?* (Vienna, 1953).

[9]Swedish Department of Justice, *Postwar Juvenile Delinquency in Sweden* (Stockholm, 1958), pp. 5–8; *Social Work and Social Legislation in Sweden* (Stockholm: Royal Social Board, 1958), pp. 259–62.

[10]Middendorff, *New Forms of Juvenile Delinquency*, pp. 11–12.

[11]Ibid., p. 12.

[12]Ibid., p. 12.

[13]Ibid., p. 14.

[14]Ibid., p. 17.

[15]Herbert Schulthess, "Zunahme der Jugendkriminalität?" (Increase in Youth Crime) *Pro Juventute* (Zurich), 38, Nos. 2–3 (Feb.–March 1957), 39–42.

[16]Middendorff, *New Forms of Juvenile Delinquency*, p. 15; Tsukuno Hayashi, "Osaka Family Court," in Dorothy Dessau, ed., *Social Work in Japan* (Kyoto: Social Workers International Club of Japan, 1969), pp. 97–194.

[17]Middendorff, *New Forms of Juvenile Delinquency*, pp. 30–31; David Reifen, "Work of the Juvenile Court in Israel," *World Mental Health*, 14, No. 3 (Aug. 1962), 131–32.

[18]Middendorff, 29.

[19]United Nations, *1967 Report on the World Social Situation*, pp. 103–4; William E. Amos and Charles F. Wellford, *Delinquency Prevention* (Englewood Cliffs, N.J.: Prentice-Hall, 1967); John P. Conrad, "Trends in European Corrections," Mimeographed report to the President's Commission on Law Enforcement and Administration of Justice, 1967.

[20]Madison, *Social Welfare in the Soviet Union*, pp. 65–72, 172–76; George Fifer, *Justice in Moscow* (New York: Simon & Schuster, 1964); Glenn G. Morgan, *Soviet Administered Legality* (Stanford, Ca.: Stanford University Press, 1967); United Na-

tions, *Report of the United Nations Consultative Group on the Prevention of Crime and the Treatment of Offenders* (New York, 1969).

[21]Middendorff, *Jugendkriminologie*, pp. 37–59; Curt Bondy *et al.*, *Jugendliche stören die Ordnung* (Juveniles Disturb the Order), (Munich: Juventa Verlag, 1957); E. H. Sutherland and Donald R. Cressey, *Principles of Criminology*, 5th ed. (Chicago: Lippincott, 1955), pp. 163–65; Albert K. Cohen, *Delinquent Boys: The Culture of the Gang* (New York: Free Press, 1951); Richard A. Cloward and Lloyd E. Ohlin, *Delinquency and Opportunity: A Theory of Delinquent Gangs* (New York: Free Press, 1960); Albert K. Cohen, *Deviance and Control* (Englewood Cliffs, N.J.: Prentice-Hall, 1966), pp. 63–73; Marshall B. Clinard, ed., *Anomie and Deviant Behavior* (New York: Free Press, 1964); A. E. Manning, *The Bodgie: A Study in Psychological Abnormality* (Sydney, Australia: Angus & Roberson, 1958), pp. 7–9, 12–13; Henri Joubel, "Une Certaine Jeunesse," *Rééducation*, No. 100 (June 1958), pp. 21–27.

[22]Walter D. Connor, *Deviance in Soviet Society: Crime, Delinquency, and Alcoholism* (New York: Columbia University Press, 1972).

[23]Henryka Veillard-Cybulska, "News of the International Association of Youth Magistrates," *International Child Welfare Review*, 13 (Apr. 1972), 54–56.

[24]Ibid., p. 55.

[25]Ibid., pp. 55–56.

[26]Ibid., pp. 56–57.

[27]Arthur Kreuzer, "Rocker-Gruppen-Kriminalität," *Monatsschrift für Kriminologie und Strafrechtsreform*, 53 (Aug. 1970), 1–25; P. Scott, "Gangs and Delinquent Groups in London," *British Journal of Delinquency*, 1 (July 1956), 4–26; W. Rasch, "Gewaltunzucht und Notzucht durch Gruppen jugendlicher Täter" (Forcible Rape by Groups of Youths), *Kriminalstatistik 1968*, pp. 57ff; Jacques Chazal, *Études de criminologie juvenile* (Paris: Presses Universitaires, 1952), pp. 96–114; Madison, *Social Welfare in the Soviet Union*, pp. 65–69; Shankar S. Srivastava, "Sociology of Juvenile Ganging," *Journal of Correctional Work* (Lucknow, India) (Sep. 1955), 72ff.

[28]Middendorff, *New Forms of Juvenile Delinquency*, pp. 46–74; Henri Joubrel, *Mauvais garçons de bonnes familles* (Bad Boys from Good Families), (Paris: Montaigne, 1957); Joseph Eaton, *Prisons in Israel* (Pittsburgh: University of Pittsburgh Press, 1964), pp. 18–23.

[29]United Nations, "Social Defense Planning," *International Social Development Review*, No. 2, pp. 24–27; Arych Leissner, *Street Club Work in Tel Aviv and New York* (London: Longmans, Green, 1969).

[30]Werner Wiesendanger, "Einführung eines umfassenden Sozialdienstes in der Strafrechtspflege" (Introduction of a Comprehensive Social Service in Criminal Justice), *Schweizerische Zeitschrift für Gemeinnützigkeit*, 110, No. 3 (March 1971), 29–37; Gibbons, *Changing the Lawbreaker* pp. 189–196; Friedlander, *Introduction to Social Welfare*, pp. 460–67; John Irwin, *The Felon* (Englewood Cliffs, N.J.: Prentice-Hall, 1970), pp. 149–200.

[31]United Nations, *1967 Report on the World Social Situation*, pp. 105–6; Malcolm W. Klein, *Juvenile Gangs in Context: Theory, Research, and Action* (Englewood Cliffs, N.J.: Prentice-Hall, 1967), pp. 1–12; Duane W. Beck, "Changing Concepts of Social Work Treatment and Prevention of Problems on a Community Level," in John S. Morgan, ed., *Changing Services for Changing Clients* (New York: National

**194**    *Violence, delinquency, and crime*

Association of Social Workers, 1969), pp. 37–54; George A. Brager, "Advocacy and Political Behavior," ibid., pp. 101–21; Jean Heuyer, "Delinquance juvénile et l'alcoolisme," (Juvenile Delinquency and Alcoholism), *Rééducation*, no. 53 (1954); Dawson, "Les Child Guidance Clinics en Australie," ibid.; Henri Chazal, *L'Enfance vagabonde* (Paris: UNESCO, 1950); Aubin, "La Délinquance juvénile outre-mer," *Rééducation*, No. 69 (1955).

[32]Dirk Schuber, "The Resocialization of Prisoners," *Inter Nations* (Bonn), (Feb. 1973), pp. 1–3.

[33]James A. Joyce, "Global Crime Wave," *Vista*, 7, No. 3 (Nov.–Dec. 1971), 19–20; 49–57.

[34]Ibid., p. 19.

[35]*National Council on Crime and Delinquency News*, 51, No. 2 (March–April 1972), 4.

[36]Abraham S. Blumberg, "Law, Order, and the Working Class," *Society*, 10, No. 1 (Nov.–Dec. 1972), 83–84.

## Selected References

*Books*

ALBINI, JOSEPH L., *The American Mafia*. New York: Appleton-Century-Crofts, 1971.

BAGDIKIAN, BEN, AND LEON DASH, *The Shame of the Prisons*. New York: Pocket Books, 1972.

BECKER, HOWARD S., *Outsiders: Study of the Sociology of Deviance*. New York: Free Press, 1963.

BELL, JOSEPHINE, *Crime in Our Time*. New York: A. Sherman, 1962.

BERNHEIM, JACQUES, *Introductory General Report of Eighth Congress of the International Association of Youth Magistrates*, Geneva, 1970.

BOHANNON, P., *African Homicide and Suicide*. Princeton, N.J.: Princeton University Press, 1960.

BROWN, RICHARD M., *American Violence*. Englewood Cliffs, N.J.: Prentice-Hall, 1970.

BULTENA, LOUIS, *Deviant Behavior in Sweden*. New York: Exposition Press, 1971.

BUSCH, MAX, AND GOTTFRIED EDEL, *Erziehung zur Freiheit durch Freiheitsentzug: Internationale Probleme des Strafvollzugs an jungen Menschen* (Education to Freedom Through Incarceration: International Problems of Infliction of Punishment of Young Persons). Neuwied: Luchterhand, 1969.

CAWAN, RUTH S., AND JORDAN T. CAWAN, *Delinquency and Crime: Cross-Cultural Perspectives*. Philadelphia: Lippincott, 1967.

CLINARD, MARSHALL B., AND DAVID J. ABBOTT, *Crime in Developing Countries*. New York: Wiley-Interscience, 1973.

COHEN, ALBERT K., *Deviance and Control*. Englewood Cliffs, N.J.: Prentice-Hall, 1966.

CONNOR, WALTER D., *Deviance in Soviet Society: Crime, Delinquency, and Alcoholism*. New York: Columbia University Press, 1972.

DRESSLER, DAVID, ed., *Readings in Criminology and Penology*, 2nd ed. New York: Columbia University Press, 1972.

ELDEFONSO, EDWARD, *Youth Problems and Law Enforcement.* Englewood Cliffs, N.J.: Prentice-Hall, 1972.

ELDEFONSO, EDWARD, ALAN COFFEY, AND JAMES SULLIVAN, *Police and the Criminal Law.* Pacific Palisades, Ca.: Goodyear, 1972.

FRANKENSTEIN, CARL, *Psychodynamics of Externalization.* Baltimore: Williams & Wilkins, 1968.

FRANKS, C. ed., *Assessment and Status of the Behavior Therapists and Associated Developments.* New York: McGraw-Hill, 1968.

GEIS, GILBERT, *Not the Law's Business? An Examination of Homosexuality, Abortion, Prostitution, Narcotics and Gambling in the United States.* Rockville, Md.: Center for the Studies of Crime and Delinquency, 1972.

GIALLOMBARDO, ROSE, *The Social World of Imprisoned Girls.* New York: Wiley, 1974.

GIBBONS, DON C., *Changing the Lawbreaker: The Treatment of Delinquents and Criminals.* Englewood Cliffs, N.J.: Prentice-Hall, 1965.

GLASER, DANIEL, *The Effectiveness of a Prison and Parole System.* Indianapolis: Bobbs, Merrill, 1969.

HENRIQUES, FERNANDO, *Stews and Strumpets: A Survey of Prostitution.* London: MacGibbon, 1961.

HOPPER, COLUMBUS B., *Sex in Prison: The Mississippi Experiment with Conjugal Visiting.* Baton Rouge: Louisiana State University Press, 1969.

JOHNSON, N., L. SAVITZ, AND M. E. WOLFGANG, eds., *The Sociology of Punishment and Correction,* 2nd ed. New York: Wiley, 1970.

JONES, HOWARD, *Crime in a Changing Society.* Baltimore: Penguin, 1969.

_____, *Criminology in Transition.* London: Tavistock, 1965.

KLEIN, MALCOLM W., AND BARBARA G. MYERHOF, *Juvenile Gangs in Context: Theory, Research, and Action.* Englewood Cliffs, N.J.: Prentice-Hall, 1967.

LEMERT, EDWIN M., *Social Action and Legal Change: Revolution Within the Juvenile Court.* Chicago: Aldine, 1970.

LEONARD, P., *Sociology in Social Work.* London: Routledge & Kegan Paul, 1966.

LUSSNER, ARYSH, *Street Club Work in Tel-Aviv and New York.* New York: Humanities Press, 1969.

MATZA, D., *Deviance and Drift.* New York: Wiley, 1964.

MIDDENDORFF, WOLF, *Jugendkriminologie: Studien und Erfahrungen* (Criminology of Youth: Studies and Experiences). Ratingen: A. Henn, 1958.

MONGER, MARC, *Casework in Probation.* London: Butterworth, 1972.

MUELLER, GERHARD O. W., *Crime, Law and Scholars.* London: Heinemann, 1969.

PHILLIPSON, MICHAEL, *Understanding Crime and Delinquency: A Sociological Introduction.* Chicago: Aldine, 1974.

PLAYFICER, GELES, AND DERRICK SINGTON, *Crime, Punishment and Cure.* London: Secker & Warburg, 1965.

POLK, KENNETH, AND WALTER E. SCHAFER, *Schools and Delinquency.* Englewood Cliffs, N.J.: Prentice-Hall, 1972.

RECKLESS, WALTER C., *The Crime Problem,* 3rd ed. New York: Appleton-Century-Crofts, 1961.

ROBERT, PHILIPPE, *Treatise on Law for Minors.* Paris: Cujar, 1969.

ROSENQUIST, CARL M., AND EDWIN I. MEGARGEE, *Delinquency in Three Cultures.* Austin: University of Texas Press, 1969.

RUMBELOW, DONALD, *I Spy Blue: The Police and Crime in the City of London From Elizabeth I to Victoria.* New York: Macmillan, 1971.

RUSCHE, GEORGE, AND OTTO KIRCHHEIMER, *Punishment and Social Structure.* New York: Columbia University Press, 1939.

SCHUR, EDWIN M., *Crimes Without Victims: Deviant Behavior and Public Policy.* Englewood Cliffs, N.J.: Prentice-Hall, 1965.

————, *Our Criminal Society: The Social and Legal Sources of Crime in America.* Englewood Cliffs, N.J.: Prentice-Hall, 1969.

SHIELDS, ROBERT W., *A Cure for Delinquents: The Treatment of Maladjustment,* 2nd ed. London: Heineman, 1971.

SIEVERTS, RUDOLPH, *Handbuch der Kriminologie* (Handbook of Criminology). Berlin: De Gruytor, 1967–69.

SOLAUN, MAURICIO, AND SIDNEY KRONUS, *Discrimination Without Violence: Miscegenation and Racial Conflict in Latin America.* New York: Wiley, 1973.

TEETERS, NEGLEY K., AND JOHN O. REINEMANN, *The Challenge of Delinquency.* Englewood Cliffs, N.J.: Prentice-Hall, 1950.

THOMAS, J. E., *The English Prison Officer Since 1850.* London: Routledge & Kegan Paul, 1972.

TULLETT, TOM, *Inside Dartmoor.* London: Muller, 1966.

UNITED NATIONS, *Rapporteur's Summary, Third Congress on the Prevention of Crime and the Treatment of Offenders* (Stockholm), Washington, D.C.: U.S. Bureau of Prisons, 1965.

VEDELER, GERDT H., *Residual Treatment of Delinquent Girls.* Oslo, Norway: Nordsik Psykologi (1969), No. 6.

WALKER, NIGEL, AND SARAH MCCABE, *Crime and Insanity in England: New Solutions and Problems.* Chicago: Aldine, 1973.

WARREN, MARGUERITE Q., *Correctional Treatment in Community Settings.* Rockville, Md.: National Institute of Mental Health, 1972.

WEBB, STEPHEN, AND JOHN COLETTE, *New Zealand Society: Contemporary Perspectives.* New York: Wiley, 1973.

YOUNGHUSBAND, EILEEN, *Social Work and Social Change.* London: Allen & Unwin, 1964.

ZIMRING, FRANKLIN E., *Perspectives on Deterrence.* Washington D.C.: National Institute for Mental Health, 1971.

ZIMRING, FRANKLIN E., AND GORDON J. HAWKINS. *Deterrence: The Legal Threat in Crime Control.* Chicago: University of Chicago Press, 1973.

*Articles*

BAYER, C. A., AND M. J. BRODSKY, "Prison Programming and Psychological Considerations," *Canadian Journal of Criminology and Corrections,* 14 (Apr. 1972), 325–34.

BRADSHAW, J., D. EMERSON, AND D. HAXLEY. "Reception to Prison," *British Journal of Social Work,* 2 (March 1972), 323–35.

COOPER, H. H. A., "Crime, Criminals and Prisons in Peru," *International Journal of Offender Therapy,* 15 (1971), 148–59.

_____ "Toward a Rational Doctrine of Rehabilitation," *Crime and Delinquency*, 19 (Apr. 1973), 228–40.

DOOTJES, INEZ, et al., "Defense Council in Juvenile Court," *Canadian Journal of Criminology and Corrections*, 14 (Feb. 1972), 122–46.

DAVIES, M., "The Objectives of the Probation Service," *British Journal of Social Work*, 2 (March 1972), 313–22.

EATON, JOSEPH. "A Cross-Cultural View on Youth," *Center for Youth Development and Research Quarterly*, 3, No. 2 (1974), 1–7.

FOSTER, JACK D., SIMON DINITZ, AND WALTER RECKLESS, "Perceptions of Stigma Following Public Intervention for Delinquent Behavior," *Social Problems*, 20 (Fall 1972), 202–9.

GUINDON, JEANNINE, "Centres de reéducations" (Reeducation Centers), *Revue des services de bien-etre à l'enfance* (Quebec, Canada), 11, No. 4, 118–26.

HANNEMANN, HARTMUT, "Jugendstrafvollzug im Ausland" (Youth Sentence Execution in Foreign Countries), *Neues Beginnen*, 21 (Dec. 1970), 215–23.

KELSEN, HANS, "The Pure Theory of Law: Its Methods and Fundamental Concepts," *Law Quarterly Review*, 50 (Oct. 1934), 474–535.

KONOPKA, GISELA, "Reform in Delinquency Institutions in Revolutionary Times," *Social Service Review*, 15 (Sep. 1971), 245–58.

KUTCHINSKY, BERL, "The Effect of Easily Available Pornography on Sex Crime," *Journal of Social Issues*, 29 (Mar. 1973), 163–81.

LUGER, MILTON, "Innovations in the Treatment of Juvenile Offenders," *The Annals of the American Academy of Political and Social Science*, 381 (Jan. 1969), 60–70.

MACCORMIK, AUSTIN, "The Prison's Role in Crime Prevention," *Journal of Criminal and Criminology* (May-June 1950), pp. 45–67.

MAKING, M., "A Psychological Study on 'Naikan Method' in Prison," *Japanese Journal of Criminal Psychology*, 5, 1968.

MILLER, W., "Lower Class Cultures as a Generating Milieu of Gang Delinquency," *Journal of Social Issues*, 14 (Jan. 1958), 5–19.

ROESTEL, GUNTHER, "Kann das Jugendgerichtsverfahren zugleich beschleunigt und erzieherisch wirksam gestaltet werden?" (Is It Possible to Speed Up the Procedure of the Juvenile Court and at the Same Time to Make It Educationally More Effective?), *Zentralblatt für Jugendrecht und Jugendwohlfahrt*, 60 (Feb. 1973), 77–82.

SANDHER, H. S., AND D. E. ALLEN, "The Prison Guard: Job Perspectives and In-Service Training in India," *Indian Journal of Social Work*, 32 (1971), 115–20.

SCHÜLER-SPRINGORUM, HORST, "50 Jahre Jugendherichtsbarkeit" (Fifty Years of Juvenile Court Jurisdiction), *Zentral-Blatt für Jugendrecht und Jugendwohlfahrt*, 60 (Feb. 1973), 41–53.

SHESKOLSKY, LEON, "The Legal Institution—The Legitimizing Appendage," pp. 294–337 in Larry T. Reynolds and James M. Henslin, eds., *American Society: A Critical Analysis*. New York: McKay, 1973.

SIMONSOHN, BERT, "Der Beitrag der Psychoanalyse zum Problem der Jugendkriminalität und des Jugendstrafrechts" (The Contribution of Psychoanalysis Toward the Problem of Criminality of Youth and Criminal Law for Juveniles), *Zentralblatt für Jugendrecht und Jugenwohlfahrt*, 60 (Feb. 1973), 65–72.

THOMAS, CHARLES W., AND SAMUEL C. FOSTER, "Prisonization in the Inmate Contraculture," *Social Problems*, 20 (Fall 1972), 229–39.

UNITED NATIONS, "Prostitution in Selected Countries of Asia and the Far East," *International Review of Criminal Policy*, 18 (Oct. 1968) 48–57.

VERSELE, S. C. AND J. SOMERS-DESMANEK, "Failure and Success in Probation" *Service Social* (Brussels), 48 (March 1970), 97–134.

WERNER, ROBERT, "Mitverwaltung als Erziehungsmittel" (Participation in Administration of Correctional Schools as Medium for Education), *Zentralblatt für Jugendrecht und Jugendwohlfahrt*, 60 (Feb. 1973), 82–103.

ZUMBACH, PIERRE, "L'enfance et la crime" (Childhood and Crime), *Revue internationale de criminologie et de police technique* (Geneva), 25 (1971–72), 1–18.

# Education for social work

## II

In contrast to mathematics and physics, education for social work differs according to the political, social, economic, and cultural conditions and to the value systems in the different countries. In spite of these differences, many nations face similar problems in the training of social workers for various kinds of social welfare services and may profit from exchanges of experiences and methodological results in other countries. In the United Nations the Social and Economic Council, the Educational, Scientific, and Cultural Organization (UNESCO), and the United Nations Children's Fund (UNICEF) have taken a particular interest in the problems of education for social work. But several private organizations, such as the International Association of Schools of Social Work, the International Council on Social Welfare, and the International Federation of Social Workers, have contributed to the training of social workers in numerous countries through courses, seminars, conferences, and publications.[1]

Social work is still a very young profession. Educational facilities were only established in the United States and Europe at the beginning of this century (first in the Netherlands), then in South America, and Australia, but they are only now developing in Asia and Africa. Social work is recognized in most countries as a "helping process" for individuals, families, groups, and communities, as a "social function" and as an "enabling process" through which individuals and communities can develop self-help activities and use available resources to their advantage.[2]

Recognition of the vital importance of unsolved social problems in foreign countries has induced schools of social work in several countries, particularly in the United States, Great Britain, Canada, France, Switzerland, Sweden, Germany, and Italy, to include the study of international problems for social work in their programs and to invite foreign scholars to join their faculties and foreign students to participate in their studies.

This trend has been vitally supported by the activities of the International Association of Schools of Social Work, the international Council on Social Welfare and the International Federation of Social Workers in cooperation with the central national organizations of social workers in participating countries such as India, Lebanon, Turkey, Israel, and some African nations.[3]

Titmuss has stated that the rich countries should feel obliged to train their own countrymen and women for the helping professions—physicians, nurses, and social workers—to enable them to serve in the poor countries, but that they should not lure scientists, doctors, nurses, and social workers from the poor countries to the industrial nations because that will deprive them of badly needed professional skills.[4]

### Training in Advanced Countries

In the United States and Britain almost all the training of professional social workers is conducted through the universities, in schools of social work or of social welfare, or sometimes in departments of social science or sociology. Most nations in South America, Asia, and Africa have followed this example. In western Europe, Spain, Portugal, Italy, Greece, and most countries of the Middle East special academies or schools of social work assume the training of social workers. There is, however, a trend in West Germany and some other countries to educate social workers in new specialized faculties in the universities.

Since social work is neither a pure science nor a technique but a profession and an art, the education of social workers has to include the preparation for a professional service with the aim of helping people as individuals, groups, or communities, to overcome difficulties and to solve their social problems. The social worker is foremost a "helping person" and should be prepared for this function, which requires knowledge of many disciplines—psychology, economics, anthropology, biology, sociology, medicine, psychiatry, political science, law, education, and philosophy, but also sensitivity for human behavior and feelings.[6]

In the Netherlands the first European schools of social work were established in the 1890s. In 1960 they were transformed into "social academies" by the addition of further disciplines to professional social work education. Their content consisted of social work education, cultural sciences, personnel management, and special educational techniques. One social academy introduced community organization as a specific field. The social academies apply United States methods of "action training" and Canadian principles in teaching "social change."[7]

### The Role of Values

Within various cultures among the nations there are different value systems. These have to be considered in social work; therefore they have to be considered in education for social work. Some cultural differences have already been mentioned in the preceding chapters. For instance, in India, the caste system, although legally abandoned owing to the teaching of Mahatma Gandhi, still influences the lives of the people. Even when a social worker does not share the prevailing caste feeling, he or she is obliged to consider the feelings of the people and has to apply his or her own egalitarian value concepts with delicacy in order not to alienate anyone and at the same time to help the so-called scheduled classes to find more just treatment in social and employment questions, and thus to overcome class differences and discrimination.[8]

Some social work goals in Western societies, such as "adjustment" or income maintenance, are strongly resented in countries like India and Japan. Value systems in different cultures often are related more to economic and political conditions than to religious and ethical principles, and are changing either to unitarian or to pluralistic points of view. But in all cultures respect for the dignity and integrity of man is recognized as the very core of social work goals. These values need to be emphasized in social work education, especially in cultures where the society does not embrace this value system and therefore is in need of social and psychological change. For a long time the major method of social work in the United States was "social casework," influenced by Freud's psychoanalysis, so this method was emphasized in social work education in most universities. In recent years, however, social group work and community organization have achieved equal importance as methods, and the latest development, an integrated "generic social work method," is considered a desirable preparation for social work practice. It also includes "social action" and "advocacy," either in the framework of community organization or as a new type, because the worker represents the interests of the client, even when they are contrary to the interests of the social agency or government that employs the worker. Social policy and community change have become major goals of social work, replacing the emphasis on individual or group therapy. At present education for social work in the United States stresses the application of democratic attitudes and helping processes for individuals, groups, communities, and society at large, thus emphasizing social policy, change, reform, and action. Stein[9] distinguishes between social work education and social work training. Social work education, he says, provides a professional knowledge that includes the basic philosophy of social work; democratic attitudes; goals of helping individuals, groups, and communities; and emphasis on the rights of clients to determine their own destinies, whereas social work training is concerned merely with the techniques and skills for specific jobs in the field of social welfare. Stein says that social work students need both types, the theoretical and practical knowledge of their profession and the specific skills for their job.

Many of these elements will be valid on an international basis, but the cultural systems of many developing countries reject the Western structure of family life and retain the extended family as the main background for social security and personal life patterns. Nor is there often the egalitarian relationship between husband and wife. Western social workers cannot take this for granted; they have to consider tribal or local customs and functions. In the United States, western Europe, Australia, and New Zealand social work is mainly oriented toward urban life, but in most developing countries the majority still lives in rural villages with different customs and values, and social workers need to consider these.

Since social workers have to apply knowledge of the social sciences and psychology in their work, they need to know that the specific culture of any people—even its subcultures, such as those of a region or neighborhood—are essential to the behavior and attitudes of the people they help. These notions have been emphasized by the United Nations as essential for international social work and should be included in the education of social workers interested in work in foreign countries. It is important that social workers learn to use the inherent strength of their clients for achieving independence and mastery of their own affairs within the framework of their cultural setting, and the social worker has to encourage them to act in view of such a goal. The economic and social conditions in most countries of the world are changing rapidly, and social work is challenged to assume the flexible strength of families and kinships to overcome the difficulties and social problems that threaten its clients.

### Social Work in the Developing World

Education for social work was started by voluntary organizations, but by the end of the Second World War most schools of social work were supported by governmental resources.[10] In the developing countries there is still a lack of professionally trained workers, so what often happens is that those with university educations soon obtain higher administrative positions and gain little experience in direct service to people in need. Some students of social work find opportunities to study in an industrial country, which has a different culture and a higher standard of living, and when they return to their native country to teach or to assume administrative positions they have not experienced the economic and health conditions of the lower classes in their home country. Consequently, in some developing nations only a small number of trained social workers have genuine knowledge of the economic and health needs of the poorer people while many persons who have no professional training are employed in the social services and are often envious and hostile to persons who have been trained in foreign countries. Developing nations are in need of well-qualified social workers who are familiar with the cultures and social structures of various groups and communities, because such people can get their governments to introduce the best programs in social policy and social planning. To meet the needs of developing countries, social work education has to stress the skills of community development and social action toward productive social legislation and services which will benefit both industrial and developing nations.

Because of the scarcity of trained professional workers in different parts of the world, in numerous countries the personnel in charge of social services have been prepared by a short, superficial in-service training or they have no proper preparation of any kind for their jobs. This condition presents a serious threat to social services and to the population they serve.[11]

### *Education for Social Work in the United States*

In education for social work the functions of public welfare organization and of voluntary agencies need to be studied, because this relationship varies widely in different cultures and nations. In the United States public welfare agencies have only become more relevant than private philanthropies and organizations since the Depression. Therefore education for social work is now primarily oriented in education for public social services, including public health, mental health activities, social policy, and social action. The strict separation in methodology for casework, social group work, and community organization is giving way to an education for "generic social work," which includes training for all three methods, and for "community development," social action and advocacy in the interest of the clients rather than that of the employing public or private agency. Education for social work in the United States used to consist of obtaining a master's degree in social work (more recently of obtaining a doctoral degree), but now there are also less time-consuming undergraduate programs of from two to four years that lead to a baccalaureate degree in social work, either as preparation for graduate studies or for social work practice. These programs came into being after the National Association of Social Workers decided to admit as members social workers with a baccalaureate degree and two years of practical experience.[12] In Great Britain, India, the Latin American countries, France, Belgium, the Netherlands, Switzerland, Italy, Spain, and Greece religious and other voluntary agencies still play an important role in education for social work since these organizations maintain most of the schools of social work (these are often independent academies rather than parts of universities, but they are still entitled to grant social work degrees).[13] In Western countries education for social work emphasizes the importance of close cooperation of social workers with related professions—social planners, doctors, nurses, health officials, sociologists, lawyers, psychologists, ecologists, and political scientists.

The Soviet Union offers no special education for social work, though after 1935 some measures of training were introduced, and in 1961 the minister of social welfare acknowledged that it was necessary to raise the professional level of social welfare workers. Since most of them are untrained trade union activists (selected for their political attitudes), teachers, public health workers, nurses, kindergarten teachers, lawyers, or social insurance inspectors, it will be rather difficult to develop any generic positive social work education for such different groups.[14]

### Education in Chile

Education for social work in Latin America may be described by the example of Chile, which established the first and most prominent South American university in Santiago in 1842 and the first school of social work in 1925, as part of the faculty of law and political science. This school was established under public auspices in connection with the social security system in Chile mainly to educate medical social workers for public health centers under the auspices of the National Health Service. It was modeled after the schools of social service in France and Belgium that the founder of the Chilean system had visited.[15]

The faculty of the Chilean "schools of social service" consists of full-time professors (mostly women) and about the same number of part-time professors. Since there is no specialized academic preparation for teaching social work in Chile, the faculty is selected from successful practitioners of social work, many of whom have studied in foreign universities. The part-time faculty is made up of physicians, psychiatrists, attorneys, civil servants, and social scientists. Faculty members often supplement their training by auditing courses in other departments of the university or by studying abroad. Field supervisors employed by the university usually also teach classes and supervise students in public and private social agencies. Greenwood suggests that valuable experience might be derived from the curriculum and the methods of social work education for schools of social work in the United States.[16]

As we mentioned before, the Soviet Union does not feel the need for training social workers in the international sense, but it has established technical schools for the training of "social security" personnel, primarily lawyers (as "claims inspectors"), physicians for the disability insurance program, and people for accounting and bookkeeping. These "social security workers" receive no special training for their "social work activities," even though they have to maintain contact with the beneficiaries of benefits and are supposed to advise and counsel them, and even though many of them are factory workers selected by their unions without social or psychological knowledge.[17] Training courses last for three months, which cannot be compared with the education for social work in the Western and most developing countries with schools of social work or social welfare.

### Education in Developing Countries

In contrast to the Russian experience, most countries of the third world have established schools of social work and recognize social work as a profession.[18] In several developing countries, particularly in Asia and Africa, social problems are not seen as individual matters but are seen instead as grounded in the society itself. Such countries therefore emphasize education in general and training for social services in particular as basic needs for their culture. In education for social work under governmental auspices, more attention is given to administrative skills; humanitarian philosophy is not often considered important. Students in schools of social work in these countries encounter lack of understanding of their proper roles and responsibilities in their field work placements and some practices that are not consistent with their theoretical studies in school. Education for social work in developing countries requires a division of training into two groups: (1) education of teachers for schools of social work and of policy-makers and leading administrators (which requires advanced training, usually a master's degree at the university); and (2) training of regular professional social workers, perhaps under a two-year program with a bachelor's degree, which would also qualify them for social welfare planning and supervision of volunteers and auxiliary staff.[19]

In addition to educated professional social workers, countries like the United States, Canada, Great Britain, India, Uganda, and Sierra Leone now use paraprofessional auxiliary personnel, and more countries are planning to do so.[20] Voluntary organizations like the Peace Corps and the International Peace Corps Volunteers also play a certain role in social services and economic development in many parts of the world, particularly in staffing rural services in Africa, Asia, and South America, without professional social welfare training.

In 1968, at the first International Conference of Ministers Responsible for Social Welfare at the United Nations in New York, the International Association of Schools of Social Work suggested that governments assume the responsibility for training social workers adequately because a high percentage of them are employed in public services and because their services are of vital importance for the well-being of the entire population. Such public support might be in the form of government sponsorship of training programs, grants-in-aid to schools of social work, the establishment of standards for social work education, or creation of facilities for advanced training. Governments should even support schools of social work that are financed by voluntary contributions, to enable them to employ qualified faculty and teaching resources to guarantee well-trained social workers.[21]

Voluntary agencies remain highly important in the employment and training of social workers in all nations since they usually represent the clients of social services as well as other citizens whose active participation in the provision of social services is essential. The participation of the "customers" of social services is one of the new trends in social work that is emphasized also in the developing nations. In most countries this trend leads to a more efficient use of social services (for instance France, Great Britain, the United States, Italy, Germany, and the Scandinavian countries) but some countries (Iraq, Yemen, Jordan, Kuwait, Lebanon, Saudi Arabia, and Syria) oppose modern concepts of social services and the presence of trained social workers because they insist on maintaining the old concepts of "poor relief," "benevolent action" and "charity," and they refuse to accept the idea that persons in need have a right to social service. In those countries the governments are hesitant to interfere with religious customs that have to do with charity and to introduce modern training of social workers and new welfare concepts.[22]

There is a consensus in all nations that education for social work needs to be responsive to national culture and local conditions, that it should include teaching of those aspects of social science, sociology, psychology, cultural anthropology, law, and administration that are of importance to social work practice. There is no single pattern of education for social work which would be fitting for all countries because their needs differ so widely. Each nation therefore needs to establish its own training policy for the various levels of social service functions, where motivation to service has to be emphasized as much as intelligence and practical experience. The leading role of the United Nations in the development of adequate personnel for the social services is now generally acknowledged.

In his Eileen Younghusband Lecture at the National Institute for Social Work Training in May 1968 in London, Professor Jan F. De Jongh of the University of Amsterdam emphasized that most Western systems of education and social work are not fitted for the cultures and value systems of developing countries, where community development, housing, adult education, and health services are considered more important than help for the individual and the family (this help seems rather the task of the extended family, the clan, or tribe). Social work in Asia and Africa is but a marginal activity within the broader social and cultural setting; reform activities, recreation, and youth training are considered more vital needs. Western social workers, therefore, will have to be careful to take a modest attitude in participating in education for social work in the developing countries, and to avoid the attitude that the new countries are inferior. Western concepts of training for self-help do not fit in these countries, and nonconformist behavior is not tolerated as excusable deviance, as it is in some industrialized nations.[23]

In a few countries, for example Norway, a systematic research has established an overview of the staffing needs of public and private social agencies and of the resources of the existing schools of social work to train the required personnel. In most countries there still exists a disequilibrium between the demand for qualified social workers and the supply of trained professionals. Advanced training in the opinion of experts is too much centered in the United States, should be available in other countries, and should include social work research.[24] For the future training and education of social workers, Eugen Pusić makes the following suggestions:

> Workers will have to go on with what they are doing today, but with better awareness of the character of the transition which we are approaching. They will have to prepare themselves for the task of being an outpost in the tremendous orientation of social education toward autonomous self-education of all people throughout their lifetime. They will have to organize for social action toward the establishment of minimal welfare standards, and toward the independent and interdependent functioning of welfare services throughout the world.[25]

To meet this challenge, social workers in all countries will need to study the international, global aspects of social services, and at the same time to recognize the specific cultural and economic conditions of the country or region they are working in.

# Notes

[1]Walter A. Friedlander, "Some International Aspects of Social Work Education," *Social Service Review,* 23, No. 2 (June 1949), 204–10; Ralph Cilento, "The World Moves Toward Professional Standards in Social Work," *Social Work Journal,* 29, No. 3 (July 1948), 99–107; Katherine Kendall, "International Developments in Social Work Education," *Social Work Journal,* 32, No. 2 (Apr. 1951), 70–77; Herbert Aptekar, "Education for Social Responsibility," *Journal of Education for Social Work,* 2, No. 2 (Fall 1966), 5–11; United Nations, *Training for Social Work: Third International Survey* (1959); U.S. Department of Health, Education, and Welfare, *Meeting Trained Manpower Needs: An International Concern of the Profession of Social Work,* Washington, D.C., 1963.

[2]Kendall, "International Developments," pp. 73–74; Parin Vakaria, "Social Work in Other Parts of the World," *Social Work Encyclopedia 1965,* pp. 745–49; Dorothy Lally, "International Social Welfare," ibid., pp. 416–17; Rachel B. Marks, "Education for Social Work," ibid., pp. 277–83; Eileen L. Younghusband, "The Third International Survey of Training for Social Work," *International Social Work,* 2, No. 4 (Oct. 1959), 30–34; United Nations, *Fourth International Survey of Training for Social Work* (New York, 1964); Lester B. Granger, "Basic Human Needs," *Social Work Journal,* 34, No. 2 (Apr. 1953), 65–70, 87–88.

[3]Werner W. Boehm, "Education for Social Work—International Social Work," *Encyclopedia of Social Work 1972* (New York: National Association of Social Workers), pp. 271–72.

[4]Richard M. Titmuss, *Commitment to Welfare* (New York: Pantheon, 1967), pp. 125–28.

[5]Eileen L. Younghusband, "The Training of Social Workers in Britain," *Social Casework,* 43, No. 9 (Nov. 1962), 494–95; Frank T. Flynn et al., *Social Services in Great Britain* (London: British Council of Social Service, 1956), pp. 3–13; Christa Hasenclever, "Problematik der Fachhochschule für Sozialarbeit und Sozialpädagogik" (Problems of the Academy for Social Work and Social Pedagogy), *Neues Beginnen,* 20, No. 2 (Apr. 1969), 45–52; Wilhelm M. Sing, "Fachhochschule und politische Bildung" (Social Academy and Political Education), *Nachrichtendienst,* 30 (Feb. 1971), 31–34.

[6]Elizabeth E. Irvine, "Education for Social Work: Science or Humanity," *International Social Work,* 14, No. 2 (1971), 53–57; Friedlander, *Social Welfare,* pp. 4–7.

[7]K. H. Roessingh, *Adult Education and Community Organization* (Rijswiyk: University of Oslo Press, 1970).

[8]Herbert H. Aptekar, ed., *An International Exploration: Universals and Differences in Social Work Values, Functions, and Practices* (New York: Council on Social Work Education, 1967), pp. 3–59; Roland L. Warren, "International Community Development," in Aptekar, *An International Exploration,* pp. 63–75; Herman D. Stein, "Different Values in Child Welfare Services," in Aptekar, *An International Exploration,* pp. 76–84; M. S. Gore, "Cultural Perspectives in India," in Aptekar, *An International Exploration,* pp. 87–107; Jane Howard, "Indian Society, Indian Social Work: Identifying Indian Principles and Methods for Social Work Practice," *International Social Work,* 12 (Jan. 1969), 16–31. Howard recommends that American methods of social work should be replaced by indigenous Indian principles and methods in order to fit into the specific Indian customs, heritage, and values.

[9]Stein, "Different Values," pp. 166–67.

[10]Eileen Younghusband, *Social Work and Social Change* (London: Allen & Unwin, 1968), pp. 123–50; Herbert S. Parnes, ed., *Planning Education for Economic and*

*Social Development* (Frascati: Organization for Economic Cooperation and Development, 1963).

[11]Younghusband, *Social Work and Social Change,* pp. 130–31.

[12]Stein, "Different Values," pp. 168–71; Arnulf M. Pins, "Changes in Social Work Education," *Social Work,* 16, No. 2 (Apr. 1971), 5–15.

[13]Arlien Johnson et al., *Social Services in Great Britain* (London: U.S. Education Commission in the U.K., 1956), pp. 5–7; 11–13; 51–54; United Nations, *1967 Report on the World Social Situation,* pp. 65–73, 93–97; Stein, "Different Values," pp. 164–67; Peter T. Brown, "Social Work Education in Zambia," *International Social Work,* 14, No. 1 (Jan. 1971), 42–47; Jona Rosenfeld, "Training for Social Welfare in Israel," ibid., pp. 48–55.

[14]Madison, *Social Welfare in the Soviet Union,* pp. 92–103.

[15]Ernest Greenwood, "Social Work Practice and Education in Chile," unpublished study (University of California, Berkeley, 1971), pp. 20–31.

[16]Ibid., pp. 29–31.

[17]Charles Schottland et al., *Social Security Programs in the Soviet Union* (Washington, D.C.: U.S. Department of Health, Education, and Welfare, 1960), pp. 101–103; Madison, *Social Welfare in the Soviet Union,* pp. 95–96.

[18]Ba Kin, "The Colombo Plan," in M. S. Gore and B. Chatterjee, eds., *Mobilizing Resources for Social Needs* (Bombay: International Conference of Social Work, 1958), pp. 151–56; Luz Yocornal de Romero, "Mobilizing Resources for Social Needs in Chile," ibid., pp. 99–112; P. P. Agarwal, "Meeting Social Needs in India," ibid., pp. 113–24; Eugen Pusíc, "Social Needs in Yugoslavia," ibid., pp. 84–98; Hla Myint, "Human and Material Resources . . . ," ibid., pp. 71–75; Florence Philpott, "The Citizen, the Volunteer, and the Social Worker," ibid., pp. 208–10.

[19]Francis Manis, "Education for Social Work: Field Work in Developing Nations," *International Social Work,* 14, No. 2 (1971), 17–20.

[20]United Nations, "Urbanization," *International Social Development Review,* No. 1 (1968), p. 95; Amitai Etzioni, *The Semi-professions* (New York: Free Press, 1969); Dorothea Cudaback, "Training and Education of New Careerists," *Public Welfare,* 28, No. 2 (Apr. 1970), 214–21; Ruby B. Pernell, "The Privilege of These Terrific Years," *Public Welfare,* 28, No. 3 (July 1970), 251–55.

[21]Leora Wood Wells, *Training Social Welfare Manpower* (New York: Council on Social Work Education, 1969), pp. 20–21.

[22]Ibid., pp. 21–33.

[23]Jan F. De Jongh, "Western Social Work and the Afro-Asian World," *Social Service Review,* 43, No. 1 (March 1969), 50–58.

[24]Younghusband, *Social Work and Social Change,* pp. 131–32.

[25]Eugen Pusíc, *Social Welfare and Social Development* (The Hague-Paris: Mouton, 1972), p. 80.

## Selected References

*Books*

ANDERSON, C. ARNOLD, et al., *Education and Economic Development.* Chicago: Aldine, 1965.

BAKER, ROBERT L., AND THOMAS L. BRIGGS, *Differential Use of Social Work Manpower: An Analysis and Demonstration Study.* New York: National Association of Social Workers, 1966.

BATTEN, T. R., *Training for Community Development.* London: Oxford University Press, 1962.

BERGER, P., *Invitation to Sociology: A Humanistic Perspective.* London: Penguin Books, 1963.

BROOKS, HARVEY, AND GARDNER LINDGEY, *The Behavioral and Social Sciences.* Englewood Cliffs, N.J.: Prentice-Hall, 1969.

BUTTON, LESLIE, *Discovery and Experiences: A New Approach to Training, Group Work, and Teaching.* Oxford: Oxford University Press, 1971.

CLARK, TERRY NICHOLS, *Prophets and Patrons: The French University and the Emergence of Social Science.* Cambridge, Mass.: Harvard University Press, 1973.

CONGROVE, S., *Science of Society.* London: Allen & Unwin, 1967.

CRAWFORD, ELIZABETH T., AND ALBERT D. BIDERMAN, *Social Scientists and International Affairs,* New York: Wiley, 1969.

DAVIS, RUSSELL C., *Planning Human Resources Development: Educational Models and Schemata.* Chicago: Rand McNally, 1966.

EIDE, ASBJORN, AND AUGUST SCHOU, *International Protection of Human Rights.* New York: Wiley-Interscience, 1968.

FRIEDLANDER, WALTER A., ed. *Concepts and Methods of Social Work,* Englewood Cliffs, N.J.: Prentice-Hall, 1958.

———, *Individualism and Social Welfare in France.* New York: Free Press, 1962, pp. 210–28.

———, *Introduction to Social Welfare,* 3rd ed. Englewood Cliffs, N.J.: Prentice-Hall, 1968, pp. 526–64.

GILETTE, ARTHUR, *One Million Volunteers.* Harmonsworth (England): Penguin Books, 1968.

HERAUD, BRIAN J. *Sociology and Social Work: Perspectives and Problems.* Oxford (England): Pergamon Press, 1970.

HOWARD, DONALD S., *Social Welfare: Values, Means, and Ends.* New York: Random House, 1969.

INTERNATIONAL COUNCIL ON SOCIAL WELFARE/ REGIONAL OFFICE FOR SOUTH-EAST ASIA AND WESTERN PACIFIC, *Progress Through Manpower.* Bombay, 1968.

JEFFREYS, M., *Anatomy of Social Welfare Services.* London: Joseph, 1965.

JEHN, D., *Learning Theory and Social Work.* London: Routledge & Kegan Paul, 1967.

JONES, KATHLEEN, ed., *The Yearbook of Social Policy in Britain, 1971.* London: Routledge & Kegan Paul, 1972.

KENDALL, KATHERINE, *Population Dynamics and Family Planning: A New Responsibility for Social Work Education.* New York: Council on Social Work Education, 1971.

KURZMAN, PAUL A., *The Mississippi Experience: Strategies for Welfare Rights Action.* New York: Association Press, 1971.

LAZARSFELD, PAUL, ed., *The Uses of Sociology.* London: Weidenfeld & Nicholson, 1968.

LEES, RAY, *Politics and Social Work*. London: Routledge & Kegan Paul, 1970.

LEONARD, P., *Sociology in Social Work*. London: Routledge & Kegan Paul, 1966.

LOEWENSTEIN, KARL, *Political Power and the Governmental Process*. Chicago: University of Chicago Press, 1957.

LYNTON, R., *The Tide of Learning: The Aloka Experience*. London: Routledge & Kegan Paul, 1960.

MARSHALL, T. H. *Social Policy*. London: Hutchinson, 1967.

MORGAN, LUCY S., *Report on Study of Role and Training of Health Workers in Community Development*. Geneva: World Health Organization, 1962.

NOKES, P., *The Professional Task in Welfare Practice*. London: Routledge & Kegan Paul, 1968.

PRIGMORE, CHARLES S., ed., *Workshop on Education for Cross-Cultural and International Social Welfare*. New York: Council on Social Work Education, 1970.

PRYOR, FREDERICK L., *Public Expenditures in Communist and Capitalist Countries*. Homewood, Ill.: Irwin, 1968.

PUSIĆ, EUGEN, *Reappraisal of the United Nations Social Service Programmes*. New York: United Nations Economic and Social Council, 1965.

ROGERS, BARBARA N., JOHN GREVE, AND JOHN S. MORGAN, *Comparative Social Administration*. New York: Atherton Press, 1968.

TIMMS, NOEL, *A Sociological Approach to Social Problems*. London: Routledge & Kegan Paul, 1967.

TOREN, NINA, *Social Work: The Case of a Semi-Profession*. Beverly Hills, Ca.: Sage Publications, 1972.

UNITED NATIONS, *Report of the Consultant Team for the Study of Schools of Social Work in Africa*. New York, 1964.

UNESCO, *Better Teachers: An Experiment with In-Service Teacher Training*. Paris: UNESCO, 1970.

VAN BENGEN, MARINUS, *Agogische Intervention: Planning und Strategie* (Agogic Intervention: Planning and Strategy). Freiburg: Lamburtus, 1972.

WELLS, LEORA WOOD, *Training Social Welfare Manpower*. New York: Council on Social Work Education, 1969.

WINDMILLER, MARSHALL, *The Peace Corps and Pax Americana*. Washington, D.C.: Public Affairs Press, 1970.

YOUNGHUSBAND, EILEEN, *Social Work and Social Change*. London: Allen & Unwin, 1964.

———, *Education for Social Work: Readings in Social Work*. London: National Institute for Social Work Training, 1968.

———, *Community Work and Social Change*. London: Longmans, 1969.

## Articles

ARAD, NAVA, "The Relief Professional Association of Social Workers in Influencing Social Policy," *International Social Work* (Bombay), 15, No. 1 (1972), 18–23.

AUSTIN, DAVID, "Social Work's Relation to National Development in Developing Nations," *Social Work*, 15 (Jan. 1970), 97–106.

BADRAN, HADRA, "Social Work Programmes in Egypt," *International Social Work* (Bombay), 14, No. 1 (1971), 25–33.

BROWN, MALCOLM J., "Social Work Values in a Developing Country," *Social Work*, 15, No. 1 (Jan. 1970), 107–12.

BROWN, PETER T., "Social Work Education in Zambia, an Integrated Approach," *International Social Work* (Bombay), 14, No. 1 (1971) 42–47.

CHANDLER, J. H., "Perspectives on Poverty: an International Comparison," *Monthly Labor Review*, 92 (Feb. 1969), 55–62.

DELCOURT, JACQUES, "Le Futur du service social" (The Future of the Social Services), *Service Social dans le Monde* (Brussels), No. 1 (Jan. 1972), pp. 2–16.

DE JONGH, JAN F., "Western Social Work and the Afro-Asian World," *The Social Service Review*, 43 (March 1969), 50–58.

EIMICKE, WILLIAM B., "Debate over Welfare in Britain," *Social Work*, 18 (Sep. 1973), 84–91.

FASOLO PAGLIA, EMMA, "Teaching Americans in America," *Education for Social Work*, 9 (Spring 1973), 31–38.

FELDMAN, RONALD A., "Professionalization and Professional Values: A Cross-Cultural Comparison," *International Review of Sociology*, 1, No. 2 (1971), 85–97.

FRIEDLANDER, WALTER A., "Labour Unions and Social Workers," *International Social Work* (Bombay), 13, No. 4 (1970), 28–31.

GANGRADE, K. D., "Conflicting Values and Social Casework," *Indian Journal of Social Work* (New Delhi), 29 (Jan. 1964), 248–56.

————, "Western Social Work and the Indian World," *International Social Work* (Bombay), 9 (July 1966), 6–16.

GINSBERG, LEON H., HARVEY L. GOCHROS, ROBERT PORTER, VICTOR L. SCHNEIDER, AND LEROY G. SCHULTZ, "An Experiment in Overseas Field Work," *Education for Social Work*, 8, No. 2 (Spring 1972), 16–24.

GORE, M. S., "The Cultural Perspectives in Social Work," *International Social Work* (Bombay), 9 (July 1966), 6–16.

HEISLER, HELMUTH, "A Reconsideration of the Theory of Community Development," *International Social Work* (Bombay), 14, No. 2 (1971), 26–33.

HERO, ALFRED O., AND EMIL STARR, "Educating Union Members Toward a World Outlook, *War and Peace*, 10 (March 1970), 9–11.

HINES, GEORGE H., "Ideals, Education, and Occupations: Attitudes of New Zealand and Asian University Students," *Pacific Sociological Review*, 16 (Oct. 1973), 449–62.

HOWARD, JANE, "Indian Society, Indian Social Work," *International Social Work* (Bombay), 13, No. 4 (1970), 16–31.

IRVINE, ELIZABETH E., "Education for Social Work: Science or Humanity?" *International Social Work* (Bombay) 14, No. 2 (1971), 53–57.

KRISHNA-MURTHI, S., "The Role of the Social Worker in Community Development—Some Reflections," *Samaj Seva* (Poona, India), 20, No. 7 (1970), 17–20.

KHINDUKA, SHANTI KUMAR, "Manpower for International Technical Assistance in the Social Field." Ph.D. dissertation, Brandeis University, 1968.

KHINDUKA, SHANTI K., AND RICHARD J. PARVIS, "On Teaching International Social Welfare," *Social Work Education Reporter*, 17 (March 1969), 35–66.

LEWIS, HAROLD, "Apology, Animation, Conscientization," *Education for Social Work*, 9 (Fall 1973), 31–38.

LONGRES, JOHN, "The Impact of Racism on Social Work Education," *Social Work Education*, 8, No. 1 (Winter 1972), 31–41.

MACAROV, DAVID, et al., "Consultants and Consultees: The View from Within," *Social Service Review*, 41 (Sep. 1967), 283–97.

MAHAFFY, MARYANN, "Lobbying and Social Work," *International Social Work*, 17 (Jan. 1972), 3–11.

MANIS, FRANCIS, "Education for Social Work: Field Work in Developing Nations," *International Social Work* (Bombay), 14, No. 2 (1971), 17–25.

MOSES, DOROTHY, "Trends in Social Work Education in Asia," *Indian Journal of Social Work* (New Delhi), 28 (Jan. 1967), 1–10.

NAGPAUL, HANS, "The Diffusion of American Social Work Education to India: Problems and Issues," *International Social Work* (Bombay), 15, No. 1 (1972), 3–17.

NURSTEN, JEAN P., AND JOHN POTTLINGER, "Social Work Training: The Consumers Views," *Social Service Quarterly* (London), 43, No. 4 (Apr.–June 1970), 152–54.

ODIA, SALOMON, "Rural Education and Training in Tanzania," *International Labour Review* 103, No. 1 (1971), 13–28.

PERNELL, RUBY B., "Perspectives of Social Development at Home and Abroad," *Social Welfare Forum 1968*, pp. 126–40.

PETERS, HELGE, "Sozialarbeit im Gesellschafts politischen Bereich" (Social Work in Connection with Social Policy), *Soziale Welt*, No. 1 (1972), pp. 41–53.

PETTIS, SUSAN T., "Whither International Education Exchange? A Social Worker's Perspectives and Recommendations," *International Educational and Cultural Exchange* (Summer 1970), pp. 57–70.

POLLAK, C., "American Social Workers and Social Welfare," *International Social Work* (Bombay), 10, No. 3 (1967), 31–36.

PRIGMORE, CHARLES S., "Use of the Coalition in Legislative Action," *Social Work*, 19 (Jan. 1974), 96–102.

REES, STUART, "International Cooperation in Community Work," *International Social Work* (Bombay), 15, No. 1 (1972), 29–33.

SHARNA, G. B., "Social Administration Toward Theoretical Standardization and Clarification," *Indian Journal of Social Work* (New Delhi), 31, No. 1 (1970), 11–23.

SHAWKY, A., "Social Work Education in Africa," *International Social Work*, 15 (March 1972), 3–16.

STEIN, HERMAN D., "Social Welfare and Development: Education and Training for the Seventies" (Manila), *Fifteenth Congress of Schools of Social Work*, 1969.

SWITZER, MARY E., "Strong Role for Public Welfare," *Public Welfare*, 27, No. 1 (Jan. 1969), 66–70.

WADE, ALAN D., "The Social Worker in the Political Process," *Social Welfare Forum 1966*, pp. 52–67.

WEISNER, STANLEY, AND CONSTANCE M. WEISNER, "Professional Social Work in Kenya," *Social Work Forum*, 11 (Jan. 1973), 3–12.

WINNICOTT, CLARE, "The Training and Recruitment of Staff for Residential Work, *The Child in Care*, 11, No. 1 (1971), 16–27.

WILLENSEN, SIGRID, "Gesundheitsfürsorge in der Ausbildung in der Fachhochschule" (Health Social Services in Education in the Social Work Academy in Germany), *Nachrichtendienst*, 51 (Nov. 1971), 312–14.

WRESCHNER-SALZBERGER, LOTTE, MONICA MOHILEVER, AND SHLOME KUGELMAN, "A Short-Term Staff Development in Israel," *Social Work*, 7, No. 4 (Oct. 1962), 73–78.

YELAJA, S. A., "Schools of Social Work in India: Historical Development, 1936–1966," *Indian Journal of Social Work* (New Delhi), 29 (Apr. 1969), 361–78.

YOUNGHUSBAND, EILEEN, "Intercultural Aspects of Social Work," *Education for Social Work*, 2, No. 1 (Spring 1966), 59–65.

———, "Which Way for Social Work," *Community Development Journal* (London), 8 (Jan. 1973), 2–5.

*Some conclusions*

$$12$$

International social welfare is concerned with the well-being of human society in all the countries of this earth as prescribed in the United Nations Declaration of Human Rights. Social work strives with other disciplines toward better standards of living for all human beings in their cultural, social, and personal conditions. Social welfare concepts recognize the importance of economic factors as a condition for health and emotional well-being, but refuse to achieve these aims through hostile competition for the sparse material resources of this earth. Our previous discussions reveal differences in the various countries in the priorities for nutrition, health standards, and housing, compared with social insurance, social assistance, and personal social services, or preventive measures in health and delinquency services, rehabilitation, and correction. But the trend in social welfare policies seems to indicate that a larger proportion of the national incomes of most countries needs to be devoted to social welfare activities and that international community development needs to be encouraged to improve health services and education, and to provide economic and political modernization of the developing countries.[1]

### The Need for a Global Approach

Our discussions show that an effective welfare system requires international cooperation without emphasis on economic and political gains for the industrial nations, and an international framework such as the United Nations and its specialized agencies (discussed in Chapter 2) or future international organizations. A global approach is required, but so far it has only developed in embryonic measure,[2] but it is to be hoped that the United Nations councils, commissions, and specialized agencies, particularly the World Health Organization, the United Nations Children's Fund, the United Nations Educational, Scientific and Cultural Organization, The International Labor Organization, and the Food and Agriculture Organization will have on their boards and staffs more thoughtful persons who are inspired by a spirit of global, international conscience and who are convinced that only with such a global concept can the world's social, political, and economic problems be solved, and the description in the Universal Declaration of Human Rights become a reality. In the area of social and economic planning, experience during the last few decades shows that despite political differences in orientation among Eastern and Western societies, economic growth and economic security can be obtained and greater economic unity of all peoples is indeed possible. Such a change requires that more than economic factors be considered,[3] although closer economic relations and intensified economic aid from industrialized to developing countries will play a certain role. But a broader sociocultural transformation of the underdeveloping countries in cooperation with the industrialized world will be needed in order to achieve the mobilization of all resources of the developing countries and a greater unification of the economy of all countries of this earth.[4]

The serious problems created by growing nationalism in the new countries and the political differences between the capitalistic and communistic nations can be solved only by a cosmopolitan orientation of economic and social policies and a general world welfare orientation. As each society constrains the egoism of its own members by regulations and moral influences, so the world community must impose similar restraints upon all countries by means of a strengthened worldwide organization (into which the United Nations needs to be developed).[5] To achieve this it is necessary to develop international economic mechanisms which are able to reconcile the desires of the rich nations for economic growth with the justified claim of the developing countries for a more egalitarian participation in prosperity and a decent standard of living. This may be achieved by intergovernmental loans, provided they do not have such strings attached as were characteristic of most postwar foreign aid programs, which were dominated by Cold War strategies, and which forced developing countries to invest substantial portions of foreign aid in military expenses rather than in economic and community development. Great Britain and France have devoted a larger proportion of their gross national products to their former colonies than the United States. If all rich countries would supply the agencies of the United Nations for a combined community development program, it would be possible to eradicate poverty and diseases in many of the developing nations and with their active participation and responsibility to achieve a healthier, more peaceful world.[6]

The biggest obstacle to international cooperation is the lack of insight into the urgency of the situation among most nations of this

world. Narrow national interests and the motivations of pressure groups
in pursuit of their policies prove the need for an enlightened citizenry in
the industrial and in the developing countries, able to create an international idealism which could establish responsible international cooperation so as to overcome the inadequacies and injustices among the
nations of this world.[7]

Until the nineteenth century all nations were composed of small,
rich ruling classes and the poor and suppressed. Now the earth is divided
into a small minority of rich industrial nations and a large majority of
poor underdeveloped countries. This applies to their economic and
health conditions, their social policy, their welfare systems, and their
community development programs. The future of this earth depends on
an international concept of progressive movement toward a development
policy and social service programs in contact with economic and technical
development in a peaceful constructive relationship between countries
which would permit survival of this planet.[8] Since with the progress of
technology a new pattern of production and occupational activities is
developing, the proportion of the population engaged in farming and
agricultural work is decreasing, and numerous rural workers in all countries are streaming into the cities and creating severe problems of slums,
squatter areas, hunger, unemployment, and crime. International social
welfare policy will have to meet these problems.[9]

International social welfare is only one aspect of the developing
concepts of global insight and concepts which are necessary to secure the
survival of this earth. U Thant, former secretary-general of the United
Nations, called attention in his "Message for Youth" in 1970 to the fact
that men and women under 25 years of age outnumber the rest of us and
will be the inhabitants of this planet in the next century. He expressed
hope that this generation would embrace a new set of values including
a deep desire for peace, and a rejection of the outdated policy of war so
that a new atmosphere of peace and cooperation would prevail.[10] As an
indication of this new spirit U Thant referred to the young volunteers
under the auspices of the United Nations who serve in many developing
countries as teachers, social workers, engineers, and assistants in many
fields without the desire for high pay or material compensation, following
the example of the American Peace Corps.

### Volunteer Agencies

In the United States there is the Peace Corps, but there are other
opportunities for volunteer service in foreign countries, particularly for
young social workers and students interested in international experi-

ences, through a group of 16 private organizations, encouraged by the International Office of the Department of Health, Education, and Welfare in Washington, D.C. Social workers with substantial experience in specific fields such as school social work, social research, or mental health services may find positions in foreign countries through the United Nations.

An International Secretariat for Volunteer Service, headquartered in Geneva, represents a worldwide organization for soical and economic development. Fifty-two governments support this agency, which encourages the establishment of volunteer organizations for the home countries and for service abroad, with the objective of training the youth of developing countries in the technical skills their nations need. There is also a Coordinating Committee for International Voluntary Services which includes about 140 national agencies and holds associate relationship and consultative status with UNESCO's headquarters in Paris.[11]

Despite the strong nationalistic trends in most developing nations which are gaining self-respect after their colonial periods, it is already evident that in this rapidly changing world no single nation is able to develop economic, cultural, and social policies for the well-being of its population alone. The nation-state is becoming obsolete, and modern technology and the recognition of a new world value system make it necessary to exchange knowledge and ideas without geographical boundaries.[12] Social policy and welfare services too are no longer the property of the industrial countries, but have been expanded to all nations. Thus a global approach to all questions of economics, science, politics, and culture becomes necessary owing to this transition from a technical, industrial age to a postindustrial, humanitarian, cultural age which requires new principles of education, politics, and social welfare which enable all peoples to live in peace in a world community.[13]

In the framework of this study we cannot attempt to elaborate fully the important function which the United Nations must play in achieving these goals, but the material in the preceding chapters should indicate that there is hope that a new global consciousness in most nations might make such changes possible.[14] The development of a social welfare policy and of responsible measures for the preservation of human dignity and protection in the international area are increasingly necessary in view of the vastly increased powers to destroy the human environment and all life on this earth by the forces of nuclear and hydrogen bombs, by nerve and nauseous gases, fever, tularemia, botulism, contamination of the oceans, and even the precipitation of earthquakes from foreign continents.[15]

In order to replace the obsolete forms of wars and destruction, human services—education, health services, cultural activities, welfare services—will have to be established all over this earth. The beginnings of these have been discussed in this study. Their systematic development remains a major assignment of the United Nations and its specialized agencies. To enable them to perform this difficult task and to secure survival for the peoples of the earth, the organization and equipment of the United Nations need to be improved. There is vast literature that examines the measures necessary to achieve this but among the recommendations for providing the United Nations and the affiliated international organizations with the required financial means, preservation of the treasures of the oceans needs to be emphasized.[16] Technology has forced us to live under a world organization, and self-management will no longer be dominated by the Western world alone, but will include a combination of Western and oriental values. Individual nations will have to give up some part of their sovereignty to the United Nations or some similar global organization under an open economic, cultural, and political order which would guarantee peace, the only form under which this earth can survive.[17]

### The Role of Social Work

The postindustrial society is just beginning. Social work, cultural activities, education, and recreation will have to play a much more important role than they have before. Greater portions of the resources of all nations, especially of the industrial countries but also increasingly of the developing nations, will be devoted to human services. In order to prepare social workers in all countries for these new tasks, schools of social work will have to give more attention to cultural activities in social work.[18]

One serious obstacle to raising the general standard of living in the developing countries is the fact that the political and economic power lies in the hands of a small ruling minority. The masses remain apathetic, seemingly satisfied with their poverty, malnutrition, and exclusion from participation in the government. This majority is rarely organized in labor or in any political party, does not feel responsible for the fate of their nation, and does not take any initiative to change its condition or to gain access to the progress which the ruling group enjoys. Frequently religious beliefs support this apathy, by preventing equalization of social and health conditions.[19]

The desire of the ruling groups in the developing countries to acquire quickly the technological advantages of the industrialized nations (autos, airplanes, heating, air-conditioning) associated with rapid industrialization involves the danger that water and air pollution, the poisoning of streams and seas and nuclear stratification may destroy all life on this earth. This danger is not limited to the peoples of the industrial nations, but encompasses all countries. To protect this earth and to allow survival of humanitarian values in religion, art, and cultures, global cooperation of all nations is needed, such as it is envisaged by the United Nations and its attached agencies.[20]

Since it is not possible to prevent the progress of industrialization and technology in this world in the rich as well as in the developing nations, there remains the hope that a revival of religious and cultural values by the arts may balance the powers of technology and succeed in restraining the dangers of destruction created by industrialization and technology. Among such constructive humanitarian forces social services will contribute as part of a new cultural emancipation of the human spirit to a civilization for all mankind.[21]

### The Need to Save the Sea

An important prerequisite for enabling the United Nations or any related global authority to function as the means for securing the survival of mankind on this earth is the achievement of an agreement on the law of the sea that requires the resources of the oceans to be used for world peace and global cooperation. The Committee of the United Nations on Peaceful Uses of the Seabed and the Ocean Floor has scheduled meetings in 1973 and 1974, but there has not yet been an agreement on essential aspects of this vital arrangement.[22]

For the further development of the analysis of the institutions and questions discussed in this study, Professor Herbert Blumer of the University of California, Berkeley, has made the following valuable suggestions: that three classifications might be made of social problems in the international scene: chronic problems persevering in numerous countries; sporadic emergency problems, mainly after natural catastrophes or in the wake of wars; and new general problems caused by changes of technology or health conditions which require international action. A stricter differentiation between international and domestic problems might be necessary, wherein international problems are those of a magnitude which an individual nation cannot handle, for instance a major health problem in an underdeveloped country that requires international action. On the other hand, there are welfare and health problems which are genuinely international in scope and which therefore need to be addressed collaboratively by nations (and probably also by international agencies) without regard for the nature and location of the problems, for example the influence of atomic radiation or a prospective world energy crisis. There are numerous indications that such international problems are growing in numbers in our modern world. In further elaboration of this study it might be desirable to examine a more intensive comparison of international governmental organizations, such as the United Nations and its affiliated special agencies, and international private organizations, such as the International Red Cross and the numerous nongovernmental organizations which are active in health and social services. It might be fruitful to investigate the different kinds of operating functions which both types use, the different types of organization, the areas in which both groups are functioning with the greatest effect, the typical problems they face, and the merits and deficiencies of each group. Such comparison would lead to a clearer picture of international problems in health and social services.

## Notes

[1]Bert F. Hoselitz, ed., *Economics and the Idea of Mankind* (New York: Columbia University Press, 1965), pp. 54–61, 94–96; M. S. Gore and B. Chatterjee, eds., *Mobilizing Resources for Social Needs* (Bombay: International Conference of Social Work, 1958), pp. 10–13, 15–29; Behrendt, *Soziale Strategie*, pp. 378–410, 479–95; Ellen Winston, "International Social Welfare—Implications for Public Welfare," *Public Welfare*, 30, No. 1 (Winter 1972), 51–57.

[2]Kenneth E. Boulding, "The Concept of World Interest," in Hoselitz, ed., *Economics and the Idea of Mankind*, pp. 53–62; Ralph Townley, *The United Nations* (New York: Scribner, 1968), pp. 288–95.

[3]Hoselitz, ed., *Economics and the Idea of Mankind*, pp. 82–94; Robert M. Hutchins, "Manhood and the Liberal Arts," *The Urban Review*, 4, No. 3 (May 1970), 3–6; Arthur Paul, "Emerging Repercussions of Economic Development," *The Asia Foundation*, (Fall 1971), pp. 2–8.

[4]Robert A. Dahl and Charles E. Lindblom, *Politics, Economics and Welfare: Planning and Politico-Economic Systems Resolved into Basic Social Processes* (New York: Harper & Row, 1953), pp. 10–18; Myrdal, *Beyond the Welfare State*, pp. 40–42, 265–87.

[5]David Felix, "International Factor: Migration and World Economic Welfare," in Bert Hoselitz, ed., *Economics and the Idea of Mankind*, pp. 97–142; Gunnar Myrdal, *An International Economy: Problems and Prospects* (London: Routledge & Kegan Paul, 1956), pp. 22–25; Elisabeth Mann-Borgese, "The World Communities," *The Center Magazine*, 4, No. 5 (Sep.–Oct. 1971), 10–18.

[6]Felix, "International Factor," pp. 137–42; Emile Benoit, "The Economics of Disarmament and Coexistence," in Hoselitz, ed., *Economics and the Idea of Mankind*, pp. 233–77; Richard Behrendt, *Zwischen Anarchie und neuen Ordnungen* (Between Anarchy and a New Order) (Freiburg: Rombach, 1967), pp. 356–74, 375–402.

[7]Myrdal, *Beyond the Welfare State*, 19–26, 282–287.

[8]Eugen Pusíc, *Social Welfare and Social Development* (The Hague-Paris: Mouton, 1972), pp. 28–29.

[9]Pusíc, *Social Welfare*, pp. 190–93.

[10]U Thant, "The U.N. Generation," *World*, 1, No. 11 (Nov. 1972), 18–19; see also John H. Kunkel, *Society and Economic Change* (New York: Oxford University Press, 1970), pp. 3–5; Gisela Konopka, "Cultural Differences and Social Work Philosophy," *International Social Work* (Bombay), 14, No. 3 (March 1971), 3–10.

[11]Violet M. Sieder, "International Volunteer Organizations," *Encyclopedia of Social Work 1972*, p. 1532.

¹²Robert M. Hutchins, "Manhood and the Liberal Arts," *The Urban Review*, 4, No. 3 (May 1970), 3–6; J. Delcourt, "Le Future du service social," *Service social dans le Monde* (Brussels), 8 No. 3 (Fall 1972), 45ff.

¹³Grant Hugo, *Appearances of Reality in International Relations* (New York: Columbia University Press, 1970), pp. 53, 64, 88.

¹⁴Charles I. Schottland, "Translating Social Needs into Action," *International Social Work* (Bombay), 14, No. 4 (1971), 3–17, especially 11–13.

¹⁵Pilisuk, *International Conflict and Social Policy*, pp. 9–22, 192–98.

¹⁶Elisabeth Mann-Borgese, *Pacem in Maribus, Ocean Enterprises*, (Santa Barbara, Ca.: Center for the Study of Democratic Institutions, 1970); John L. Lofue, "What is the Ocean Problem?" *World Federalist*, 17, No. 104 (Apr. 1972), 6–7; Silvin Brucan, *The Dissolution of Power* (New York: Knopf, 1971). See also Eugen Pusíc, "Levels of Social and Economic Development As Limits to Welfare Policy," *Social Service Review*, 45, No. 4 (Dec. 1971), 400–413.

¹⁷Fred W. Neal, "A New Foreign Policy Based on Core Interests," *The Center Magazine*, 5, No. 3 (June 1972), 61–66; Elisabeth Mann-Borgese, "The Promise of Self-Management," ibid., pp. 54–60.

¹⁸Daniel Bell, "The Year 2000—The Trajectory of an Idea," *Daedalus*, 96 (Summer 1967), 644; Werner W. Boehm, "Education for Social Work," *Encyclopedia of Social Work 1972*, p. 272.

¹⁹Otto A. Jaeger, *Probleme des Gesundheitsdienstes in Entwicklungsländern* (Problems of Health Services in Developing Countries), (Stuttgart: Enke, 1963), pp. 10–12.

²⁰Behrendt, *Soziale Strategie*, pp. 337–47, 488–90; United Nations, Department of Economic and Social Affairs, "Evolution of the United Nations Approach to Planning for Unified Socio-Economic Development, An Introduction," *International Social Development Review*, No. 3 (1971), pp. 1–14; Hans W. Singer, "A New Approach to the Problems of the Dual Society in Developing Countries," ibid., pp. 23–31.

²¹Jean A. Legrand, "Psycho-Sociologie in Communications," *Service social dans le monde* (Brussels), No. 1 (Jan. 1967), pp. 31–41.

²²Michael Tanzer, "Oil over a Barrel," *Vista*, 8, No. 6 (June 1973), 414; Kay Rainey Gray, "UN Notebook," ibid., pp. 5–49; UNESCO, *Main Trends in Research in the Social and Human Science* (Paris: Mouton, 1970); Harold Gershinowitz, "Applied Research for the Public Good—A Suggestion," *Science*, 176, No. 4044 (Apr. 28, 1972), 380–86; Elisabeth Mann-Borgese, "Who Owns the Earth's Resources?" *Vista*, 9 (Aug. 1973), 12–48.

## Selected References

*Books*

BEHRENDT, RICHARD F., *Soziale Strategie für Entwicklungsländer* (Social Strategy for Developing Nations). Frankfurt a/M.: Fischer, 1968.

———, *Zwischen Anarchie und neuen Ordnungen* (Between Anarchy and New Orderly Arrangements). Frankfurt a/M.: Fischer, 1968.

BELL, DANIEL, *The Coming of Post-Industrial Society: A Venture in Social Forecasting*. New York: Basic Books, 1973.

BENDIX, REINHARD, *Nationbuilding and Citizenship: Studies of our Changing Social Order*. New York: Wiley, 1964.

BERELSON, BERNARD. ed., *Family-Planning Programs: An International Survey.* New York: Basic Books, 1969.

BROWN, LESTER R., *Seeds of Change.* New York: Praeger, 1970.

CLAWSON, MARION, *Natural Resources and International Development.* Baltimore: Johns Hopkins Press, 1964.

COWAN, C. D., ed., *The Economic Development of South-East Asia.* New York: Praeger, 1964.

DAHL, ROBERT A., AND CHARLES E. LINDBLOM, *Politics, Economics, and Welfare.* New York: Harper & Row, 1971.

FAIRBANK, JOHN K., EDWIN O. REISCHAUER, AND ALBERT M. CRAIG, *East Asia: The Modern Transition.* Boston: Houghton-Mifflin, 1965.

HOSELITZ, BERT F., ed., *Economics and the Idea of Mankind.* New York: Columbia University Press, 1965.

JACOBY, NEIL H., *The Progress of Peoples.* Santa Barbara, Ca.: Center for the Study of Democratic Institutions, 1969.

JENKS, C. WILFRED, *The Common Law of Mankind.* New York: Praeger, 1958.

KLINEBERG, OTTO, *The Human Dimensions in International Relations.* New York: Holt, Rinehart and Winston, 1964.

LIPSET, SEYMOUR MARTIN, *The First New Nation: The United States in Historical and Comparative Perspective.* New York: Basic Books, 1965.

McCORD, WILLIAM, *The Springtime of Freedom.* New York: Oxford University Press, 1965.

MAIER, JOSEPH, AND RICHARD W. WEATHERHEAD, eds., *Politics of Change in Latin America.* New York: Praeger, 1964.

MANN-BORGESE, ELISABETH, *Pacem in Maribus: Ocean Enterprises.* Santa Barbara, Ca.: Center for the Study of Democratic Institutions, 1970.

MASON, EDWARD S., *Foreign Aid and Foreign Policy.* New York: Harper & Row, 1964.

MONTGOMERY, JOHN D., AND WILLIAM J. SIFFIN, *Approaches to Development: Politics, Administration, and Change.* London: Oxford University Press, 1966.

MYRDAL, ALVA, ARTHUR J. ALTMEYER, AND DEAN RUSK, *America's Role in International Social Welfare.* New York: Columbia University Press, 1955.

MYRDAL, GUNNAR, *An International Economy: Problems and Prospects.* London: Routledge & Kegan Paul, 1956.

———, *Beyond the Welfare State.* New Haven: Yale University Press, 1964.

———, *The Challenge of World Poverty: A World Anti-Poverty Program in Outline.* New York: Pantheon, 1970.

———, *Challenge To Affluence.* New York: Pantheon, 1963.

PEARSON, LESTER B., *The Crisis of Development.* New York: Praeger, 1970.

PLISCHKE, ELMER, ed., *Systems of Integrating the International Community.* Princeton, N.J.: Van Nostrand, 1964.

RAPAPORT, ANATOL, *Strategy and Conscience.* New York: Harper & Row, 1964.

SINGER, HANS W., *International Development: Growth and Change.* New York: McGraw-Hill, 1964.

TOWNLEY, RALPH, *The United Nations.* New York: Scribner, 1968.

YOUNGHUSBAND, EILEEN, *Social Work and Social Change.* London: Allen & Unwin, 1964.

*Articles*

BEHRENDT, RICHARD F., "Die Zukunft der Entwicklungsländer als Problem des Spätmarxismus" (The Future of the Developing Nations as a Problem of Late Marxism), *Futurum, Zeitschrift für Zukunftsforschung,* No. 4 (1970), 547–616.

GABLE, RICHARD V., ed., "Partnership for Progress: International Technical Co-operation," *Annals of the American Academy of Political and Social Science,* 323 (May 1959), entire issue.

KENDALL, KATHERINE A., *Social Work Values in an Age of Discontent.* New York: Council on Social Work Education, 1970.

KRAUS, HERTHA, ed., "International Co-Operation for Social Welfare—a New Reality," *Annals of the American Academy of Political and Social Science,* 329 (May 1960), entire issue.

MANN-BORGESE, ELISABETH, "Human Nature Is Still Evolving," *The Center Magazine,* 6 (March-Apr. 1973), 4–9.

TITMUSS, RICHARD M., "International Aspects of Welfare," pp. 125–28 in *Commitment to Welfare.* New York: Pantheon, 1967.

VON VORYS, KARL, "New Nations: The Problem of Political Development," *Annals of the American Academy of Political and Social Science,* 358 (March 1965), 1–179.

# Index